MW00648057

SIDES

SIDES

Peter Straub

CEMETERY DANCE PUBLICATIONS

Baltimore

❖ 2007 ❖

Cemetery Dance Publications
132-B Industry Lane, Unit #7
Forest Hill, MD 21050
http://www.cemeterydance.com

First Limited Edition Printing

ISBN: 978-1-58767-165-4

Cover Photograph © 2007 by Marni Horwitz
Dust Jacket Design by Michael Fusco
Interior Design by Kathryn Freeman

To John Clute

To live is to be someone else.
—Fernando Pessoa

Table of Contents

Author's Note

Sides collects most of the non-fiction I have written since moving from an extremely presentable house in Westport, CT, into my brownstone in New York City. Since that move took place in 1985 and it is now 2006, the attentive reader will observe that my non-fictional output has been shamefully slender, especially since a good third of this book consists of the ravings of Putney Tyson Ridge, my self-invented human speed bump and alter ego, and therefore could be considered fiction, if of an odd ventriloquial sort, after all.

It is true, I much prefer writing fiction to non-, and was persuaded to try my hand at the following projects, which tend toward the essayistic, largely because a number of editors and/or publishers dangled projects before me that I found irresistible. A new edition of *The Stepford Wives* gave me a chance to describe what I thought were really admirable and underappreciated qualities in Ira Levin's work; Peter Crowther let me express my appreciation, which has since doubled or perhaps even re-doubled on itself, of Graham Joyce's writing; Barry Hoffman encouraged me to think about the reasons I found myself so persuaded by the work of Caitlin R. Kiernan and Poppy Z. Brite; editors at the Modern Library invited me into their comfy, book-lined purview to mull over two great classics of horror; and a terrific guy at the Book-of-the-Month Club, now Bookspan, asked if I would consider doing a piece on Stephen King that would serve as the Introduction to a nice fat volume of his previously uncollected articles and interviews that dealt with the subject of writing. Lawrence Block himself, a friend, asked if I would write a short Intro to a UK small-press edition of his then latest Matt Scudder novel, *Hope to Die.* He did not ask me to think about the Scudder series as a whole, but that's what I wanted to do, and so I did, temporarily confounding the small press. Once they picked themselves up off the floor, everything worked out fine.

"The Fantasy of Everyday Life" was my Guest-of-Honor speech at the 1998 International Conference of the Fantastic in the Arts, and can serve as a perfect example of the goofy, homespun surrealism which seems to be my default response to an invitation to express myself in public. As "Looking Back," the essay entitled "Mom" appeared in a book that combined short stories written by mother-son partnerships with essays written by male writers about their mothers.

The "frivolity" here, "Why Electricman Lives in New York" was written for an anthology celebrating the twenty-fifth anniversary of New York is Book Country. Two executives of DC comics attended the reading NYIBC had organized for the publication of their handsome volume, and as we filed out of the room, these gentlemen promised to reward me for my efforts on behalf of superheroes with the gift of several boxes of "cool stuff." About three weeks later, two huge cartons from DC arrived at the downstairs gate. They had sent me hundreds of graphic novels large and small, earnest and perverse, comic and tragic, sunny and embittered—the boxes kept me occupied for months. They were right: it was cool stuff.

Peter Straub

Encounters:
Introductions and Afterwords

The Stepford Wives
Introduction to the Perennial Editon

The *Stepford Wives*, along with almost everything else written by the admirable Ira Levin, does honor to a demanding literary aesthetic that has gone generally unremarked due to its custom of concealing itself, like the Purloined Letter, in plain view. Polished and formal at its core, the aesthetic can be seen in James Joyce's *Dubliners*, the novels of Ivy Compton-Burnett, the work of California Gothic writers like Richard Matheson and William F. Nolan, and in Brian Moore's last, drastically underappreciated six novels. Clearly adaptable over a wide range of style, manner, and content, it emphasizes concision, efficiency, observation, accuracy, effect, speed, and the illusion of simplicity. Fiction of this kind rigorously suppresses authorial commentary and reflection in its direct progress from moment to moment. This emphasis on a drastic concision brings with it a certain necessary, if often underplayed, artificiality that always implies an underlying wit, although the individual works themselves may have no other connection to humor. Such fiction possesses the built-in appeal of appearing to be extremely easy to read, since the reader need do no more than float along on the current, moving from a paragraph centered around a sharp visual detail to a passage of dialogue, thence on to another telling detail followed by another brief bit of dialogue, and so on.

In fact, *The Stepford Wives* is so effortlessly readable that it has been persistently misread, which is to say misunderstood, over the thirty years since its original publication. As a novel that can be devoured nearly in one gulp, its very efficiency deflects attention from the controlled composure of its prose and the jewel-like perfection of its structure. (Readers of popular fiction tend anyhow to ignore the construction of the books that push their buttons and, even more noticeably, to disregard stylistic niceties; gripped by a compelling, or at least exciting, narrative, readers of popular fiction generally overlook the essential qualities of the actual writing that delivers the story, whether it shines or stinks.) Levin's prose is clean, precise, and unfussy specifically in order to be as transparent as possible: he wishes to place no verbal static between the words on the page and the events they depict. One great difference between good writing that readers overlook and bad writing that they fail to notice has to do with the number of rewrites and revisions usually required by the former. It isn't at all easy to write clear, declarative prose—transparency evolves from ruthless cutting and trimming and is hard work—while lumpy, tangle-footed writing flows from the pen as if inspired by the Muse.

Reading *The Stepford Wives*, we gradually recognize that an inexorable internal timetable lies beneath its action, and that each of the novel's hints, breakthroughs, and miniclimaxes—the stages of its heroine's progress toward final knowledge—have been exquisitely timed against the imperatives of that underlying schedule. It is like a great clock, ticking away from September 4 to just before Christmas. After moving to the suburban village of Stepford, Joanna Eberhart soon befriends two women refreshingly unlike the house-proud, polite, but seemingly brainless women married to the local men. Bobbie Markowe, "short and heavy-bottomed," with "small hands and dirty toes," instantly suggests that they try to drum up interest in a local NOW chapter. The only woman in town to display any interest is Charmaine Wimperis, an avid tennis player, who babbles about astrology and her husband's depraved sexual tastes, as evidenced by his recently having presented her with a heavily zippered, whole-body rubber garment. Charmaine moved to Stepford in July, Bobbie in August. Wives in Stepford become Stepford wives after the period of time necessary for their husbands to prepare the ground, or four months after arrival. In November, therefore, Charmaine abruptly tears up her tennis court to install a putting green for her husband, now understood to be "a wonderful guy." At this point we do not share the author's awareness that Bobbie has one month left before the dread transformation, Joanna two. Like our heroine, we become aware of the timetable only after Bobbie Markowe returns from a brief marital vacation with enhanced breasts, a slimmer bottom, and a newfound passion for ironing.

Although in longer works of fiction time is always a besetting problem—a conundrum that demands constant attention—a narrative built atop a four-month clock must be even more careful in its handling than as is the case in other novels, and Levin manages with beautiful economy the business of moving us from September to November, when the noose tightens, by listing specific events that carry us through the days: "Pete took a fall on the school bus and knocked out his two front teeth. Joanna's parents paid a short-notice three-day visit on their way to a Caribbean vacation...The dishwasher broke down, and the pump; and Pete's eighth birthday came...She saw Bobbie almost every day...By the end of October, Walter was getting home for dinner again...They carved a huge pumpkin for Halloween, and Pete went trick-or-treating as a front-toothless Batman...On the first Saturday in November they gave a dinner party..."

And there we are again, located within a dinner-party scene bristling with apprehension that will come to a climax a mere 900 words later, with Charmaine blandly going on about cleaning her house, while workmen cut up the metal fence around her already demolished tennis court.

A wicked, deadpan humor lies at the heart of this tableau with Bobbie and Joanna staring in mingled disbelief and horror at their former fellow-rebel, while the workers below deal the coup de grâce to what once had been a sign of grandiose over-privilege. ("It's a *clay court*!" Joanna wails.) If *The Stepford Wives* were the easy satire on the banality of suburban housewives that it is commonly taken to be—a misconception that has installed its title in our language as shorthand for those homemakers who affect an uncanny perfection—this humor would seem wildly out of place. Yet it fits the moment so accurately that it slips by almost unnoticed, for it is the same subversive humor that shapes the entire book. This is a novel that satirizes its oppressors and their desires, not their victims, within a context that satirizes its very status as a thriller.

A coven of high-tech, randy suburban men conspire to replace their wives with compliant sex-robots dedicated to sparkling floors and clean grout in the bathrooms—whatever we are dealing with here, it isn't mimetic fiction. Levin created the same kind of deliberately genre-parodic, over-the-top exoskeleton for *The Boys from Brazil*, where Nazi scientists breed little Führer clones and adopt them out to families akin to Hitler's. Oblivious to his satire, lots of heavy-footed thriller writers immediately began to imitate precisely what he had been lampooning. Similarly, not a single reviewer of *Son of Rosemary*, Levin's most recent novel, understood that it, too, satirized the excesses of its own supposed genre.

Levin's Olympian humor emerges primarily in his depiction of the Stepford husbands. Until the last fifteen pages, almost everything these men do is hilarious. At parties, Stepford husbands talk only to one other, like clueless boys. Like teenage boys, they yearn to translate their fantasies of sex with Playmate-style lollapaloozas into reality, so they spend as many evenings as possible in the steamy atmosphere of the Men's Association, where groin and brain unite to whip up the latest walking, talking sex toy. (When not bent over the workbench, they goggle at porn flicks.) These men are so single-mindedly, comically lubricious that they barely attempt to disguise their intentions, drawing portraits of the new prospects and having them read endless lists of vowel-consonant combinations into a tape recorder. Actual women irritate and bore them, and the busty robots are useful only as concubines and maids.

The funniest revelation of wholehearted male piggery occurs very early in the book, when the Eberharts have been in town no more than a few weeks. At two in the morning, after Walter Eberhart has returned from his first visit to the Men's Association, the shaking of the bed and the squeaking of bedsprings awaken his wife. Joanna quickly realized that her husband is…masturbating! "Well next time wake me," she says, and before long they are enjoying the best sex they've had in years. Something has ignited Walter's fuse, and not until much later do we realize—as Joanna never does—that it was the world-class fantasy object described to him by the grinning lads up on the hill.

Without at all belaboring the point, Levin pinpoints the origins of the husbands' scheme by having Joanna leaf back through old issues of the local paper to discover that the Men's Association came into being shortly after Betty Friedan, author of *The Feminine Mystique*, gave a well-attended talk to the Stepford Women's Club. The same club soon suspended meetings—due to lack of attendance, no doubt.

In 1972, the year *The Stepford Wives* was published, Betty Friedan helped found the National Women's Political Caucus, and *The Feminine Mystique* had been in print for nine years. That same year, Congress passed the (ultimately doomed) Equal Rights Amendment. To conservative-minded males, the feminist movement had just become something a great deal more than a minor nuisance. I don't know if *The Stepford Wives* can properly be called a feminist satire, but Levin's timing was impeccable, a thing of beauty all in itself. Like nearly everything else he has written, this book, resembles a bird in flight, a haiku, a Chinese calligrapher's brushstroke. With no wasted motion, it gets precisely where it wants to go.

The Siege of Leningrad
An Introduction to *Lenningrad Nights*

Once upon a time, or if you wish for more specificity at the end of October, 1984, the excellent, smart and goodhearted Stephen King happened to find himself seated at a long table before a microphone and a sizable audience in a ballroom-sized space within the handsome old Claremont Hotel in Oakland, California, where he had been panelizing about one or another of the usual topics in the course of a World Fantasy Convention. I know this because I was sitting next to him, along with a number of our fellow horrors. After we panelists had vented our customary grouchy set-pieces, someone in the audience stuck up his hand and inquired as to the future of our genre, thereby offering King the opportunity to exercise his talent for pithy sound-bites by uttering a sentence which has been quoted probably thousands of times since that nice, sunny afternoon, this sentence: "I have seen the future of horror, and its name is Clive Barker." At the time, Barker was largely unknown in the United States, where The Books of Blood had just begun to be published, but of course he soon demonstrated both a depth of imaginative power and a capacity to stretch and redefine the boundaries of horror literature that more than justified King's remark.

All along, English writers—more accurately, writers from throughout the United Kingdom and Ireland—have enriched and expanded the central definitions of horror, a literary category particularly, maybe even uniquely, open to the erasure of its own boundaries. Stoker and LeFanu were Irish, Arthur Machen was born in Wales, Mary Shelley, M. R. James, Algernon Blackwood, W. H. Hodgson, H. H. Munro (Saki), Walter De La Mare, Robert Aickman, and Angela Carter were British, as are Barker, Ramsey Campbell, James Herbert, Brian Lumley, Brian Hodge, M. John Harrison, and many others. Some of these people established or formalized horror's commanding tropes, others colonized them, and some blithely investigated the fresh territories suggested by their own imaginations. Horror writing blessedly accommodates a well-nigh infinite range of approaches, styles, and subjects. Because it is rooted in an apprehension of the unknown and thrives on detail-by-detail representations of contexts which imply other, wider contexts, horror is always resisting its own tendencies toward the kinds of narrative conventions that irrevocably determine the structure of mystery novels.

As Stephen King had the prescience to observe fifteen years ago, Clive Barker was taking horror writing into worlds previously unmapped, and during the latter half of this decade, Graham Joyce, a resident of Leicester, England, has, with astonishing panache, been doing the same.

When I say 'the latter half of this decade,' I am speaking purely subjectively, because the first Graham Joyce novel I read was *Requiem,* published in the UK in 1995 and in the US a year later, after it had won the British Fantasy Award. Joyce had been given the same award for his previous novel, *Dark Sister* which is at last to be published in the United States this year. Two earlier novels,

Dreamside and *House of Lost Dreams,* had preceded *Dark Sister,* so by the time I came to Joyce, he was completely in charge of his gifts. (Maybe he was in charge of his gifts when he wrote *Dreamside,* too, and one day I hope to be able to read it so that I can find out, but most working novelists, at least those who produce anywhere between eight to thirty or forty books over the course of their careers, are still growing into their talents during the first two or three.) I read *Requiem* because several English friends of mine, among them the publisher of this novella, Peter Crowther, had recommended Joyce's work strongly, even passionately.

I hate to admit this, but my typical response to suggestions that I read a new horror novel by an unknown writer (meaning one unknown to me) could be described as genial dismissal: I smile, I nod, I say, "Sounds great, I'll look for it," then promptly forget the name of both author and book. I have read far too many crappy so-called horror novels, at least half of them recommended by friends, to put much faith in other people's temporary enthusiasms. Also, and this is even harder to admit, my innocent trust in the one-to-one correspondence between awards and value wilted after I'd seen a couple of dim-witted productions beat out fictions I thought more deserving in every way. However, when Pete Crowther became the second person to tell me I ought to read Graham Joyce, I remembered that Tor Books had sent me a copy of *Requiem* months before, and I pulled it off the shelf and started reading.

The first thing I noticed was that Joyce paid attention to the shape of his sentences, their cadences and rhythms, and that the details he selected always contained an emotional message that moved the scene forward. He was a direct, plain-style, presentational writer—which is no piece of cake, let me assure you, to do that well demands hard work and a rare kind of selflessness—and he put real human dialogue into the mouths of his characters, another capacity far less common than it would be in an ideal world. The book kept getting better and better, more suggestive and mysterious, more open to its own unpredictable impulses. By the time I came to the last page, I was entirely grateful to those who had recommended the book to me: Joyce was one of the best new writers I had read in years, the real thing, fearless, observant, and deeply imaginative.

I do not have enough space here to describe my response to *The Tooth Fairy,* so I'll say only that I thought it was a breathtaking step forward, even more accurate in its representation of ongoing, daily human predicaments and their physical and social locations, even more fearless and imaginative when dealing with the archaic and the unknown, with Otherness.

Leningrad Nights is one of those works of fiction that seem to arrive unmediated from a space located at an oblique angle slightly above the earth's surface. The novella form, of which I am particularly fond, seems to me to move instinctively into this rewarding space, because novellas grant enough room to stretch out one's arms and breathe, to execute a couple of hand-springs if one likes, while being brief enough to avoid the dutiful, long-term, developmental necessities that come into play the moment a story declares the intention of meandering on for more than 50,000, 75,000, 100,000 words. With a novella, you can 'play', you can cut loose and see where you wind up without having to worry about next month's mortgage or the kids' tuition. (Novels, alas, take so long to write they inevitably encroach upon everything else.)

Here, Graham Joyce uses the novella's unique mixture of liberating length and liberating brevity to evoke a phantasmal, haunted version of Leningrad, "a city so old and so beautiful and so terrifying that no-one knows its true name," under siege during the Second World War. An orphaned boy named Leo dodges through the rubble, doing whatever he must to survive. This is simultaneously a Christmas tale, a doppelganger story, a reflection of the limitations of religious faith in which the sacrament of Communion becomes alarmingly literal, a frame narrative that questions its own resolution, and an account of an experience marked by tremendous uncertainty, grief, extremity, and madness. We have come a long and frightening way from the comforting satisfactions of *A Christmas Carol,* described by its energetic, profoundly complicated author as "a whimsical sort of masque intended to awaken loving and forbearing thoughts."

In our world, literary expressions of loving and forbearing thoughts generally appear within the direly sentimental fantasies written by self-deluded frauds like Robert James Waller and Alice Walker, which are quickly translated into filmic buttermilk by 'sincere', 'thoughtful' uplift merchants like Stephen Spielberg and Robert Zemeckis. Charming Tom Hanks ambles into the frame, broadcasting the sweet, goofy, tender-hearted, perhaps even mildly brain-damaged quality we enjoy in our heroes. When the emotions Dickens sought to awaken surface authentically, within tougher, more truthful works of art, they come as hard-won moments of grace. Our popular entertainment culture, and to a great extent our literary culture, has been so debased by their social and intellectual contexts that an astonishing number of people imagine that if Dickens were living now he would be writing screenplays and directing blockbuster movies. Yeah, sure, and he'd have a wonderful little place in Malibu.

Let us take a moment to consider the imaginary, present-day Dickens, a contemporary of ours whose internal structure literally demands the relentless creation of one ambitious, wide-ranging, vastly successful work of fiction after another. He lives in his native country, forget California, he cannot abandon everything that ties him to England. Three or four times a year, he flies to California to meddle with the movies being made from his books.

He has acting roles in most of them, because the guy truly gets off on performing. As soon as possible, he escapes LA to go home. He's all over the place, supporting left-wing political candidates and social causes, but most of the time he is planted in front of his computer, writing, should he have evolved sufficiently, some work of fiction responsive to his own most honest insights, something daring, fluent, and unpredictable, something, we well as might say, not unlike *Leningrad Nights.*

I don't know if Graham Joyce is the future of horror, but I want to think that he, and those few writers of his generation who share his visionary imaginative capacity, might be exactly that. Horror, 'horror', a remarkably expansive category willing at any time to erase its own hypothetical boundaries, depends for its survival on artists like Graham Joyce.

Peter Straub
January 1999

Tales of Pain and Wonder

Caitlin R. Kiernan

Caitlín R. Kiernan strides into a room with a look in her eye that says you had better come up to the mark, because you won't get much slack from this quarter. Her shoulders are back, her spine is straight, and she projects the charismatic confident self-sufficiency seen only in tall people who learned long ago that the only way to carry off their height is not to slouch—as weaker souls do—but to suggest by their posture that they are even taller. (I don't know how tall Caitlín actually is, but I'm 6'2", and I'm pretty sure she looks at me straight-on, face-to-face. In fact, there are times when Caitlín appears to gaze down at me from a position located several inches above eye-level, even under conditions that render it physically impossible, as, for example, when I am seated comfortably but inelegantly in a chair and she has deployed herself on the floor.) Let's go back to the moment Caitlín enters our hypothetical room—she is wearing attractive gear layered with a kind of stylish bohemian panache that suits her down to the ground, party clothes for a party a bit more louche than those to which you are accustomed, especially if you are over forty. She moves from person to person, making the sort of remarks that are called "asides," her manner modulating from the confidential to the disengaged to the amused as she progresses, all the while ignoring the rude fact that most of the other people in the room, in varying degrees of obviousness, happen to be looking at her.

The word "striking" has been applied to Caitlín Kiernan so often that it has ceased to be anything but irritating, and with good reason. "Striking," an otherwise harmless pat on the back, implies the refusal to articulate any definition more nuanced; it's a cop-out. Caitlín is striking; she's the sort of person who instantly compels attention, but so are Madonna, George Hamilton, Dennis Rodman, Placido Domingo, RuPaul, Sandra Bernhart, Iggy Pop, and the late Duke Ellington. We need, and Caitlín deserves, more specificity.

Caitlín Kiernan is first of all a writer distinguished by certain unique gifts; from that everything else flows. Like all worthwhile writers of fiction, she is in urgent possession of a vision, a point of view communicable only through representation in an ongoing series of short stories and novels. For those who find themselves under this obligation, fiction presents itself as a kind of aperture. The aperture provides a means of both expression and focus, but it is narrow and infinitely difficult to negotiate. Supple, exploratory access to its resources is given only to those whose internal structures render such access crucial to psychic survival, and in most cases the discovery of how best to use it arrives after years of unrewarding slog. No one unaffected by this weird process could be expected to understand it, a matter which results in a widespread delusion amongst the civilian populace.

If you happen to be a writer, during the course of almost every social situation, some vainglorious, well-meaning idiot is going to plant himself before you and explain that had he not gone into brain surgery, real estate sales, pork belly futures, or the importation of black-market domestic servants, he'd be a writer, too, because he is a creative-type person, just like you, only he never had the time to put his ideas on paper. (The best response to this kind of thing is, "You know, that's interesting. I always knew I could be a brain surgeon, but I was too busy writing to get around to it.") A good part of Caitlín's presence is grounded in the awareness of having successfully evolved a distinctive voice and manner all her own, which, with unerring instinct, she turned to the investigation of a fictional territory ideally suited to their particular resonances.

That landscape haunts the stories in Tales of Pain and Wonder, a perfect title for this collection. The setting changes from Athens, Georgia, to Los Angeles, New York City, New Orleans, Atlanta, San Francisco, and a Hudson River island near Storm King mountain, but the nature of the territory, the essential landscape, remains the same. Kiernan's characters inhabit a worn-out, exhausted world long since degraded by pollution and neglect into a uniformly oppressive bleakness.

...the asphalt ended in sticky red mud and pine trees, pothole alley behind the shopping center. Much darker back there, tree shadows, whispering needles and dumpster shadows, wet garbage stink.

("Superheroes")

Salmagundi Desvernine...stares through broken panes across the corrugated rooftops toward front gates padlocked and chained against the world outside....strains to steal a gimpse beyond the road that winds through other abandoned industries, disappears, finally, between high gneiss and granite bluffs, boulders pollution-scarred and spray-paint tagged, wrapped in fog the color of rust.

("Glass Coffin")

Stinking maze of loading docks and wholesale butchers: diesel fumes, fresh blood; knives and meat hooks for everything down here. Past concrete and greasy plastic drums marked Indedible—Do Not Eat…

("The Last Child of Lir")

The interiors of the rooms, clubs and theaters where the characters sleep, eat, have sex and pursue their obsessions, and through which they drift in search of amusement or enlightenment, offer an only slightly domesticated version of the devastation outside. Broken glass litters the concrete floors; the windows are either filthy or cracked; the furniture is junk; elevators reek of urine, and staircases threaten. Rubbish accumulates. We are located well below the poverty line, and all living arrangements are temporary. Hopeless squalor has become a common condition, as if in the wake of some apocalyptic catastrophe.

Lost and passive, the affectless boys and girls who populate these stories, too childish to be called men and women even when they are approaching thirty, unquestioningly accept the hopelessness of their surroundings and live within its paralyzing terms. All but three of these characters seem to have entered the world unburdened by the presence of mothers and fathers, and for an excellent reason: Were we to be introduced to their parents, the larger, more explanatory psychological framework in which we would instantly begin to locate Deacon, Magwitch, Rabbit, Glitch, Erica, Lark and Crispin is utterly irrelevant to Kiernan's concerns. Psychological insight, which permits a kind of description in fact detached from judgement, is none-the-less often experienced as judgmental, as are other neutral forms of description. Even the hint of conventional judgement, however misapplied, would interfere with our appreciation of these stories. We must take Kiernan's disenfranchised protagonists on their own terms, as her fiction presents them to us. Once we have done so, we are free to notice what matters, what is important about them.

These lost children know they have the life expectancy of moths, and that predators, human and otherwise, lurk and hover, yet an instinctive gallantry prohibits them from feeling anything like self-pity. They seldom whine. In the absence of other structures, they have chosen their own elective families, to which they are deeply loyal. These people are fellow-travelers, they're in it together, and for all their mutual bitching, they care for the well-being of their companions. They stick up for and defend each other, sometimes at tremendous cost. Marginalization, poverty and precarious health have not stripped them of a kind of valor, a kind of courageous readiness. Although by conventional standards nearly everything about their circumstances conspires to make them seem dismissable—their aimlessness, squalor, drug usage, crazy sexual tropisms and pathetic ambitions, if they have ambitions—they are in no way to be dismissed. Kiernan's characters have adapted to their surroundings so thoroughly that they might as well have been produced by it, and are not so much without ambition as beyond it. In the most basic way, they are getting on. For all their fragility, they are open to the extraordinary experiences lying in wait for them. Their receptivity to the extraordinary, a category which here involves horror, monstrosity, mystery, enigma, ecstasy, revulsion, and the sense of the sacred, depends upon their vulnerability.

A symbiotic connection between revelation and alienated protagonists in ill health resonates throughout the Romantic tradition. (More about this later. Kiernan's attachment to the essentially Romantic, early-Modernist poets William Butler Yeats and T. S. Eliot adds another, extremely interesting, layer to these stories.) This connection, long ago became so thematic as to be nearly reflexive, can these days be found in the work of M. John Harrison, Ramsey Campbell, Thomas Tessier, Poppy Z. Brite, and plenty of others, including me. For writers, who always feel marginalized, the notion that wounded outcasts are uniquely equipped to receive deep-level transmissions cannot help but be seductive. (There's some truth in it, as the lives of many gifted writers, musicians and other artists indicate. Think of Harte Crane and Poe, think of Charlie Parker.) Kiernan's remarkable contribution to our literature has been to mold this theme into an expressive vehicle by embedding it within her narrative technique, thereby creating the aesthetic which gives these stories their expressive and individual form.

The most significant characters in *Tales of Pain and Wonder* appear and reappear throughout the collection, surfacing in one location or another over time. Deacon "Deke" Silvey moves to Birmingham, Georgia, from Atlanta; the twins Crispin and Lark drift from Los Angeles to Seattle and San Francisco, then back to LA; Jenny Haniver finds her way from a derelict New Jersey shipyard, inherited by Salmagundi and Salammbo Desvernine, to a basement apartment in Greenwich Village; a homicidal drug dealer extravagantly named Jimmy DeSade pilots an old Lincoln from Georgia to Mexico, New Orleans, Los Angeles and New York; but no matter where they travel none of them ever change or grow. Moving around is merely a literalization of the aimlessness and passivity that render them suitable for their essential task. They are to serve as witnesses. In story after story, Kiernan's protagonists are led into variations on the theme of a shattering encounter with profound Otherness, a revelation of hideous and seductive powers which enforce an increased helplessness and passivity upon those with whom they come into contact.

In their obdurate purity of means, their dream-like refusal to yield any more information than is necessary for the creation of the central effect, the stories themselves echo the condition of the characters within them. Only a handful—"Breakfast in the House of the Rising Sun," "In the Water Works," "San Andreas" and perhaps "Estate"—unfold in the manner common to short stories from Chekhov to Flannery O'Connor, by suspending details and events along a narrative arc like that of a novel in miniature. Kiernan can martial her material into that kind of form whenever she feels like loosening up and getting expansive, but the nature of her vision customarily demands a more compressed, elided and enigmatic narrative technique. Cinematic pans and jump-cuts from character to character are cut to the bone, along with back-story explanations; plot has been distilled down to movement toward encounter and encounter; in the absence of familiar narrative comforts, details take on a surreal glow, and the trappings of rationality evaporate; a fetishistic, entranced eroticism prevails; meaning is devoured by mystery, and coherence can be glimpsed only in terrifying, myth-like fragments.

The fragmentation of coherence and the disappearance of meaning reduce value, as generally understood, to loyalty to one's companions and the awareness of exhaustion and despair. The world is dying, and faith is dead. Human behavior is seen to be parodic and empty. The human body, formerly an emblem of value, has become deeply distasteful, a revulsion, an object best treated with mutilation, injury, deliberate wounding.

Yet fractured coherence speaks of a larger, genuine coherence existing either in memory or immediately beyond human apprehension. Uniquely qualified for the role, Kiernan's characters are led to their moment of witness—their perception of alien Otherness—and find in it an enigmatic but persuasive transcendence. Certain scholarly or scientifically-disposed characters, collectors of oddities preserved in glass jars and fishtanks, have devoted themselves to research into explanatory Otherness; the rest, aided or not by the efforts of the former, stumble upon it. In both cases, revelation typically occurs in the rich psychic terrain invoked by journey downward and inward, movement beneath the earth's crust, movement into secret passages, mineshafts, hidden realms.

"They were keeping her in a subbasement, Deke."

Abandoned warehouses, basements, subbasements, crypts, sewers, underground rivers, subterranean caves… the ultimately authoritative lurks underground, often in a cavern with access to water. Water-creatures of all kinds, being cold-blooded and inhuman, imply its presence, for there is a wavering yellow-green light beneath the water, the gaudy drab light of things which have never seen the sun and have learned to make their own ("Tears Seven Times Salt.") In "Paedormorphosis," Annie, a half-heartedly aspiring musician disaffected with her "baby dyke" bandmates, encounters "riot grrrl" Elise, a paleontologist's daughter who seduces her on a "shimmering carpet like all the colors of autumn lying beneath still and murky waters," then entices her through underground vaults to a black lake inhabited by "fetal" salamanders "the pinkwhite of an old scar," and provides the most humane, intimate revelation of an underlying Otherness in these stories by raising her arms to expose the presence of gills, "crimson slits where her armpits should be, the feathered edges bright with oxygen-rich blood, gasping slits like twin and puckered mouths." Ever after, Annie is haunted by a vision of "vast and empty spaces."

Vastness, emptiness, and coldness are the touchstones of the mysterious and alien set of forces to which the disenfranchised elect are given access. "Postcards From the King of Tides," one of this collection's most effective stories, moves like a series of snapshots depicting the progress of hapless Lark and Crispin, twins marked with "the stain of protracted innocence," from a stalled car across a stream to signs advertising MERMAIDS AND MIRACLES! and into a seedy trailer smelling of saltwater and rot, where a sinister caretaker offers, what else, ranks of pickled curiosities floating in jars and at last thrusts aside a curtain and displays his final exhibit. Arctic cold pours from the opened space. The old man recites Tennyson on the Kraken:

> There hath he lain for ages, and will lie
>
> Battening upon huge sea worms in his sleep,
>
> Until the latter fire shall heat the deep…

Lark yields to a swooning sense of immanence that threatens to engulf her within "this perfect, absolute cold and darkness…and the thing swimming through the black." When Crispin wrenches her away, a "sudden emptyhollow feeling…like waking from a dream of heaven or someone dead alive again" pierces her—she has been given a vision of a destructive purity.

"The Long Hall on the Top Floor" extends the moment of revelation into an account of its emotional consequences. Sadie, a zombie-like young woman with "boiled fish eyes," brings the wasted psychic Deacon Silvey to an old warehouse and leads him upstairs to a hallway. Again, the visionary encounter begins with an immersion into coldness that "isn't just cold, it's indifference, the freezing temperature of an apathy so absolute, so perfect." Undone, Silvey collapses, keeping his eyes helplessly on the tiny window at the corridor's end, where a "dim shadow," a "fluid stain," resembles wings "or long, jointed legs moving fast through some deep and secret ocean." These images are mere approximations, he understands; what he has glimpsed is beyond his comprehension and neither wishes nor is meant to be seen. Sadie refuses to play along. Awed recognition has shocked her out of zombie-hood, and she insists on putting into words the stages, one by one, of her recognition. We can paraphrase the steps of her recognition in this way:

1) Whatever I saw was beautiful.

2) The power of its beauty forced me to find out if that thing was real, and I did find out. It was real, all right.

3) Even though it was horrible and frightening, I am grateful for its reality. Everything else is so empty of meaning that only fear reminds me I am still alive.

Transcendence, in this world the single escape from a pervasive death-in-life, has become inextricably dependent upon the shock of fear.

And now there's writing there, sloppy words scrawled in something black; runny, black words…

We have arrived at a point not far from Rilke and the visionary insights at the beginning of the first Duino Elegy:

Denn das Schöne is nichts

als des Schrecklichen Anfang, den wir noch grade ertragen, (For beauty is nothing/ but the beginning of terror, which we are still just able to endure,) and

Ein jeder Engel ist schrecklich. ("Every angel is terrifying.")

Nothing could be further from the reassuring New Age oatmeal ladled out by beloved "uplift" merchants like Marianne Williamson, Deepak Chopra, and their myriad clones, who want us to know that if only we were to cast off our negativity we would wake up mystically fulfilled in a paradisal garden. A search for "Angels" in any on-line bookstore turns up an endless list of books about personal encounters with warm-hearted celestial beings always prepared to step in and offer assistance, as Della Reese does every Sunday evening, right after "60 Minutes." (Ms. Reese and her fellow-angels are terrifying, all right, but not in the way Rilke meant. Television angels, and the ones in cuddly best-sellers, behave like the know-it-all relatives you dread seeing at Thanksgiving.) The kind of people who benignly think of themselves as "spiritual" never understand this, but sublimity incorporates a substantial quantity of terror, and mystery, being by definition inhuman, ruthlessly violates rational order. Violence shares a border with the sacred. Mystery accommodates awe and fear, emotional majesty and emotional devastation. Kiernan's title, *Tales of Pain and Wonder,* instantly locates us within an educated point of view, one which has been defined by her responses to both personal experience and the experience of literature.

The idea of literature, representing art in general as our most accurate and comprehensive means of expression, haunts this collection like a despairing ghost. Matthew Arnold's "Dover Beach," Eliot's "The Waste Land," and the poetry of Yeats float beneath the surface of the prose, their resonant summations of lost faith, lost coherence, lost innocence in a fragmented, brutally degraded world with "neither joy, nor love, nor light, Nor certitude, nor peace" invoking the painful recognition of their own lost usefulness. Only a very few of the characters in these stories call upon the resources of art, and those that do meet with frustration. Here, a deeply literary sensibility seems to turn against itself and declare its own central touchstones no longer valid. Salmagundi Desvernine, who escapes the self-imprisonment of the typical Kiernan protagonist by fleeing from ruined Pollepel to San Francisco and becoming an avant-garde artist, laments the death of poetry—and, by extension, all of literature—in two of the collection's most finely developed stories, "Salmagundi" and "...Between the Gargoyle Trees." On both occasions, she uses the same words, condemns the same villain, and refers to the same iconic figure of now-unattainable verbal authenticity, William Butler Yeats.

Poetry isn't just dead, it was killed, done away with by contemporary poets who "eviscerated" poetry by making "emotion almost completely inaccessible through language." Salmagundi disdainfully calls these murderers they, thereby turning them into a faceless crowd, a kind of lynch mob. They consist of "Everyone after [or since] fucking Yeats and T. S. Eliot [or fucking William Yeats]." "Salmagundi" gives us a little more specificity by referring to "The Poet-citizens,'" but it's still difficult to identify the villains. The category "everyone after Eliot and Yeats" includes an enormous number of poets of wildly differing techniques, approaches, value-systems, and poetics. Was Wallace Stevens a "poet-citizen"? (Yes, probably.) Were Robert Lowell, John Berryman, and Elizabeth Bishop? (Dubious.) Or Anne Sexton and Sylvia Plath? (Even more dubious.) Frank O'Hara, John Ashbery, and James Schuyler? (Not at all, although Salmagundi Desvernine might find them guilty of having done a gene-splice on the traditional relationship between words and feelings. In 1922, a lot of people accused T. S. Eliot of the same offense.)

Of course, in the end these quibbles mean nothing—I bring them up only because Kiernan is using her artist-savant to express a blanket condemnation she herself knows better than to share. Salmagundi Desvernine, that extraordinary character, progresses toward immaculate failure and abandonment of the human realm; her creator is shoring fragments against the widespread ruin, bringing into being a condemned universe shot through with golden threads.

Are You Loathsome Tonight?
Introduction

The inspiration of killing that man came to me out of the blue on the day I realized that one of my two different lives was making me crazy.

• • •

Poppy Z. Brite never really goes where you expect her to. While circling over certain common themes, she is waiting to sink her teeth into her obsessions. Every fiction writer worth reading for more than the sake of a momentary distraction hovers over the chosen territory in precisely this manner, hawk-like, obsessed, awaiting the opportunity to plunge.

• • •

Until the moment inspiration settled its divine hands on my shoulders and pushed me out of my frame, I had been proud of my little balancing act. No other girl in my school could float like me—that's what I said to myself.

No boy could, either. Pride like that wraps a blindfold over your eyes and plugs your ears with wax.

• • •

The simple sexual act is different from eroticism; the former is found in animal life, whereas human life alone admits of an activity defined perhaps by a "diabolical" aspect, aptly described by the word eroticism.

—*The Tears of Eros,* Georges Bataille

I am control and the uncontrollable.
I am the union and the dissolution.
I am the abiding, and I am the dissolution.
I am the one below, and they come up to me.

—"The Thunder: Perfect Mind," in *The Nag Hammadi Library*

• • •

What does not partake of consciousness is not human, and yet even an ape can grieve.

• • •

See that half-naked girl smoking a joint on the river bank between two guys wearing nothing but their grins? See the girl on the back of the Harley with her arms around the mountain-man? That's me.

And here I am in my Junior English class, raising my hand to inform the dazzled Mr. Froelich that *Their Eyes Are Watching God*, a novel by Zora Neale Hurston, progresses through constant reference to a particular organic metaphor.

In this one I appear to be dead but have been merely rendered unconscious by a drug administered by the saint-like Denny Watters, who died of gunshot wounds three days later; this is me dressed up to go to the prom with Tommy Deutsch, who got into Brown on early admission.

This is the limousine that drove us around all night. Our driver thought we were disgusting.

This is the hovel I went to after I ditched Tommy Deutsch, and these are the people who lived there: fat, fantastic Toomey, his lover Jerome, and Jerome's female hanger-on, Hilly, a succubus. Their band was called Duino Elegy. About an hour after I took this picture, we were resting up in a huge tangle on their mattress, and I remember thinking that Jerome would be much nicer if he settled down and stayed gay all the time, like Toomey. Jerome had the perfect body for a gay boy, almost like a girl's body. Next to Jerome, Hilly looked like an evolutionary dead end.

• • •

The Daoist is listening for the mystical voices which rise in him and sing in his viscera. He visualizes ethereal breath produced by the distillation of the juices of his entrails: it is at the paroxysm of the organic and at the lowest and most quotidian level that the body is decanted, that matter is transmuted into essence and that sublimation takes place. But this is made possible only because the organic functioning is sacred: because the inside of the body, where crude secretions are developed, is the vessel of delicate spirits.

—"The Body: The Daoists' Coat of Arms," Jean Levi

• • •

In a world where the body's crude, functional secretions speak of sacred essence, the tissue of social interactions and the stabilizing consensus of judgments derived from these interactions dissolve into weightlessness. When the literally internal is recognized as the literally central, a radical democracy asserts itself on all sides, and we occupy an egalitarian universe. Persons of the deepest conventionality, persons absent of any insight whatsoever, carry within themselves a quantity of divinity—of access to divinity—equal to that within the most enlightened. Everyone occupies the same spacious rung on the food chain; everyone is a potentially sacramental meal.

The same can be said of narrative, also of the version of narrative known as history.

• • •

During my year and a half at the State University, I followed my old pattern of living half in banal light, half in rich darkness. No one suspected, apart from the few other students doing the same thing, and most of these were girls who knew how to keep their mouths shut. To maintain two separate lives, you have to tend your fences.

It wore on me, though, it undermined my assumptions. The death of an assumption always breaks your heart. No sooner did I exchange a complicitous glimmer with a classmate in Art History 101, whom twenty-four hours before I had glimpsed in the tropical atmosphere of the hidden universe, than our mutual project seemed shallow and misguided. These doubts concerning my authenticity came to a head late one Saturday night when a girl named Abbey Pullman materialized beside me. Slinky, darkly gorgeous and corrupt to the core, Abbey Pullman came from New York City, and she existed within an aura of private schools, family trusts, and discreet holidays in detox-rehab facilities supplied with chefs instead of cooks. Abbey put her heart-shaped mouth to my ear and whispered, "Sweetie, do you have a beeper number for that sexy little beast you saw talking to me last night?" I packed my shit and got out of there the next day, sorry.

• • •

"All three saw a young child on the altar, and when the priest started breaking the Host, it seemed to them that an angel came down from Heaven and divided the child in two with a knife, and collected his blood in the chalice. And when the priest divided the Host into several parts to give Communion to the people, they saw that the angel was also dividing the child into several small parts. And when, at the end of the Mass, the hermit went to receive Communion, it seemed to him that he alone was given a part of the bloodied flesh of that child. Seeing this, he was filled with such dread that he screamed and said: 'My Lord, now I really believe that the bread which is consecrated on the altar in Your holy body and the chalice, that is to say the wine, is Your blood...'"

Believers, particularly in earlier centuries, confusedly understood God's sacrifice as a prodigy of abominable grandeur, and were quite conscious of the bloody fragment of divine flesh that descended into their stomachs in the guise of the Host...The child slaughtered by the angel, his flesh cut up into small bloody bits...reflects this profound attraction-repulsion toward the sacrificial mystery...

—"The Consecrated Host: A Wondrous Excess,"
Piero Camporesi

• • •

Certain cities and certain moments in time offer themselves to the imaginative eye. New York; Calcutta; Los Angeles; Shanghai before the Japanese invasion; the Sarajevo of 1914, in which a boy named Gavrilo Princip assassinated Archduke Ferdinand and Countess Sophie;

1918 New Orleans, where a murderer calling himself "The Axeman" advised the readers of the *Times-Picayune* that he was "invisible, even as the ether that surrounds your earth;" 1967 London, where in an Islington terrace a failed actor named Kenneth Halliwell committed suicide after murdering his lover, the playwright Joe Orton; Jeffrey Dahmer's Milwaukee of 1993, glistening with the multiple snail-tracks of his obsessive progress; any place and time elevated by a distinguishing act of violence. Or any city, like Amsterdam, receptive to such an act by reason of its tolerance of what elsewhere is condemned as deviation.

• • •

I had a gig in Boca Raton where I put on a headset, dialed numbers all over the country and said, "Hello, Mr. (Name.) I hope I have not reached you at an inconvenient time. You have been selected to participate in a nation-wide survey which will take only a few minutes of your time. After you have answered a few simple questions, you will be eligible to participate in our Grand Prize Giveaway." I was living in an A-frame in Aspen with a ski instructor who had to snort half a gram every morning just to get out of bed. I transferred to Barnard, and this uptight guy in the next apartment paid me $100 for every Harlan Ellison first edition I could steal from the Columbia library. I took a bus to Montana, talked myself into a job on a local newspaper, and, you could have fooled me, married a rancher. When Gainesville got risky, I took a bus to Palm Beach, where I screwed up big time and almost went to prison. I worked in a Minneapolis massage parlor, where I rubbed peppermint oil into guys' backs, dipped between their legs, ran my fingers over their balls and asked if they cared for a relief massage, which of course they always did, never mind the extra $35, you never saw so many bananas yearning upward, and when at the last moment the bananas did that thing where they locked into their yearning, they were filled with an essence having nothing to do with humanity.

At that moment, I attended to the descent of the sacred. I watched the muscles in the arms and legs stand out like ridge-poles. I observed the arching of the back, the tightening of the face as the inner man flew toward the surface. It was an effort, it was a labor. The body struggled toward a violent surrender. There were groans and curses. Then at last the inner man came leaping from the body, flowing from what seemed a bottomless well.

After that, most of those guys turned right back into assholes.

• • •

The Gnostic texts known as the Nag Hammadi Library were unearthed in a cave near the end of 1945 by two brothers, Muhammad and Khalifah Ali, from the Egyptian village of al-Qasr. They were looking for *sebakh*, a particular kind of soil used as a fertilizer, but instead discovered a tall jar which they imagined might hold either treasure or evil spirits. Frightened but hoping to find gold, they shattered the jar with a pick-axe and discovered that it contained rolled-up manuscripts, which they brought back to their village.

Some months earlier, their father, a night watchman for the village's irrigation fields, had surprised and killed an intruder. In accordance with the tradition of vendetta, he was murdered the next day. A month after the library had been brought to al-Qasr, Muhammad Ali was told that a man who had fallen asleep near his hut, in fact an innocent dealer in molasses, was his father's killer. Muhammad, Khalifa and their mother attacked the sleeping molasses dealer, murdered him and dismembered his body. They removed his heart, cut it into sections and divided it amongst themselves.

After the murder of the molasses salesman, the police often visited Muhammad's house. He blamed the library for his difficulties and lodged some of the volumes with a Coptic priest. His mother burned others for fuel. Some were sold for pennies to neighbors. A one-eyed local criminal named Bahy Ali managed to buy up most of the remaining texts and brought them to Cairo, where they were eventually acquired by the Coptic museum. In the meantime, the substantial Codex 1 had been smuggled out of Egypt by one Albert Eid, a Belgian art dealer who feared its confiscation by Nasser's new government. Eid hawked the Codex to the Bollingen Foundation and the Bibliothéque Nationale, to no effect. In 1952, after Eid's death, the Codex was acquired by the Jung Institute and presented to Carl Jung. Later, it, too, passed into the hands of the Coptic museum in Cairo. The next twenty years were a disgraceful, ignominious battle between rival groups of scholars. All of this is par for the course when it comes to sacred objects and sacred texts.

• • •

Gnõsis is a knowledge possessed of a revelatory force and rooted in a recognition of one's true self.

• • •

The night before inspiration told me that I had to save myself, find *salvation*, by bidding farewell to my false life through the murder of that man, I dreamed that I was embracing the corpse of the Savior.

• • •

Not long ago, Poppy Z. Brite ruffled a feather or two by publishing in her newsletter a lengthy meditation on the subject of an erotic encounter between herself and the mortal remains of William Burroughs. Burroughs, one cannot but think, would have been delighted.

• • •

At the center of its anarchic heart, the idea of narrative yearns simultaneously for wholeness and fracture. We begin in one place and time, we shift to another. Roughly, imperiously, we shift back. We catch up with ourselves, or we do not. It is satisfying when we do, but better, far better, when we scrap thoughtless versions of coherence. Jokes, anecdotes, and shaggy-dog stories, undermine lazy expectations, so let us sprinkle in any number of bafflements to the humorless. For the literal-minded, let us float the suggestion of a "theme:" the "theme," say, of "possession." We may safely assume the failure on behalf of the literal-minded to recognize that every encounter with a text represents an act of "possession." As the reader devours the text, the text inexorably colonizes the reader, who is, unlike the devouring text, altered by this process, in large part by means of that truest, most infallible expression of "theme," the detail. As a result, every vibrant detail contains an erotic component.

• • •

There is much more in eroticism than we are at first led to believe.

Today, no one recognizes that eroticism is an insane world whose depths, far beyond its ethereal forms, are infernal.

...Eroticism is first of all the most moving of realities; but it is nonetheless, at the same time, the most ignoble. Even after psychoanalysis, the contradictory aspects of eroticism appear in some way innumerable, their

profundity is religious—it is horrible, it is tragic, it is still inadmissible. Probably all the more so since it is divine.
—*The Tears of Eros,* George Bataille

• • •

"God is in the details," wrote Flaubert, who once took the time to have a pharmacist named M. Homais take in the billowing of Emma Bovary's clothing before the glow of a wood stove.

Here are three details from these stories:

It was a semi-automatic pistol with a six-inch sighted barrel and a checkered grip of heavy rubber, nearly three pounds of sleek steel filled with little silver-jacketed bullets like seeds in a deadly fruit. ("Saved.")

It was like some enormous steaming bowl of stew, full of glistening meat, splintered bone, great handfuls of tubes torn loose from their moorings, and everywhere the rich coppery sauce of blood. The sewer smell of ruptured bowel rose in shimmering waves from his body. ("Saved.")

In the streets, the harsh reek of exhaust fumes was filled with a million subtler perfumes: jasmine, raw sewage, grasshoppers frying in peppered oil, the odor of ripe durian fruit that was like rotting flesh steeped in thick sweet cream. ("Self-Made Man.")

In "Vine of the Soul," a shaggy-dog story, the crowd on a street in Amsterdam moves in the "peristalsis" of waste through the intestines; "In Vermis Veritas," a bubble of pure inspiration written as an Introduction to a graphic novel, presents the rapturous meditations of a "connoisseur of mortality," a highly conscious maggot devoted to the piquant memory-sensations embedded within "the translucent rose of fresh viscera, the seething indigo of rot" of those who died fearfully and in pain. The maggot is a reader for once gloriously empowered to stand in the place of the writer.

Are You Loathsome Tonight?

• • •

Who, if I cried out, would hear me among the angels' hierarchies? and even if one of them pressed me suddenly against his heart: I would be consumed in that overwhelming existence. For beauty is nothing but the beginning of terror, which we are still just able to endure, and we are so awed because it serenely disdains to annihilate us. Every angel is terrifying.

—"The First Elegy," *Duino Elegies*, Rainer Maria Rilke, translated by Stephen Mitchell

• • •

I dreamed of embracing the dead Jesus in that Tomb, no more than a cave, actually. His small, wounded body seemed extraordinarily beautiful to me, for it registered every trace of his journey toward crucifixion: the hard calluses on the foot-soles, the legacy of anger written across the forehead, the harsh, knife-like furrows at the corners of the eyes, the grime embedded into the folds of the knuckles. And, of course, the wounds.

I touched every inch, every micro-millimeter of his body, and under my hands, his body spoke. The language in which it spoke was *Braille*. His body was a *sacred text*. By slow explorations of my fingertips, tongue, eyelids, lips, by awed, sensitive tissue of my cheeks and my nipples, also the aureolae and undersides of my breasts, also by the delicate kiss of my labia, I read of an *abominable grandeur*.

His body was sturdy, banded with muscle like the body of a mule, a peasant's body, its Mediterranean complexion tinged with the green of a Levantine olive. His coloring, lightest on the palms of his hands, darkest about the knees, elbows and scrotal sack, was that of a meal prepared over a desert campfire, and the smell of his flesh suggested sand, blazing sun, smoky cook-fires built on the sides of salty lakes.

That was the most erotic dream I've ever had, even though it was all about *knowledge*.

Braille is a two-way street.

Transfigured, I woke up to a transfigured world.

• • •

The world is a corpse-eater. All the things eaten in it themselves die also. Truth is a life-eater. Therefore no one nourished by [truth] will die.

...God [...] a garden. Man [...] garden. There are [...] and [...] of God. [...] The things which are in [...] I wish. This garden [is the place where they will say to me, "...eat] this or do not eat [that, just as you] wish." In the place where I will eat all things is the tree of knowledge.

—"The Gospel of Philip," in *The Nag Hammadi Library.*

Secret Windows
Introduction

Let us deal with a potential embarrassment, or what may seem at least a conflict of interest, right away. In this companion book to *On Writing,* my name pops up often enough to suggest that Stephen King may have adopted the remuneration system perfected by the late Pee Wee Marquette, a diminutive, klaxon-voiced gentleman long ago employed by a jazz club called Birdland to announce the names of the musicians onstage, and who gleefully performed this function as long as the musicians in question slipped him a couple of bucks. In "Horror Fiction," excerpted from the thoughtful *Danse Macabre,* King devotes a lengthy run of pages to Ghost Story, a novel I wrote in my boyhood. During the course of the 1998 interview at the Royal Festival Hall, King responds to a question about the uncharacteristic eroticism in *Bag of Bones* by alluding to an ancient remark of mine, made in his presence, that "Stevie hasn't discovered sex yet." (He also calls me "a really good friend" and mentions that he once got lost while trying to find my house in Crouch End,

London N8, an experience he found so unsettling that he wrote a story in which that amiable little pocket of London is transformed into a Lovecraftian Hell.) My name is invoked in a couple of other pieces, too. Under the Pee Wee Marquette system, all of this would have set me back an unimaginable amount of money, an incalculable fortune, probably something like twenty-five smackers.

Of course, it set me back nothing at all, although I have no doubt that a number of King's fellow-writers would be delighted to give him a couple of dollars for uttering their names on the sorts of occasions represented by the pieces in this collection. The very fact of this book testifies to Stephen King's extraordinary popularity and the influence of his works and opinions upon the reading public. He is one of the very few living novelists—among them, Tom Clancy and John Grisham—with a mass following so devoted that its individual members may be addressed as "Constant Reader," and the only one actually to do so.

King's habit of directly addressing the reader is noteworthy for several reasons. Every writer blessed with an enormous, true-blue readership made up of people who will buy each new work of his or her fiction as it tumbles from the presses, who will buy anything that has their favorite author's name stamped on the cover and in fact have been checking their calendars and lining up at the bookstore to badger the clerks as to the exact day and hour of the latest tome's arrival, has earned this devotion by giving the fans precisely what they most want. If you want patriotic derring-do swaddled in the niceties of high-tech weaponry, you buy the new Tom Clancy; if you are looking for entertaining hugger-mugger involving a lot of attorneys, you pick up the new Grisham. (Clancy's formula is so impersonal that it has been successfully farmed out to the other writers responsible for the "Clancy's Psy-Ops" series; John Grisham executed a very different but no less difficult feat, that of getting better and better as he went along without alienating his admirers.) On four or five occasions in the present book, Stephen King pauses to explain that, at heart, he really does like to scare people, no matter how strange it might sound, and we could easily assume that his millions of fans faithfully purchase his books because they enjoy being scared.

It's true, King does like the idea of frightening people—while making the movie *Maximum Overdrive,* he told me that he wanted the audience to crawl out of theaters with Jujubes in their hair. And lots of people get a kick out of spicing up their lives with controlled doses of safe, manageable fear. Yet King has always been after bigger game than Clancy, Grisham, or any other bestselling brand-name author, and he moved on from writing immediately classifiable horror fiction two decades ago, with *The Dead Zone.* Since then, his work has bounced from genre to genre, taking in fantasy (the *Dark Tower* books and *The Eyes of the Dragon*), and science fiction (*The Tommyknockers*), mainstream fiction (*Misery, Gerald's Game,* and *Dolores Claiborne*), and the coming-of-age story ("The Body"), as well as departing from any known genre altogether in wild-eyed, mythic excursions like *Insomnia* and *Rose Madder.* Of course, every one of these novels was categorized as horror immediately upon publication, because that is what reviewers are like: they think in terms of categories and straight lines, and once they have you labeled, you might as well be branded, because you will wear that label forever. Leaving aside for a moment the question of King's larger ambitions, which are robust, and granting that his audience has been cozied into the assumption that his primary objective is to deliver terrors the way Danielle Steel dishes out molasses, we might consider the many other reliable terror-deliverers now busily writing away and wonder why their careers are not as spectacular as Stephen King's.

The obvious answer, merit or quality, is not helpful, since some of these writers, like Jack Ketchum, Thomas

Tessier, Ramsey Campbell, and Graham Joyce, are deeply persuasive, in their individual ways as good as any writer can be. In his Introduction to *The Girl Next Door,* Steve describes Ketchum as "a kind of hero to those of us who write tales of terror and suspense...His work lives in a way that the work of his better-known literary colleagues cannot even approach—I am thinking of such disparate novelists as William Kennedy, E. L. Doctorow, and Norman Mailer." (A little while later, he throws in the aside that "other than poetry, the suspense novel has been the most fruitful form of artistic expression in America's post-Vietnam years," a comment rooted in a point of view central to our present concerns.) If Jack Ketchum's work is more vibrant, more living than Kennedy's, Doctorow's, or Mailer's, why hasn't he achieved their popularity, if not that of King, to whom he is "a kind of hero"? Of course, those three writers never came close to achieving King's level of popularity, either. For all their indisputable strengths, they were either unable to connect, or uninterested in connecting, with their readers as directly as King, with his startling immediacy. When this writer speaks to "Constant Reader," legions of people take it personally. They look at the phrase and see their own names.

The catchword for King's approach to the reader used to be "accessibility," but "immediacy" rings truer. Robert B. Parker and Lawrence Block are entirely accessible, but neither of them seems to drift up from the page and wrap an arm over the reader's shoulders, as King does. For their own reasons—Parker's adherence to a greatly modified "hard-boiled," Chandleresque model, Block's aestheticism—they adopt other stances. In King's case, the illusory obliteration of the inevitable distance between narrator and reader is an instinctive gesture that creates a companionable, avuncular tone. We could say, the tone of a pure storyteller, unpretentious to the core, apparently selfless, emotionally incapable of lying and therefore utterly trustworthy. This voice is one of King's most potent inventions and may be part of what he had in mind when he told me, on two or three occasions in the early eighties, that he always knew he had this big, big cash register in his head, and all he had to do was figure out how it worked. (We'll get to the question of cash registers later.) Take the two-sentence paragraph at the beginning of the third piece in this book, the Foreword to *Night Shift.*

Let's talk, you and I. Let's talk about fear.

With its deliberate repetition of the first two words, its gliding but insistent rhythm, and its movement from the colloquial contraction of "Let's" to the abrupt shock of the final noun, this flourish is literary to the core. We could be listening to a nice bit of introductory throat-clearing on the part of some great Victorian stage manager like Thackeray or Wilkie Collins. However, these two short sentences do not sound at all literary because they represent that friendliest of all communications, the invitation. The next two sentences extend the invitation by welcoming us into the writer's house:

The house is empty as I write this; a cold February rain is falling outside. It's night.

In the next paragraph, our host takes us into the kitchen, pours us a drink, hands us a bowl of nuts, rolls up his sleeves, and gets confidential in a low-key, supremely unthreatening way.

> My name is Stephen King. I am a grown man with a wife and three children. I love them, and I believe the feeling is reciprocated. My job is writing, and it's a job I like very much...At this point in my life I seem to be reasonably healthy. In the last year I have been able to reduce my cigarette habit from the unfiltered brand I had smoked since I was eighteen to a low nicotine

> and tar brand, and I still hope to be able to quit completely. My family and I live in a pleasant house beside a relatively unpolluted lake in Maine; last fall I awoke one morning and saw a deer standing on the back lawn by the picnic table. We have a good life.

All right. So here is a working joe named Stephen King, who has a family, an okay house, and a satisfying job, sort of like meter-reading or muffler repair, except it involves writing. He could live a couple of houses down the street, if your street were contiguous to a large body of water in the state of Maine. The point of the drink, the nuts, and rolled-up sleeves is their comforting distance from *fear*, the last word of the first paragraph, but a remarkable quantity of unease peeks out from behind the comfort. Any assertion akin to "I am a grown man…" instantly evokes its own contradiction by supplying a silent "not," especially when the assertion is extraneous. (Don't the wife and three children automatically make him an adult?) He "seems" to be "reasonably healthy," although his cigarette habit (now conquered) represents the threat of death by cancer. The nice lake is only "relatively" free of contamination. Fear has already entered the conversation, for this down-to-earth, homespun fellow, our host, had no choice but to let it in.

Although most readers and a surprising number of writers cherish a literary version of free will, from early on, King understood that subject matter selects the writer instead of the other way around. This determinism is experiential, not pessimistic, and realistic, not fatalistic. It is grounded in deep common sense, like a sense of humor. King knows that the only sensible answer to the question as to why he wishes to squander his talent on topic like brutalized women and possessed automobiles is, as he says here, *Why do you assume that I have a choice?*

The idea of *having been chosen* extends to both writing, described first as a "hobby," then, more frankly, as "obsessional behavior," and it its underlying aesthetic principles. King tells us, *My obsession is with the macabre,* and *I am not a great artist, but I have always felt impelled to write.* "Always"; "impelled"; an almost undetectable trace of fear hovers about these words—what would happen if one day he found he could not write?; and, were it not for King's straightforward disavowal, they would seem to point to a conventionally Romantic conception of artistic creativity. But King, for whom truth is a complicated and essential matter, is merely going about the unusual business of telling it as well as he knows how, and what he is really pointing to comes out with the authority of deep conviction:

> All my life as a writer I have been committed to the idea that in fiction the story value holds dominance over every other face of the writer's craft; characterization, theme, mood, none of those things is anything if the story is dull. And if the story does hold you, all else can be forgiven.

King is hardly kidding around here—not only is he being as direct and honest as it is possible to be, he is advocating an aesthetic which is itself based on honesty and directness. What he calls "story value" is the foundation of all narrative ventures, the bedrock upon which everything else is constructed. A dyed-in-the-wool fundamentalist at least in this one regard, King has no patience with writers who foreground technique, style of one kind or another, thematic play, misdirection, ambiguity, or even depth of characterization at the expense of narrative's most basic element. What matters most is story, story, story. A vital, entertaining story renders bad or clumsy writing irrelevant. I guess this means that *Sister Carrie* makes a more valid claim than *The Wings of the Dove* and that *The Good Soldier* cannot measure up to *The Postman Always Rings Twice.* I cannot agree with this value system, but I have no problem with it, either. Writers and works of fiction should be considered on their own internal merits, not ranked like tennis players, and King has, in any case, merely inverted the conventional and inherently restrictive concept of literary value, which he is more than entitled to do.

A short passage from the essay "Turning the Thumbscrews on the Reader," picks up a theme from the Foreword to *Night Shift,* King's refusal to define himself as a "great artist," and pushes it toward an explicit statement of its embedded significance.

> I'm not any big-deal fancy writer. If I have any virtue it's that I know that. I don't have the ability to write the dazzling prose line. All I can do is entertain people. I think of myself as an American writer.

The last, stunning sentence permits us to paraphrase this passage as follows:

> My greatest virtue is that I know better than to evade my responsibilities by the useless exercise of trying to write fancy prose. I entertain people by giving them good stories dealing with the content of ordinary American lives, which is in the best, truest tradition of American fiction.

The tradition, that is, of Frank Norris, the late-nineteenth-century American Naturalist and author of *McTeague,* whom King praises twice in this collection. Like Norris, King is absorbed by the nuts and bolts of ordinary American lives, those defined by the "iconography" of the "housing developments, TV dinners and McDonald's."

Show-offy prose is the province of the rootless effete; story, the meat and potatoes of fiction's meat and potatoes, radically democratizes all it touches. King knows perfectly well that he can write dazzling prose anytime dazzle is called for. Here are some examples:

> The warm October wind gusted strongly and great shades of light and shadow seemed to pass across the world.
>
> —*The Dead Zone*

> The hole opened and Paul stared through at what was there, unaware that his fingers were picking up speed, unaware that his aching legs were in the same city but fifty blocks away, unaware that he was weeping as he wrote.
>
> —*Misery*

> She does not come here to worship or to pray, but she has a sense of rightness and ritual about being here, a sense of duty fulfilled, of some unstated covenant's renewal.
>
> —*Rose Madder*

And, my favorite, this extraordinary bit of observation from the terrified victim of an attack by a huge, maddened dog:

> Starlight ran across Cujo's mad eyes in dull semicircles.
>
> —*Cujo*

The first time I read that, I forgot to breathe for a couple of seconds. Shortly after finishing the book, I wrote Steve that *Cujo* amounted to an excellent battering ram, if you had something you felt like battering, but I have remembered that sentence ever since. It may not be dazzling prose, exactly, yet to have your frightened heroine take in the movement of starlight reflected in her crazed attacker's eyes represents a pure act of imagination, and if such visionary feats do not inform one's conception of superior prose, the conception is insufficient.

As it began, the *Night Shift* Foreword ends with an invitation. In a nice touch of craftsmanship, it refers back to the beginning before leading Constant Reader into engagement with the book's contents in a way that combines reassurance with a well-modulated menace.

> Where I am, it's still dark and raining. We've got a fine night for it. There's something I want to show you, something I want you to touch. It's in a room not far from here---in fact, it's almost as close as the next page.
>
> Shall we go?

Of course we will go, for the next room is the true interior of the household, its center, our host's workshop. The short stories contained in the workshop are the reason we purchased the book, but besides that, in the paragraph preceding his final invitation King has cemented the bond between us by thanking, with his characteristic directness,

> each and every reader who ever unlimbered his or her wallet to buy something that I wrote. In a great many ways, this is your book because it sure never would have happened without you. So thanks.

He thanks us for buying our admission ticket. The book we will read is our book, and but for us it would never have been written. Performers of a certain (pre-MTV) cast like Tony Bennett and Rosemary Clooney invariably end their shows by saying, "You've been a great audience," an assertion that pleases and warms each successive crowd of spectators despite their knowing that Tony and Rosie said the same thing the previous night, when other people occupied their seats. Marilyn Manson and Trent Reznor, I'm sure, rarely tell their paying fans they've been great, but Frank Sinatra and Duke Ellington always did, and so do all kinds of jazz musicians whose work, for all its pungent immediacy, may be less accessible for a general audience.

Writers, on the other hand, never do this kind of thing. They shake hands and mutter thanks at book signings, and that is about as far as it goes. When asked, bribed, or coerced, writers will tell other writers how great they are in introductions and afterwords to small-press productions, in the process adding value to the books in question, but direct stage-to-audience, or in this case, desk-to-armchair, communication is usually considered out of bounds, a no-no. It feels faintly undignified, since fiction is supposed to make its case by itself. Also, it destroys the mysterious but crucial fourth wall, the one that keeps the rabble from trampling into the workshop. King's blithe dismissal of the typical punctilio establishes an unprecedented intimacy between himself and his readers. One effect of this intimacy has been that his fans feel as close to him as J. D. Salinger's do to their idol, in fact so close that King had to erect a tall iron fence around his property in Bangor to keep people from strolling in through the front door with boxes of books they wished to be autographed, preferably with a comradely inscription.

Another consequence of this intimacy has been the deep loyalty of King's readers. His expressions of gratitude resound with a sincerity as genuine as Liberace's, who after parading onstage in a floor-length ermine coat and twirling around to a chorus of admiring sighs used to say, "Do you like this? I wore it for YOOUUU!," and meant every single word. Those middle-aged and elderly women in the audience knew that the fur-swaddled, jewel-bedecked gentleman before them, who had begun as a working class Polish boy from Milwaukee, was delighted to share his success with the fans who had made it possible. It is not difficult to imagine Liberace saying something like, "I have enough sense to recognize that I'm no big-deal pianist, but I know how to entertain."

What is at stake is a granite-ribbed populism that inspires identification. Steve King wears T-shirts instead of floor-length ermine wraps, and although he does possess many handsome sports jackets, his brand of sartorial magic turns them into lumpy resale-fodder the second he rams his arms into the sleeves. He has other ways of sharing his success, of which he is justifiably proud, and the unprecedented essay entitled "On Becoming a Brand Name," originally an introduction to a critical examination of his work, lays them out in plain view.

Success is a validation second to none, a proposition that holds true everywhere except in artistic circles. The Dave Brubeck Quartet fell out of critical favor soon after Brubeck appeared on the cover of *Time* magazine. (Paul Desmond, the quartet's alto saxophone player and most vital musician, said, "We used to play for jazz fans, now we just play for people.") Somerset Maugham's literary reputation declined relentlessly as more and more people bought his books, and by the time he complained of being in "the first rank of the second-raters," most critics had in fact consigned him to the third or fourth rank, where the makers of potboilers dwell. Now, Brubeck was always a mediocre jazz piano player, and even at his best Maugham was never anything more than an extremely skillful second-rater, but Paul Desmond, a very great and idiosyncratic artist, was tarred with the same brush as his employer-partner and failed to gain adequate critical recognition until years after his death. In the arts, commercial popularity has no direct bearing on quality, but neither, despite all evidence to the contrary, does it guarantee inferiority. This assumption, that success = meretriciousness, has dogged King all of his writing life and lies behind much of the Aw Shucks attitude he expresses here and there in this volume.

(The funniest of the Aw Shucks moments occurs in "How *It* Happened":

> I'm not a bright novelist, no Graham Greene or Paul Bowles…I'm a storyteller, my virtues are honest, good intent, and the ability to entertain people of my own level of intellect.

Stephen King for Dummies, now available at your local megamall? The fact is, Steve is one of the smartest people I've ever met, one of the smartest people on the *planet*, and he knows that saying stuff like this will keep category-minded critics at bay even while it serves as comfort food to his fans. Still, the equation written above cannot help but rankle him, and you can find a number of passages here in which he permits himself to sound off.)

Writers open their account books in public even more rarely than they thank readers for pulling out their wallets, and King's frankness in "On Becoming a Brand Name" would make this essay unsettling were it not for the unhurried confidence of its voice. It should be called "With Figures." I can't think of another novelist, especially a world-famous one, who would open up his own professional history so thoroughly. The essay, King says, "is an attempt to explain how it happened that I made a great deal of money writing novels about ghosts, telekinesis, vampires, and the end of the world." Success is a surefire validation of itself, anyhow, and King takes pride in his capacities as a proven breadwinner. As the essay makes clear, he did not begin that way: he is as honest about the conditions of his early penury as he is about the size of the checks that rescued him from it.

King's instincts are right, as they say, on the money. We *should* know that in the first year of his marriage he had an infant daughter and $60-a week job in a Laundromat, and that his wife, the glorious Tabitha Spruce King, came home from her shift at Dunkin' Donuts "smelling like a cruller." When he finally managed to get a $6,400-a-year teaching position, his family, by then expanded to four, occupied a trailer. He drank too much; he could not pay his bills; they lost their telephone. He wrote four unpublishable novels. *Four* of them. Imagine the unrelenting effort, eked out an hour at a time when the papers had been graded and babies had fallen asleep; imagine the thousands of sheets of cheap typing paper cranked into the old Underwood, its ribbon, daily, growing grayer and fainter. Imagine the sheer willpower. Imagine the compounding heartbreak. (No wonder King likes Frank Norris. When you think about his life at that time, you can smell the dirty diapers, not to mention the electrical-fire stench of desperation.) King came to his populism honestly, and his satisfaction at putting food on the table was earned the hard way. No one raised poor, as King was, and who endured poverty through early adulthood, can (1) ever forget it; (2) ever make enough money; (3) ever think he is better than anyone else just because he finally made a lot of it.

King gives us the amount of his advances for his first four published novels ($2,500 for the Doubleday hardback of *Carrie,* $400,000 for its New American Library paperback reprint), their sales figures, the places they reached on bestseller lists, and their prices in hardback and softcover editions. He describes the origins of the novels, thereby answering for once and all time the eternal question, "Where do you get your ideas?" The whole endless, private process of conceiving a novel, beginning to write, losing faith, trying again, giving up, trying yet again, talking things over with your closest companion, getting sudden descents of inspiration, dealing with editors and the whimsical vagaries of publishers, comes through from a consistently sea-level perspective, inch by inch, as if painted by Jan van Eyck. King's account of working with the brilliant Doubleday editor Bill Thompson is one of the best descriptions of the quirky editor-author relationship I have ever read. Of Thompson's initial work on *Carrie*, King says:

> [His] ideas worked so well that it was almost dreamlike. It was as if he had seen the corner of a treasure chest protruding from the sand and unerringly driven stakes at the probable boundaries of the buried mass.

I know that to be true, because a few years later Bill Thompson migrated over to Putnam, where he performed the same sorcery on one of my books. When I learned that Bill was going to be my editor, I called Steve for a consultation. He told me, "Bill can see what's wrong, and he knows how to fix it." No writer can ask for more from an editor, and most settle for much less.

"On Becoming a Brand Name" democratizes the process of writing and publication by means of radical demystification. King raises the hood and lets us see the engine at work. He describes publishing lunches, conferences with New American Library's art director, and the completely unglamorous realities of a working novelist's life. In words that should be blazoned across the blackboard at the beginning of every creative-writing course, whether undergraduate or part of an MFA program, he writes, "You keep pretty regular hours—that is, if you want to get anything done." The fundamental assumption of this dead-level remark is that writing fiction is a job like any other, and must be done honestly and well. And the basis of any such conviction is that writing done honestly and well carries its own weight, regardless of genre or (vulgar) popularity. Quietly, at the level of the lowest frequencies, King is offering an implicit rebuttal to a notion he finds elitist, absurd, and insulting, that successful commercial fiction *by definition* must be inferior to fiction of other sorts. Truthfulness—truthfulness of a specific kind—grants any work of fiction authenticity, strength, and dignity, King believes, and a popular commercial writer faces a greater temptation to fudge than his more "literary" colleagues, due to his consciousness of how an artificial turn or change of direction would gratify his audience, should he impose it upon the living story.

Truth is a loaded concept to writers of fiction, who are always aware that their occupation consists of telling one flagrant lie after another. At a conference in Florida where I was a guest of honor a few years ago, I mentioned in the course of my laborious post luncheon vaporings that nothing I said should be taken very seriously, because after all I told lies for a living. (Unconsciously, I was quoting Steve King. A decade earlier, our families had met in Boston to spend Thanksgiving together, and at one point, while we were all leaving the hotel to walk over to the Aquarium, Steve's son Joe asked me who I thought was the greatest person who ever lived. "It's a toss-up," I said. "Either Louis Armstrong or Warren Spahn. You can hardly tell them apart, anyhow." With a disaffected glance at me Steve said, "Remember, Joe—that man tells lies for a living.") After I had finally shut up and wandered away from the podium, Brian Aldiss, who is several inches taller than King and about a foot taller than I am, besides being twice as distinguished as either one of us, came barreling up to me, looking even more disgruntled than Steve on that November day in Boston. "What d'ye mean," Brian thundered, "saying you lie for a living? Don't you agree that we are meant to tell the TRUTH?" I assured him, with no sense of contradicting myself, that I did agree, of course.

The answer to this conundrum lies in the difference between invention and discovery. Let us say that you are beginning the third chapter of a novel called *Death in Ventura,* or maybe *The Magic Mole Hill,* concerning the descent into crime and ill-health of a poor fellow named Hansi Ashbach. Hansi embarked upon the long slide downhill in the previous chapter, number Two, in which he failed to tip the waiter who served his lunchtime *choucroute garni* and deliberately gave the wrong directions to a crippled Tibetan monk. Now he is ready for terrorism on a slightly larger scale. In his left hand, he is carrying a plastic bag containing a half pound of ground chuck and a small box of rat poison. Hansi feels a bit giddy, and so do you. You know what is going to take place in your big climax, when Hansi make a savage escape from the hospital ward where his illness had landed him, and you know what happens at the end, when Hansi dies at sunset on the beach at Ventura, coughing feebly as from the depths of a folding beach chair he ogles a strapping young female volleyball player. All you have to do is work out the in-between bits.

This is your big chance. You feel it in your bones, your gut. Previously, you have published little: two stories on the Internet, another in a fugitive horror'zine called *Whatever You're Doing Up There, Stop It Right Now!,* and a poem in the college lit mag. But this book…boy, if you don't mess it up, this book is going to change your life. You'll be able to get a famous agent, like Lynn Borchardt or Georges Nesbit, who right away will sell it for a half-million-dollar advance to a famous publishing house like Farrar, Simon & Collins or Harper, Holt & Giroux. George Spielberg will buy the film rights for two million big ones even before it jumps onto the bestseller list.

Peter Straub

You've captured lightning in a bottle, you have a tiger on a leash! From here on out, life is going to be cocktails with John Amis and Irving Theroux, chummy dinners with Stephen Koontz, Clive Dean, and Anne Rampling!

Chapter Three, you type at the top of your screen, trying to imagine what Hansi does next. What *is* he doing? He is walking down the street, that's what, on the way to the house of his ex-girlfriend, Gretel, whose drooling, rheumy-eyed, fang-equipped bull terrier, Maximillian, he intends to put out of its misery. Type, type, type. In a series of deft little strokes, you march your tragic hero up the street to the end of the block, where, for some reason, you notice the presence of an attractive young female in Capri pants and a halter top standing, her back to your hero, on the curb and waiting for the light to change. Cars stream by. Hansi advances; he moves to within a foot of the young woman, who continues to stare straight ahead.

You know in your heart of hearts that it is too early for Hansi to murder someone. These things must be prepared for, they must be built up to. On the other hand, he's going to starting killing people sooner or later, and might as well begin with a nice-looking young woman in Capri pants. On the same other hand, readers, at least the kind of readers you want to ensnare, enjoy murders, the more bloodshed they get, the jollier they are, just look at the career of Thomas Barker King-Harris, for heaven's sake. You type, and Hansi raises his hand, not the one holding the plastic bag, the other one. You raise your own hands, stare down at the keyboard, then touch the keys again.

If what you write is:

> Hansi tucks his lower lip between his front teeth and pushes his hand into the cross-web of the halter top, shoving the girl off the curb and into the traffic.

you are inventing, and should you ever manage to get your book published at all, it will be via a scandalous, money-grubbing, low-rent outfit called something like Donner Pass Press, and you will squander your two-thousand-dollar advance on crack cocaine and wind up living on the street.

If, on the *other* other hand, you write:

> Hansi holds his hand three inches from the strap of her halter top and watches it tremble like a mouse cornered by a snake. The girl sighs and shifts her weight to one foot, causing the subtle misalignment like a gently slanting curve to the spinal indentations in the suntanned skin rising out of the waistband of her Capri pants. A current, a series of sparks, runs from a starfish-shaped area in the center of the girl's back and into the palm of his hand. His palm tingles under the bombardment of the invisible sparks. He tucks his lower lip between his front teeth and closes his hand, then lowers it to his side.
>
> The girl glances over her shoulder. "Don't you just hate this darn light?"
>
> "No," Hansi says. "I'm quite fond of the color red."
>
> "Hey, you have a cute accent!" the girl says. "Where are you from, like, Europe?"
>
> "Swabia," Hansi lies. "It is in Europe, yes. Rather near the vicinity of Herzegovina."

then you are discovering, not inventing, and within a minute or two you will realize that the reason the girl was standing on that corner was to become not a nameless murder victim but your hero's companion and love interest, and a valuable new element in your story. You may not get rich and famous, but at least you permitted yourself to tell the truth.

In two of the three transcribed interviews collected here, "Banned Books and Other Concerns," and "A Night at the Royal Festival Hall," King addresses the question of truth and uses the same accurate expression both times.

Virginia Beach, 1986:

> In other words, what I'm talking about is telling the truth. Frank Norris, who wrote *The Pit, McTeague,* and other naturalistic novels that were banned, said: "I don't fear; I don't apologize because I know in my heart that I never lied; I never truckled. *I told the truth."* And I think the real truth of fiction is that fiction is the truth; moral fiction is the truth inside the lie. And if you lie in your books, you are immoral and have no business writing at all.

Royal Festival Hall, 1998:

> You have to be brave to do this job. If you're not going to tell the truth, why do it? My God, fiction is a lie. If you can't find the truth inside the lie, you're being immoral. You're not being true to yourself.

The truth inside the lie, a phrase Stephen King carried around within himself during the twelve years between these speaking engagements, can be found only in fiction, which is the best reason for reading it. Since his adolescence, King has understood that fiction's enthralling tissue of lies represents one of mankind's surest paths to the spiritual windows which look out onto the specific, soul-enlarging realities of our shared humanity. Why did dull semicircles of starlight run across the gigantic dog's mad eyes? Because the dog was twisting his head, a detail you must strip yourself naked to see.

Hope to Die
An Appreciation of the Scudder Series

The fifteenth of Lawrence Block's crime novels to be centered on the idiosyncratic private investigator Matthew Scudder, *Hope to Die* represents all the remarkable and various strengths of this ongoing series through a kind of understatement available only to an absolute master of the genre. That Block had indeed achieved mastery of his form was given symbolic recognition by his receipt of the Mystery Writers of America's greatest honor, the Grand Master award, in 1994, by which time his protean talent had distinguished him as among the finest writers in his field for something like two decades.

Very early in his career, Block decided to express himself through a number of different protagonists, each with his own individual voice and persona. He may not really have known that Matt Scudder, Bernie Rhodenbarr, Evan Tanner, and Keller, to name only the most prominent of his series heroes, would occupy him for longer than a single book, but it is certain that he wished to avoid the confinement, not to mention the probability of eventual boredom, of spending his entire life writing about the same person in book after book. Boredom and a sense of confinement—of possibilities diminishing within a calcifying formula—threaten any writer wedded to a single series hero or heroine. Rex Stout managed to stay crisp as a snap-pea for five decades of annual visits to Nero Wolfe's brownstone, but his level of consistency over time is matched only by P. G. Wodehouse, whose Drones' Club and Blandings Castle have more in common with Stout's changeless brownstone than may be immediately apparent.

Sooner or later, most writers who choose to work within the limitations enforced by the narrow aperture of a single protagonist wind up feeling restricted, especially if their ambitions go beyond the kind of serene domesticity many readers find profoundly reassuring. It is the responses to their dissatisfactions that define them. Some writers fall silent, some jump ship, and some, the saddest, most dispiriting cases, lapse into reflexive self-parody. (Seeing a once-interesting writer hollowing out his own name book by book is pretty gloomy, but it's nothing compared to the misery of realizing that he can't tell what is going on and supposes everything to be just dandy.) Raymond Chandler addressed his growing dissatisfaction with Philip Marlowe by means of a magisterial act of imagination: while writing *The Long Good-Bye*, Chandler vaulted over his self-imposed limitations and gave Marlowe a greater depth of emotion than ever before, and his world a far richer and sadder palette. A brutal sense of loneliness spun out over a series of escalating betrayals elevates the book to that plateau where genre fiction and literature breathe the same air.

The most beautiful, most heartbreaking paragraph Chandler ever wrote is in *The Long Good-Bye*; it can be found on page 645 of the Library of America's *Chandler: Later Novels & Other Writing* and begins with Philip Marlowe feeling "as hollow and empty as the spaces between the stars." As he watches the traffic on Laurel

Canyon Boulevard, Marlowe and his author meditate upon "the big angry city":

> *...Twenty-four hours a day somebody is running, somebody else is trying to catch him. Out there in the city of a thousand crimes people were dying, being maimed, cut by flying glass, crushed against steering wheels or under heavy tires. People were being beaten, robbed, strangled, raped and murdered. People were...cruel, feverish, shaken by sobs. A city no worse than others, a city rich and vigorous and full of pride, a city lost and beaten and full of emptiness.*

I am tempted to say—Want to keep your detective series alive and vital? Simple. Write like that.

I am also tempted to say that the writers of crime novels divide into two opposing camps, those who have the sense to appreciate *The Long Good-Bye*, and those who see the book as a bloated, sentimental falling-off. These people usually prefer the less writerly, less humane Dashiell Hammett to Chandler. This, I am tempted to say, is an error, and the same people probably think that *Clifford Brown With Strings* is sentimental because it has violins on it—but setting aside temptation, the issue is more complicated than that; different kinds of temperament invoke differing tastes and standards; and the expressionistic minimalism of the Hammett-aesthetic is of course equal in validity to the warmer, more expansive Chandler-aesthetic. However, Larry Block is a friend of mine, and I know he really likes *The Long Good-Bye*. He is also fond of John O'Hara, in whose work sorrow is seldom farther away than the next bar stool.

Block is not temperamentally suited to fireworks, however downbeat, although he could undoubtedly pull them off if he ever felt like doing so. The Scudder novels contain a dozen or more passages in which the prose warms up momentarily, and for the space of a paragraph or two, and lifts itself out of context. Yet the customary ambient weather of a Scudder novel is cool and dry, and the customary attitude is one of observant, live-and-let-live detachment. It is all the more surprising, then, that the Scudder series should have evolved into the most emotionally powerful, and in fact, the most spiritually resonant, crime novels from the mid-eighties to the present day.

The Scudder books accumulated their resonance by being the repository for Lawrence Block's central feelings and concerns. If he chose to use different lead characters for the variety they permitted him, none of the others permitted anything like an equal access to himself. Evan Tanner ping-pongs around the globe, putting to use in compulsively addictive adventures the contacts and information acquired during the twenty-four hours of consciousness daily given him by a relentless sleep disorder; Keller, the meditative hit man, exists primarily as a tool for scraping away preconceptions about the moral lives of professional killers, also for indulging in a sort of pastel Blockian whimsy. (Because it's Blockian, the whimsy often opens its mouth to reveal alarmingly pointed teeth in jagged rows, like a shark's.) Bernie Rhodenbarr's exploits, the "Burglar" books, are overtly comic jabs in which the inversion of conventional morality serves as the foundation for hilariously Rube Golderg-like narrative structures. The Matt Scudder novels take place in another, much darker, universe.

Now we are faced with an odd paradox, that crime novels distinguished by a singular degree of detachment should take on an emotional resonance attained only very seldom—as in *The Long Good-Bye*—in this kind of fiction. One explanation lies in Block's prose style, which seems effortless in its deliberate restraint. A quiet, nearly transparent voice is speaking, generally in simple declarative sentences. Here are some examples from *Hope to Die*:

> *We ate at home and walked up Ninth to Lincoln Center.*
> *Mike ordered a Heineken's and I said I'd have a glass of Coke.*
> *I put the phone down and decided it was just as well he'd brushed me off.*

In a long-ago interview with Melvyn Bragg, Martin Amis said that the only thing that marred his admiration for his father's novels was Kingsley's tendency to produce sentences like "I picked up my drink and walked to the door." Saul Bellow and Vladimir Nabokov, his alternative, self-selected paternal figures, would never have settled for such mediocrity, he said, and neither, of course, would he. Martin Amis has great taste, and he's a wonderful writer, one without a trace of Lawrence Block's instinctive restraint. Twice, the first time during a Mystery Weekend at Mohonk Mountain House and several years later, I think in the midst of a party on Don Westlake's terrace, Larry told me that he had given up trying to read Dickens novels because every time he started one, the repeated phrases and tags annoyed him so much that he couldn't go on. All that verbal extravagance made him feel seasick. If Dickens had filled his pages with sentences like "Bill Sykes picked up his pint and staggered to the jakes," he would have had no trouble at all.

The truth is that the point-to-point aspect of Block's prose has a direct relationship to the level of feeling in his fiction. As Hemingway's first, radical stories famously made clear, stylistic simplicity is capable of communicating extremely powerful emotional states almost without reference to their causes. In Block's case, the march of declarative sentences in their journey down the page carries with it a freight of melancholy. The melancholy is unstated, but a lambent sadness colors every phrase, giving an emotional topspin to the pervasive sense of detachment.

In the first four Scudder novels, this melancholy seems to be the product of the hero's aimlessness—after having shot and killed a child named Estrellita Rivera, Scudder quit the police force, left his wife, children, and the family house on Long Island, and moved into a cheap hotel room in Hell's Kitchen, there to drift into investigative jobs while meandering from drink to drink. Alcohol soaks the pages, and Scudder frequents his heavy-drinking author's favorite bars. These books are worthy detective novels of the hard-boiled school, among the best of their kind, but they pale beside the fiction their author began to create once he declared himself an alcoholic and gave up drink for good.

At first, Larry once told me, he thought he would have to abandon Scudder as well, since his investigator seemed thoroughly embedded in the world he himself had just escaped. Speaking of the breakthrough that enabled him to retain the services of his favorite series hero, he said, "Then I figured out how to do it." *Eight Million Ways to Die* and *When the Sacred Ginmill Closes*, the following two Scudder novels, represent a high water mark in detective fiction and stand as testimony that crime writing, in this case the humble P.I. novel, can still attain the level of literature—that it can move beyond craft into art.

What Block figured out was that he could treat drinking retrospectively, by describing older cases from the standpoint of sobriety. In *Eight Million Ways to Die*, Scudder is mutely attending AA meetings and counting days while looking for the murderer of a prostitute who wanted out of the business. Alcohol is a constant and corrosive presence throughout the book; one of its emotional centerpieces is a horrifying account of Scudder's increasingly irrational justifications for a long slide into drunkenness that leads to blackout and hospitalization. Beginning by allowing himself two drinks a day, he soon figures out that if twelve hours has elapsed since the first one, he is in effect starting fresh, then rewards himself for his insight by making his new drink "a respectable one." He fills a water glass to within an inch of its top with bourbon and realizes that number, not size, is the crucial element, which means that his first drink was far too small. After redressing the shortfall, he feels too elated to stay in his apartment. A Coke at one bar and a ginger ale at another prove that he has his drinking under control, don't they? He goes into another bar and orders a double bourbon. "I remember the bartender had a shiny bald head, and I remember him pouring the drink, and I remember picking it up. That's the last thing I remember." Reading this passage is like watching someone decide to play Russian Roulette with a revolver that, instead of one full cylinder, has only a single empty one. Dread makes you want to avert your eyes. We no longer have need of Estrellita Rivera, who from here on out puts in merely token appearances in the Scudder books.

The world that surrounds our struggling detective in *Eight Million Ways to Die* is almost too frightening to reckon with when sober. The title refers to a brilliant series of paragraphs depicting weirdo homicides in the city of New York, murder by exploding television being the ripest example. Scudder himself nearly shoots a teenager who drives his car too close, and, in another of the book's emotional centerpieces, savagely beats and cripples a thug who picked the wrong victim. Violence and the threat of violence darken everything. Without the psychic protection of alcohol's comforting haze, the alcoholic feels as unprotected as a snail without a shell. Not even Scudder's tiny apartment is safe; at the book's climax, a naked, sexually aroused madman bursts out of his bathroom and charges towards him, brandishing a machete.

Unsurprisingly, the details of the plot recede into this atmosphere of raw desperation. Discovering the details and progressing step-by-step toward a final knowledge feels less like the actual center of the story than a metaphor for the narrator's own progress. The true center of the story is Scudder's helpless tropism toward alcohol and his fearful, deeply embattled vision; and the true climax comes in the novel's last sentence, when Scudder begins to weep after introducing himself as an alcoholic at an AA meeting.

In *When the Sacred Ginmill Closes*, the details of the plot carry more emotional weight, since two of the plot's three strands are rooted in taverns and after-hours bars. In fact, this triple plot is one of Block's best inventions, growing directly out of his detective's troubled existence in the days before his epiphany at the end of the previous novel. Scudder and the secondary characters spend hour upon hour getting drunk and then getting even drunker, especially when transfixed by the sodden wisdom of Dave Van Ronk's "Last Call," the song that provides the title. When Scudder hears Van Ronk sing

> *I broke my heart the other day*
> *It will mend again tomorrow.*
> *If I'd been drunk when I was born*
> *I'd be ignorant of sorrow.*

he immediately says, "Play that again."

Alcohol is both an occupation and a preoccupation. It is a therapeutic tool, a kind of medicine, a mystery, a sacrament. Its proper measure is the overdose. The act of drinking is voluptuous, luxurious, sacramental; in other words, sacred. Here, Scudder has not yet reached the unpeeled condition in which the previous book has found him, and AA meetings are still well in his future. He spends much of the book wandering from bar to bar, trying to work out the meanings of the narratives happening around him. And although the reverential boozing slows him down, Scudder does finally puzzle out the actual narrative that, underlying all the stories whirling about him, is their meaning, and lays it out for his fellow-characters and the reader in a You-may-be-wondering-why-I-asked-you-here moment that echoes, I think deliberately, the confrontation scene that concluded nearly every Nero Wolfe novel.

This scene resolves two of the novel's threads; Block resolves the third strand of the plot through a device unthinkable to most of his fellow private-eye novelists but perfectly consonant with the tone of his own work. The device is frankly criminal. When Scudder realizes that Tommy Tillary, a blowhard drinking buddy, has used him to disguise Tillary's culpability in the killing of his wife, he takes advantage of the suicide of Tillary's girlfriend to frame him for her murder. We are left in no doubt that the primary justification for the detective's skullduggery lies in his victim's offensiveness. Had Tillary not been a loudmouth and a heel—and had he left our narrator out of his machinations—he would very likely have stayed a free man. Scudder's morality incorporates a good deal of aestheticism. So, of course, did Hemingway's.

A novelist's moral sensibility tends to embed itself in his style, helplessly, and a style as chaste and conversational as Block's announces its aestheticism immediately. A morality grounded in aesthetics ignores conventional social judgments and classifications, so much so that it may appear perverse, topsy-turvy, and amoral. (On his American lecture tour, Oscar Wilde delighted his audiences because they thought his epigrams were ironic—which they were, but not in the way the silver miners in Leadville imagined.) Keller, after all, murders people for a living, and Bernie Rhodenbarr swipes trinkets from other people's houses. Their jobs are presented so neutrally that assassination and burglary become vehicles for the rebuke or condemnation of hypocrites, fools, poseurs, pretenders: the second-rate, like Tommy Tillary.

When the Sacred Ginmill Closes, perhaps Block's most powerful work, ends in a stunning reversal akin to the conclusion to a conversion narrative. With a smooth, sudden transition from the woozy past to the clear-eyed present and a burst of understated lyricism that expresses an overwhelming gratitude for the salvation of sobriety, Block manages also to suggest the sorrow of all that has been lost. Half of that sorrow is for the loss itself, no less than that of a familiar, well-known self and all its rituals, therefore devastating. When the old self has been discarded, its world goes with it.

So a new world must be created, furnished, and peopled around the new self with its new habits and rituals. For a while, apart from incorporating a good many AA meetings in church basements, Scudder's universe remains focused on his tiny hotel room and the bars scattered along seamy Ninth Avenue, but he drinks his coffee at a little restaurant called the Flame and in Greek diners, and he takes it without bourbon. And the people with whom he chooses to spend his time are quite different from his previous acquaintances.

• • •

Every contemporary detective series I can think of involves an ongoing cast of supporting players who re-enact their essential roles in book after book. As well as serving as foils to the hero, these characters provide a reassuring continuity to the reader. Like members of a family, they continually reiterate their primary traits; because they are not members of the reader's family, these traits work like comfort food. When Scudder's drinking buddies fall away, Block replaces them with three primary recurring characters, Mick Ballou, Elaine Mardell, and T. J. That is, in Blockian fashion: with a homicidal gangster, a whore, and a black teenage hustler from Times Square.

The most important of these, the gangster, appears simultaneously with sobriety in *Out on the Cutting Edge*, and Mick Ballou's capacity for implacable violence determines its tone and that of the next three Scudder novels. Ballou gives Block precisely what he most needs, a vehicle to express the rage aroused by everything that has been lost. (This comfort food comes laced with razor blades.) A cold, vivid anger unlike anything else in detective fiction animates these four novels, little by little granting their hero access to his own capacity for violence and sociopathy. A stunningly amoral darkness speaks from them, and Block's instinctive readiness to violate the conventions of his genre is a large part of what makes them so good.

Ballou, a huge man who drinks whisky non-stop, oversees numerous criminal enterprises, and murders people on a regular basis, fascinates Scudder, excites his admiration and his love. For Ballou lives as, with a considerable portion of his soul, Scudder wishes he could. Utterly fearless, Ballou cannot be intimidated. Recognizing no laws but his own, he escapes society's restrictions and obligations by having all of his properties and possessions listed in other people's names. Ballou is something like the last of the Westies, the Irish gang that once ruled Hell's Kitchen, and a legendary violence surrounds his history. To make a point, he once carried an enemy's severed head, in a bowling bag, through the bars on Ninth and Tenth Avenue. When feeling particularly savage, he adorns himself in his father's old butcher's apron, which is covered with bloodstains old and new. It is this man who becomes the best friend of the newly sober Matt Scudder.

Warned off Ballou by well-meaning acquaintances, Scudder turns noncommittal and evasive. Why are he and this monster such good friends? He can't say, it just happened. When they sit up all night swapping stories in Ballou's bar, something profound but not quite capable of articulation passes between them. Their bond goes deeper than words, certainly deeper than superficial judgments about criminal homicide. Block renders this male bonding guff so well that its spell endures for the length of each individual book and only afterward seems as specious as every other unexamined rationalization. Scudder seeks out Mick Ballou because he secretly yearns for his matter-of-fact sociopathy. Scudder thrills to his friend's completely business-like savagery; the savagery mirrors the repressed violence in himself.

Because of this linkage, the books are Ballou's as much as Scudder's. At the climax of *A Dance at the Slaughterhouse*, Scudder all but *becomes* Mick Ballou and, in a stunning moment of moral negation, commits an entirely gratuitous murder. He decided, as he explains later, to get some blood on his own apron. Olga Stettner, the unarmed woman he kills, richly deserves to die, but he does not shoot her because of her vileness. Nothing about this choice frames it as a moral act. Scudder pulls the trigger in the same spirit that inspired him to join Ballou's gang as a working criminal before the murder and after it to partake of the Host at a Catholic mass: the spirit of the dilettante. He wants to know how it feels to commit these acts, but in no way supposes that they will mark him permanently. (Indifferent to the murder, Ballou understands that taking Communion unshriven will zap him into hell for sure.) Seen this way, murder itself becomes aestheticized.

Only, however, in Scudder's consciousness, for Block knows more than his hero. Olga Stettner's murder and its surrounding uproar rise to a level of violence that can only be called stunning. Alone in American crime fiction, I think, the Scudder series from *Out on the Cutting Edge* through *A Walk Among the Tombstones* presents violence in its most ideologically troubling form, as a variety of ecstasy. Though you would never guess it from reading the average crime novel, violence and the sacred share a common seam, they walk hand in hand, for both invoke the ultimate things. At its heart, the ultimate is that which overwhelms our capacity to categorize, classify, comprehend. Here, rage for the lost self and its lost world, too destructive, too *great*, to be acknowledged directly, converts the massive sorrow of the two preceding books into perfectly cathartic, deeply satisfying, because actually transcendent, violence.

• • •

Although *Everybody Dies*, the novel immediately before *Hope to Die*, moves irresistibly toward another explosive Ballou-moment, this one so infused with anger and regret that a valedictory feeling surrounds the bloodbath, Block had by then worked through the second great movement in the Scudder books. He must have understood that he had accomplished the most serious task presented to genre writers, one most of his colleagues decline even to contemplate, that of reshaping their chosen field to their own design, and that his work had become canonical amongst mystery readers. The sorrow of his hero's first stage and the rage of his second having receded into the emotional background, he now could work with a Scudder more balanced and generous in his responses than previously. This evolution toward a more mature and sophisticated temperament does not eliminate Scudder's idiosyncrasies; it merely enables him to move deeper into the daylit world than had been permitted by the alienation resulting from alcoholic despair or sociopathic rage. This change in Matthew Scudder's world brings into greater prominence Elaine Mardell and T. J., the two remaining principal characters in the supporting cast.

• • •

In the progress from *A Ticket to the Boneyard* to *A Walk Among the Tombstones*, a countermovement to the implications of the transcendent violence has all along been setting itself in place. This countermovement has centrally to do with attachment, and in these novels attachment is felt first of all as the antidote—really, the cure—for pathological alienation. (Mick Ballou, unsurprisingly, has underlings but no soulmates or fellow-travelers, apart from Scudder.)

At the beginning of their relationship, Elaine Mardell's job is her primary attraction for Scudder. Although she has invested her money in a number of residential properties in Queens, that she makes her living on her back denies her any real claim to respectability at the same time as it prohibits emotional intimacy between her and Scudder. Their attachment is sordid and functional—Elaine is a slap in the face to conventional judgments. Sobriety brings with it a fresh assessment of her character, and in *A Ticket to the Boneyard*, the second of the "violence" novels, Block has his hero appreciate her good taste, intelligence, business acumen, and courage. By the end of that book, he has saved her from a feral ex-con and begun the progress into a deeper intimacy that one book later, in the grandly violent *A Dance at the Slaughterhouse*, results in Elaine's calling him a "big old bear" and alluding to the possibility of marriage. In the next book, *A Walk Among the Tombstones*, which winds toward an unblinking description of torture and dismemberment, Elaine answers Scudder's admission that he has long been troubled by her visits from other men, and his straightforward confession of love, with the revelation that she has not entertained another man for months, has in fact quit her profession, and of course loves him, too.

To reduce the sugar content, Scudder remarks that "The whole thing is very fucking Gift-of-the-Magi, isn't it?" It almost, though not quite, works. What does rescue the pair's mutual admissions from a fatal sentimentality is (1) that we have read, only a few pages earlier, that graphic account of torture, and (2)—even more importantly—that Elaine immediately informs Scudder he will very likely be unfaithful to her in the future, a matter of no consequence as long as he remembers to come back to her at night. Her prediction becomes fact as soon as is possible, i.e. in the next Scudder novel, *The Devil Knows You're Dead.* This book inaugurates the third stage of the series, more domesticated than the preceding two and animated by an even more authoritative aesthetic impulse.

With *The Devil Knows You're Dead*, *A Long Line of Dead Men*, *Even the Wicked*, and now *Hope to Die*, we move closer towards the territory of the classic mystery, in which one of the writer's crucial tasks is to keep inventing, in book after book, fresh crimes, contexts, and situations. In such fiction, a kind of deliberate formal, artificiality indistinguishable from playfulness, determines the rules of the game. Previously, Scudder had held center stage—now, the novels tend to use him as an instrument for the solving of entertainingly eccentric or unpleasant murders. With one exception, the five most recent novels in the series present a hero much less threatened and driven, less *exposed*, than ever before, and the tone of these books, similarly less drawn to the exposure of extremity, smoothly matches this shift in circumstance. (The exception is of course *Everybody Dies*, the blazing violence of which nonetheless manages to communicate a sense of leave-taking, of the backward glance.) This *is* only a tendency, and should not be overstated. If anything, it has the effect of underscoring the level of mastery Block has attained—it's a pleasure to see him clear his own bar on occasion after occasion.

Although these books essentially focus more on the homicides than their investigator, the basic quirkiness of the series as a whole remains undiminished. Neither Block nor his detective has lost the ability to surprise, even to discomfit, the reader. *The Devil Knows You're Dead* revolves around what turns out to be a hideous error in identification that makes a mockery of detection: if the victim, whose wife is the client, was murdered *by mistake*, how on earth is Scudder supposed to find out who killed him? After some digging, Scudder gives Mick Ballou a free pass for the murder, because he would have had an excellent motive; besides, Scudder likes Ballou more than he did the victim, with whose widow he has begun to be unfaithful to Elaine. Although this infidelity appears to be remarkably passionless, an intermittent whim, that the widow happens to be re-enacting childhood scenes of sexual abuse, albeit absent penetration, *with her father* demonstrates that Block's uncanny talent for unsettling the reader remains intact. Does Scudder understand that he is continuing her father's exploitation? If so, does he care? Of course he understands; of course he does not care. The issue has been framed altogether differently, as harmless mutual comfort, and he is absolved.

At the end of the novel, Scudder and Elaine have moved into an upscale apartment in the Park Vendome building located on rapidly gentrifying Ninth Avenue. They are soon to marry. Two wonderfully off-beat murders have been solved without recourse to mayhem. Every thread has been knotted. Matters, that is, have reached the stabilizing condition of formal satisfaction to be found at the conclusion of a Golden Age mystery, with the added pleasure of our Lord Peter, formerly a drunk, being soon to wed our Harriet Vane, formerly a whore. In this case, however, the last lines of the novel reveal our hero in tranquil contemplation of yet another tumble with his former client. We are an unimaginable distance from the moral and narrative assumptions of *Gaudy Night*, much less those of a clockwork bit of machinery like *The Greek Coffin Mystery*.

Scudder's next outing, which floats between giddy playfulness and true, vindictive nastiness, even more pointedly upends the tradition it celebrates and extends. *A Long Line of Dead Men* invokes a device that seems to come straight from Rex Stout's hermetic world: the detective's clients make up a small, exclusive, radically private men's club whose current roster of thirty-one members is being killed off one by one. The Club of Thirty-One differs from others of its kind in the purity of its minimalism. Without a fixed clubhouse, professional affinities, or any of the usual amenities, its only function and sole commitment is the annual dinner meeting currently held in an upstairs room at Keens Chophouse on West 36th Street. Every one of the club's living members is theoretically obliged, despite the inconveniences inevitable over time, to attend the meetings until death subtracts him from the rolls. These men represent the most recent links of an associational chain stretching back to the sixteenth century, perhaps even to the first, when Babylonians and Essenes may have joined separate branches of the same club. What goes on at these meetings, like the facts of the meetings themselves, are tacitly but firmly understood to be shared only within the upper room on West 36th Street.

At their gatherings, the members speak of the changes in their lives over the preceding year and remember those who have died. The last man left alive recruits thirty new candidates, who go on to enjoy the satisfactions of their unusual alliance. These satisfactions have primarily to do with the growing intimacy and presumed safety of their mutual association, which soon becomes a valuable form of attachment. For each new group, the dinners acquire the warm familiarity of family reunions. The anonymity to the world outside, as well as the shared assumption that confidences will be protected, gives the dinners an even greater resemblance to AA meetings. By now, these meetings have become something like the moral center of the series, and the unstated connection charges the unknown murderer with a heightened villainy.

Late in the book we learn that, by tricking Scudder into taking him to several AA meetings, the murderer has literally, not merely metaphorically, violated the sanctuary. It is a profound betrayal. The outrage and loathing aroused by his exploitation of Alcoholics Anonymous and Scudder's faith in its efficacy magnifies the killer's wickedness, therefore his need for punishment. In its icy malignity, the solution to this problem surpasses all of Block's previous body-blows to his readers' expectations, and although no less an act of vigilante frontier justice than the railroading of Tommy Tillary and the killing of Olga Stettner, does so without any trace of emotional dissociation or Olympian illegality. The murderer's fate—lifelong, unofficial solitary confinement chained to the floor in a barren room with the means of suicide close at hand—seems strikingly ingenious, breathtakingly cruel, and entirely appropriate. In this instance, the reader assents to Scudder's subversions of conventional morality with no hesitation whatsoever. We have, by virtue of a narrative satisfaction both moral and aesthetic, become Scudder to Scudder's Mick Ballou.

• • •

The brilliance of this endgame solution emerges from what I can only call a hard-earned, deep-seated confidence as to effects. For a fiction writer, confidence of this sort is wondrously enabling. It gives access to freedom of invention, an instinctive level of control, and a maturity of thematic play that allows for the kind of understatement found in *Hope to Die*. Understatement and narrative ease go hand in hand, and speak of authentic mastery, that condition to which all novelists aspire.

In *Hope to Die*, familial attachment has become the central theme, to be examined and explored in a number of different contexts. Now a secure married couple, Scudder and Elaine inhabit the conspicuously civilized milieu shared by the book's victims, the Hollanders, a lawyer and a novelist who own a three-million dollar brownstone on the Upper West Side. Patrons of the Mostly Mozart program at Lincoln Center, both couples attend the concert and private dinner that precede the Hollanders' murders. Barbara Walters and Beverly Sills hover in the background; their fellow-patrons enjoy white wine and hors d'oeuvres on the second floor of Avery Fisher Hall, then a catered meal, before taking their orchestra seats for the *Prague* concerto. Although the geography in fact remains unchanged, this atmosphere of cultured privilege seems a great distance from the Irish bars and after hours clubs of the earlier novels. Like Ninth Avenue, Matt Scudder has come up in the world; Elaine's apartment houses bring in all the money they will ever need.

The other figure in the supporting cast, T. J., serves as a surrogate son within their family. Adaptable and observant, T. J. has become Scudder's legman, researcher, and deputy; by variations of manner, speech, and clothing, he is capable of moving effortlessly back and forth between the street and, say, the campus of Columbia University, where his habit of auditing humanities classes has put him in touch with the Hollanders' niece. Scudder, Elaine, and T. J. make up an ideal family unit, capable of meeting all challenges to their common well-being with equanimity and humor.

The other two family structures in the book illuminate the idealized quality of the first by demonstrating the ancient grievances, suffused angers, emotional murkiness, conflicting motives, and manipulative ill-will of troublesome ordinary human families. Scudder's first wife has died, and very early in the novel he drives to Long Island to attend her funeral and spend time with Michael and Andy, his two grown sons. A sense of guilt and loss soaks these scenes, and when the alcohol comes out, old grievances and misunderstandings contaminate the atmosphere. Block handles this material superbly, counterpointing Andy's resentful, increasingly drunken attacks with Scudder's growing weariness as he rises grimly to the occasion. In a moment of lacerating honesty, he says to himself, "I wanted this little talk to be over and I knew it was going to go on forever." Near the end of the book, Scudder's attitude becomes even more bracing in its refusal to allow sentimentality to obscure the dire facts. When Andy squeaks away undamaged from his latest self-created catastrophe, his father implicitly suggests that death might be preferable to a life so wayward.

In a lifelong fog of self-pity, Andy Scudder creates problems for himself, then waits for other people to bail him out. Too sleazy to be honest, too lazy to be an effective criminal, he moves from town to town, embezzling from his employers. He will undoubtedly wind up in jail one day, true—but would imprisonment be worse than death? Except in cases of great mental or physical suffering, how can a parent think of a child, *better off dead*? In its own way, this moment is as shocking as the murder of Olga Stettner in *A Dance at the Slaughterhouse*. Scudder denies his son any prospect of emotional maturity or reformation. Yet the Andy we see in *Hope to Die* is an unlikely candidate for change; he appears set on an unalterable course to an increasingly pointless and embittered life. Scudder's dismissal may be self-protective (Andy being one too many in human form), but its sadness contains an unhappy wisdom beyond the scope of the "violence" novels.

The connection of the novel's third family to the plot eliminates it from detailed description, but its dynamic is based on innocence, illusion, and manipulation. If

Scudder's present family represents a well-nigh impossible ideal and his former one a heartbreaking mess from which self-awareness and brutal frankness provide the most effective rescue, here no rescue is possible. Actual active evil is at work, binding the unsuspecting victims within its cold, mad grandiosity.

The villain who embodies that evil is one of Block's best inventions, and he takes full advantage of the character's quirks by the unprecedented step of putting him on display, center stage, in lengthy italicized passages that report his thoughts as he moves around the city in pursuit of his shifting goals. For the first time in a Scudder novel, we enter the killer's mind, an inspiration that nakedly reveals his vanity, his pleasure in scheming and pride in his cleverness, his unbridled madness and selfishness, also his lunatic ambition, increasing recklessness, and accelerating desperation. The result is to humanize the villain by enriching our perception of him: we take in his odd pettiness and his habit of grotesque misjudgment, and these traits help define his monstrosity.

Scudder's progress towards identifying the preening villain takes the form of a deeply satisfying mystery novel that is nearly meta-fictional in its self-awareness. Block establishes false leads that culminate in a classic locked-room puzzle; Scudder's elaborate explanation of the puzzle reads like the denouement of an old-fashioned murder mystery. Red herrings abound. Minor characters float in and out of view, suggestively. In a nice inversion of convention, our detective clings to a logical but false solution until a homicide cop persuades him otherwise.

Throughout, Block, now so confidently at home in this universe that he can afford to indicate his own presence in it, makes reference to the central role of imagination, specifically novelistic imagination, in detective work. Scudder opens the book by stepping into the place of his author, consulting his fictive imagination, and *writing* the

Hollanders' murders. As he tells us, "it's my imagination. I guess I can do what I please with it." I guess he can—no one in his right mind would want to stop him.

The Island of Dr. Moreau
Foreword

What sort of book is it, this *Island of Dr. Moreau*? As one races pell-mell through the narrative, moving smartly from one nasty shock to another on the way toward revelation and resolution, it seems like nothing so much as a boy's adventure novel adapted to the field of science fiction, a then-infant genre invented at least in part by its author, H. G. Wells. Our hero, Edward Prendick, is shipwrecked, then rescued by another ship only to be unceremoniously ejected by its drunken captain onto a remote, forested island where he must overcome an escalating series of perils before his final rescue and return to civilization. Much of the novel's action concerns Prendick's repeated escapes from the perceived dangers of the human society offered by the island into the wild, where he encounters even greater threats. Characteristically, Prendick is seen in flight, charging through thickets, changing course at the snap of a stick, ripping his clothes on thorny spines, in every way doing his utmost to supply us with the obligatory thrills. For the most part, the tone of the narrative is that of reliability and assurance, blandly professional in its assumptions about the contract between reader and writer.

Peter Straub

Dear reader, this tone seems to say, *come along with me, for I guarantee an entertaining journey and a safe return to shore.* Something along these lines must have been what its original readers anticipated when they picked up the new book by the author of *The Time Machine*, Wells's first great success.

To Wells's enormous credit, they did not find anything so reassuring. On publication in 1896, reviewers recoiled from the book as if it carried a contagious disease, excoriating Wells for the horrors to which he had exposed the tender reader, the chief among them being blasphemy. At this point, the contemporary reader, conversant with AIDS, crack babies, drive-by shootings, half a dozen enthusiastic attempts at large-scale genocide, and the emergence of an entire tribe of serial killers—a reader who has merely to stroll to the nearest bookstore to come upon any number of respectable theologians asserting that Christ was the product of a normal birth, performed no miracles, uttered no more than a fifth of the remarks attributed to Him, and was not resurrected—steps back and in wondering tones utters, "Blasphemy?" It seems an absurdly far-fetched charge, but what outraged Wells's reviewers was his refusal to honor conventional distinctions between human beings and beasts and his inability, it seems to me despite himself, to suppress his own perception of the absolute partiality and fragility of all human knowledge, especially that version of knowledge produced by rational thought.

The sickly child of domestic servants who had gone into "trade," apprenticed at fourteen to a draper, Wells learned early on to summon the intellectual stamina and ceaseless effort necessary to escape his background, no ordinary achievement in Victorian England. Because Wells continued his productive life until 1946, no one thinks of him as a product of the era of Dickens and Trollope, but he was born in 1866, when Victoria emerged from her three-year seclusion following Albert's death and one year after the publication of *Our Mutual Friend.* Twenty-one years later, at the time of Victoria's fiftieth Jubilee and still two years before the death of Wilkie Collins, Wells was close to completing his hard-won education at the University of London. By the time of Victoria's sixtieth Jubilee, he had already published *The Time Machine, The Island of Dr. Moreau,* and *The Invisible Man.* Wells was educated as a scientist under the influence of T. H. Huxley, the grandfather of Aldous Huxley and the most prominent English Darwinist of his day, who proposed that evolution was an upward progress. Blessed with an ethical sense unknown to animals, mankind was destined ever more increasingly to conquer nature with civilization as it marched toward that ideal truth embodied in the scientific method. At a time when Darwinism itself could provoke a reflexive outrage (as, among those happy souls who call themselves Creationists, it continues to do), Huxley's reassuring formulations won him considerable recognition, even celebrity. As a popular novelist of pseudoscientific fancy, Wells was a natural candidate to support these assumptions, rather avant-garde for their day, and cloaked in the brisk unassailability of science. Since vivisection—the dissection of animals—was a controversial method of research, a novel with an antivivisection bias should have had no problem with general acceptance; but a fable in which religion appears to be a manipulative sham, science a poisonous threat, and mankind in general so thoroughly implicated in a Mad Vivisectionist's savagery that man himself is a ravening beast was another matter.

With the advantage of hindsight, we can see that Wells's vision was never simple or sunny. As soon as he came into focus it was clear that he was a rare and energetic character indeed, a pessimistic idealist who wished to sweep away the last remaining traces of Victorianism, promote sexual freedom and world peace, and alert his readers to the grave dangers represented by political instability and modern scientific development. He lived through two World Wars and understood the dangers represented by nuclear fission long before most of his peers. Wells wanted to make a difference in his own time, and he did, but not the one he had desired. Through endless exertion and a vast number of books he became a sage, a teacher of difficult truths who spoke with the authority of the man who had written the million words of *The Outline of History*. Yet all of his energy and intelligence could do nothing to prevent or even forestall the horrors to come, and his last book was titled *Mind at the End of Its Tether*. By that time the pessimism and the idealism within him were in an unequal struggle, and the dread one often feels in Wells spoke plainly.

In various ways, that dread inhabits *Dr. Moreau*, and one reason the book continues to be vital is that Wells can be seen throughout to resist and deny the implications suggested by his own imagination. The text often seems at war with itself. Some of its bleakest overtones appear to have leaked out of the pen while the busy author was thinking of something else. The resulting tension makes of the book a more complex, layered, and irresolute performance than Wells ever intended or his most hostile critics ever took in—the knowing craftsman in Wells, willing to provoke and disturb his public only to a self-protective point, could not suppress the artist in him, an occasion all the more remarkable for his skepticism about the claims of art. No aesthete, Wells so discounted what he saw as the pretensions of those who presented themselves as artists that he made one of the greatest errors of his life by ridiculing his old friend Henry James in the novel *Boon*, thereby provoking the bewildered James into a memorable defense of himself and his methods.

This episode deserves a moment's consideration, as it illustrates an aspect of Wells's character more apparent to his contemporaries than it can be to us. Wells was an irreverent working-class boy who became a successful writer by challenging received ideas, and at least to some extent science-fantasy tales must have appealed to him because they represented a poke in the eye to the notion of literary seriousness. A part of him that was eventually concealed behind the sage-historian-prophet remained a small boy armed with a snowball. James was twenty-three years his senior and already a considerable literary figure when they met. Though James had treated Wells with unfailing generosity and honesty, the younger man eventually could not contain his resentment at the Jamesian manner, and the small boy stepped forth and fired the snowball at his elder's top hat from what he must have hoped was the safe psychological distance of two removes. *Boon* supposedly represented the literary remains of one George Boon as edited by Reginald Bliss, with an introduction by Wells. Upon reading that his work resembled an empty church in which the altar displays a dead kitten, an eggshell, and a piece of string, James wrote Wells that he found it difficult to put himself fully in the place of a fellow writer who found him "futile and void," and that the loss of the assumed common ground between them felt like the collapse of a bridge. Wells's embarrassed reply dismissed the novel as a journalist's "wastepaper basket." Unpacified, James wrote back, "I live, live intensely and am fed by life, and my value, whatever it be, is in my own kind of expression of that. Art *makes* life, makes interest, makes importance…" Their friendship was at an end. Henry James died a year later. Even after, Wells's condescending allusions to James only barely masked his enduring hostility.

Here we reckon with a writer of tremendous will and ability, in sometimes imperfect command of his imaginative and emotional impulses, prone to trusting that his assertions will be taken at face value and subject to the tendency, calamitous in daily life but fruitful in novels, of saying more than he knew. *Dr. Moreau* is a much happier instance of unconscious revelation than *Boon* and its aftermath. The cheeky small boy is present in the depiction of the Sayer of the Law and his absurd litany—Wells clearly intended to mock the clergy, and likely took pleasure in the thought of offending Victorian sensibilities—but what the artist in Wells smuggled into the novel is a pattern of confusion and uncertainty which undermines its gestures toward resolution, generic satisfactions, and narrative confidence.

As we have seen, his narrator endures harrowing trials, uncovers a secret (a treasure is also a kind of secret), and returns to the civilized world in apparent emulation of his counterparts in the most unreflective of adventure stories, and we follow his several escapes into the perilous wilds during the journey toward homecoming with entranced, eager involvement—its success as a compelling yarn has always been the principle reason for the continuing popularity of *Dr. Moreau*.

The Platonic model for any such story, *Treasure Island*, had been published thirteen years before Wells's book. It is worth remembering that Robert Louis Stevenson, dead two years by the time Wells met Henry James, had been a cherished friend of the older writer's. (We might also remember that Wells and James spent considerable time with their neighbors Stephen Crane and Joseph Conrad, and that Ford Madox Ford, soon to be Conrad's collaborator, was a constant presence. Wells, James, and Conrad celebrated the dawning of 1900 at Crane's residence and contributed to a play at the local school in which one character was named Peter Quint Prodmore Moreau. In terms of literary accomplishment, this association of writers—James, Crane, Conrad, Wells, and Ford—casts a long shadow over the Bloomsbury Group.) Given its infusion of the adventure tale with deep, pervasive doubt, *Dr. Moreau* can be seen as a unique and compelling alliance of *Treasure Island* and Joseph Conrad.

Certainties of every sort dwindle into hopeful suppositions when a shared language, consensual history, and common belief systems are undermined; when authority is seen as a despotic sham, authoritative statement turns hollow and empty; under these circumstances the nature of fact, the very fact of "fact," becomes fluid and mysterious, threatening and open to the suggestion of the uncanny; stripped of its familiar supports, the mind despairs and seeks escape, even the ultimate escape. (*Dr. Moreau* must be the only *Treasure Island*-style adventure tale, at least until its late twentieth-century variations at the hands of Umberto Eco, John Barth, and others, in which the hero prays for his own death, twice contemplates suicide, and at journey's end suffers a barely disguised nervous breakdown.) This destabilization begins with the bland self-contradiction of the first sentence and continues with the remarks which immediately follow. "I do not propose," Prendick says, "to add anything to what has already been written concerning the loss of the *Lady Vain*," meaning that he intends to do exactly that. "As everyone knows," a clause containing a built-in irony, the ship collided with a derelict, leaving only the seven survivors in the longboat whose dreadful tale has become legendary—a glimpse of an unreadable because unwritten book. Common knowledge has it that "the four men who were in the dinghy perished," but this is wrong on two counts: there were only three of them, and only two of these "perished," so ten, not seven, survived the wreck, and one of the three, not four, in the dinghy survived to give us his account of what happened after.

If we must presume that the captain of the *Lady Vain* was an incompetent seaman, Davis, the captain-owner of the absurdly named *Ipecacuanha* is even worse, an abusive drunk whose own inevitable shipwreck and death will much later provide the mechanism for Prendick's timely escape from Dr. Moreau's island. Davis describes himself as "the law here...the law and the prophets," sounding the first note of false and delusional authority framed in scriptural terms which will reappear in the grotesque of the Sayer of the Law, will later be amplified by the novels' ultimate figure of unreliable leadership, Dr. Moreau, for whom science is an obscenely lunatic religion, and still later come to full, corrosive expression in Prendick's manipulative adaptation of religious language, liturgical cadences, and the resurrection myth as a means of controlling the Beast People between the time of Moreau's death and the degeneration of his half-human creatures into fearful, unreasoning animality. Moreau "is not dead," he bellows. "Even now he watches us…The House of Pain is gone. It will come again. The Master you cannot see. Yet even now he listens above you." Prendick's self-disgust at the use of this maneuver causes him to deny the reality of his having now supplanted the hated Moreau and claim that "the folly of [his] cowardice," by keeping him from grasping "the vacant scepter," had made him no more than "one among the Beast People on the island of Dr. Moreau." (Ford Madox Ford's *The Good Soldier* and James's *The Sacred Fount* soon would make conscious use of the unreliable narrator, fiction's central case of false authority; but here, as elsewhere in *Dr. Moreau*, nothing suggests that we are not intended to take Prendick's self-evaluations at face value. Of course it is also literally true that Prendick *is* becoming one among the Beast People.) The final and most unsettling appearance of this theme occurs after the return to civilization, when the shaken and unstable Prendick discovers to his horror that even an authentic clergyman evokes the memory of the Ape Man's pathetic and pompous efforts to communicate meaningless "Big Thinks."

Language expresses accurate meaning in its passing from hand to hand like a coin, its nuances of weight and value instantly comprehended; and as soon as Prendick enters the world of Dr. Moreau we meet hints of the unreadable and obscure, suggestions of impenetrable meaning. Language works at cross-purposes, at its least translatable level reduced to the screams of pain which persuade the narrator that his host is torturing human beings and provoke him into his first wild flight. (His second attempt at escape results from his so misreading the sights and sounds around him that he imagines himself the next victim.) The suggestion of the inaccessible is established near the beginning of the seventh chapter, "The Locked Door," when Moreau admits Prendick into the residence cum laboratory unvaryingly called "the enclosure," a structure whose purpose is less to provide shelter and comfort than to conceal the secret within. Much is made of keys, of locking and unlocking of doors. Within "the enclosure," Moreau directs the narrator to a small "apartment" consisting of a single room with an "inner door" leading to a courtyard which Moreau promptly also locks, announcing that henceforth it shall be fastened on the outer side. Prendick notices "an array of old books, chiefly, I found, surgical works and editions of the Latin and Greek classics—languages I cannot read with any comfort—on a shelf near the hammock." Everything surrounding the narrator is like a language imperfectly and partially understood, and when he quizzes his rescuer from the dinghy, Moreau's assistant Montgomery, about his unsettlingly hairy aide and the deformed-looking beings he had observed on the beach, he is given transparent evasions. Beyond the inner door, a puma issues harrowing screams. Troubled by these "exquisite expressions of suffering," Prendick throws aside "a crib of Horace"—another imperfectly apprehended text—and flees into its metaphoric equivalent: "the world was a confusion, blurred with drifting black and red phantasms." In short order, he comes across a group of Swine People and overhears speech in which all content is untranslatable and opaque, locked firmly behind an unbreachable door. "The speaker's words came thick and sloppy, and though I could hear them distinctly I could not distinguish what he said. He seemed to me to be reciting some complicated gibberish."

The world was a confusion…

Almost exactly halfway through the novel, in the chapter entitled "Dr. Moreau Explains," Prendick, for the moment literally if not figuratively out of the woods, again is listening, this time to a peroration which stands as the antithesis of swinish gibberish. Moreau's explanation of the island's puzzles—that he is a creative vivisectionist of unprecedented skills working to mold an ideal being—rises to a parody of Huxleyan theory. Evolution implies an upward progress through the gradual elimination of primitive traits toward a perfect rationality uncontaminated by instinctual animal cravings. When the atavistic illusions of pleasure and pain have been excised, with them will go those benchmarks of the bestial nature—anger, hate, and fear. Moreau's experimental creations have as yet persistently mocked his ambitions by gradually sinking back into the lusts of their original animal nature, but he cherishes fond hopes for the puma currently on the operating table….This fantasy of a scientifically created *Übermensch* is wholly evil, and both Prendick and Wells know it. Two chapters later, when the distinctly unevolved Leopard Man kills Moreau, no grief is wasted on his departure from the text.

Two points, the first related to its assumptions and the second to its language, should be made about Moreau's "explanation." Though cogent, his self-justification, being insane, is no less a form of gibberish than the utterances of the Swine People. When Moreau leaves him for the night, Prendick responds with the exhausted depletion characteristic of one forced to endure the "explanations" of the deranged: "weary emotionally, mentally, and physically…I could not think beyond the point at which he had left me. The blank window stared at me like an eye." And for all its conviction, Moreau's speech regularly stumbles, halts, breaks down, and falls into the wordless coma of ellipses.

> "As soon as my hand is taken from them the beast begins to creep back, begins to assert itself again…"

> "…see into their very souls, and see there nothing but the souls of beasts, beasts that perish—anger, and the lusts to live and gratify themselves…It only mocks me…"

What reduces the language to silence is the acknowledgement of failure, and the failures are what undermine it; but although narrator and author both draw back numbed from the abyss, they share Moreau's sense of an absolute distinction between man and beast which apportions bravery and self-respect to mankind, the humiliations of fear, servility, and credulity to brutes. At the moment of Moreau's final confrontation with his subjects, Prendick takes in their "wincing attitudes and the furtive dread in their bright eyes" and wonders "that I had ever taken them to be men." Animals cringe in dread, men do not. Insofar as animals may become men, they may be granted a partial and qualified dignity; when their animality begins to reassert itself, they are to be feared. Much of the latter half of the book records Prendick's increasingly apprehensive awareness of the Beast People's "reversion."

A central signal of the creatures' relapse into beast-like savagery is the erosion of their verbal skills. The narrator describes the process with an eloquent horror:

> My Monkey Man's jabber multiplied in volume, but grew less and less comprehensible, more and more simian. Some of the others seemed

> altogether slipping their hold upon speech, though they still understood what I said to them at that time. *Can you imagine language, once clear-cut and exact, softening and guttering, losing shape and import, becoming mere lumps of sound again?* (My italics.)

Instead of being particular to beasts, dread lays its cold hand on those men who witness the corruption of human capacities into hideous travesties.

Prendick's need to maintain essential distinctions between man and animal causes him to look askance at Montgomery's fondness for the Beast People, a failing he readily attributes to the latter's history of dealing with swarthy traders in African ports—wogs aren't really human. "He hardly met the finest type of mankind in that seafaring village of Spanish mongrels." Spaniards may be dogs, but Englishmen are made of finer stuff. Later, his inherited assumptions drive him further into rigidity: "My first friendship with Montgomery did not increase. His long separation from humanity, his secret vice of drunkenness, his evident sympathy with the Beast People, tainted him to me."

If the walls between man and beast had remained as high as this thoughtless and thoughtlessly racist revulsion erects them, none of the previous implications of the instability of authority and language would be more than interesting curiosities and the book would have met with a cheerful reception married only by some cavils at its macabre glimpses of the unhappy puma's torments. Wells' imagination was too powerful to allow such an easy course, and in withdrawing from Moreau's abyss he promptly opened one of his own.

That things may not be as they ought properly to seem to right-thinking Englishmen first surfaces in the narrator's face-to-face encounter with the most "reverted" of the creatures, the murderous Leopard Man. His baffled shock compels a response of great psychological accuracy. The passage begins with a wonderfully dismissive throwaway:

> It may seem a strange contradiction in me—I cannot explain the fact—but now, seeing the creature there in a perfectly animal attitude, with the light gleaming in its eyes, and its imperfectly human face distorted with terror, I realized again the fact of its humanity. In another moment another of its pursuers would see it, and it would be overpowered and captured, to experience once more the horrible tortures of the enclosure. Abruptly I slipped out my revolver, aimed between his terror-struck eyes and fired.

Looking at the creature in the instant before it can spring, he has a full apprehension of its savagery and terror, and what most comes home to him is its humanity. Strange, contradictory, inexplicable, indeed; to this sequence we might add the final term, *unbearable.* Disguising the execution of this secret sharer as an act of mercy (to which "slipped" adds a note of gentlemanly courtesy) serves mainly to emphasize the magnitude of the "strange contradiction" and the speed with which the unbearable is put to death. Not surprisingly, our narrator quickly suffers the fate of those who misread, however cleverly, their own psychic texts: "I fell…into the morbid state, deep and enduring, alien to fear…I must confess I lost faith in the sanity of the world when I saw it suffering the painful disorder of this island."

He *lost faith in the sanity of the world.* Here, already, is a mind at the end of its tether, moving toward the tragic conclusion that it has witnessed "the whole balance of human life in miniature, the whole interplay of instinct, reason, and fate, in its simplest form." At this point the narrative shrinks away from recognition by declaring an "abhorrence" for the hybrids and the disavowal of Montgomery, who "was in truth half akin to these Beast Folk, unfitted for human kindred." Montgomery's death at the hands of a wolf creature comes as a restoration of balance, and Prendick clasps whip and revolver to his bosom, re-invents Christianity in Moreau's image, and thunders his mock-sermon to the bestial flock. In doing so he performs a bold self-rescue entirely appropriate to the heroic narrator of an adventure tale, supplants the Mad Scientist, and submits to the transformation of his own language into gibberish.

Nearly at the end of his story, Wells now abandons his plot entirely and compresses Prendick's remaining ten months on the island into a few perfunctory pages. Language, always problematical, completes its descent into repulsive "lumps of sound." Our narrator cannot bring himself to describe the specifics of the simultaneous deterioration of monogamy into "public outrages." What follows the account of this regression is meant as simple clarification of his remark about becoming "one among the Beast People on the island of Dr. Moreau": like any castaway, he cannot properly groom himself: but the busy pen admits another reading as it glides across the page.

> I too must have undergone strange changes. My clothes hung about me as yellow rags, through whose rents glowed the tanned skin. My hair grew long, and became matted together. *I am told that even now my eyes have a strange brightness, a swift alertness of movement.* (My italics.)

The first sentence weakens the bland amelioration of "must have" with the insertion of "strange," a word persistently associated with the Beast People. The next two, ostensibly marking the unremarkable signs of an inevitable process, strengthen the association by alluding to the rags and matted hair which delineate them; more tellingly, the glow of his skin evokes their dangerous vitality. The final sentence gives the game away completely. Throughout, "bright eyes," eyes which "sparkle" and "shine with a pale green light," and unusual quickness of movement announce the presence of the original animal self. Prendick will soon be forced to recognize that, to a much greater extent than Montgomery, he, too, has become "unfitted for human kindred."

Wells's great triumph lies in his courageous reversal of these valences. In the novel's most beautiful and imaginative passages—those concerning what ordinarily would be the resolution of homecoming—the implications of the "strange" insight that the Leopard Man's gleaming eyes reveal its humanity render the narrator unfit for society: he cannot escape the perception that civilization is but a larger version of the island. Wells has so liberated himself from the conventions and underlying consolations of the adventure tale that his subtext floods up onto the page. The optimistic Edwardian world softens and gutters into fresh horrors, gibberish, and intimations of death. Author and narrator have come to the heart of darkness, and it is…London.

> I could not persuade myself that the men and women I met were not another, still passably human, Beast People, animals half-wrought into the outward image of humans souls, and that they would presently begin to revert, to show first this bestial mark and then that.

Unable to yield to the pressures of his own imagination, Wells frames unacceptable despair as mental illness. Fearing for his sanity, Prendick consults "a mental specialist" and claims substantial relief. Wells's diligent efforts to persuade us that his narrator's nihilistic dread is a temporary affliction already fading under the applications of healthy thinking and country air ring false and hollow. In fiction, the energy, conviction, and heat of the words on the page always speak for themselves, rebelliously subverting the intentions of any mere misguided author trying to pull rhetorical wool over his own eyes. After Prendick tells us that he knows his fears are illusory and the men and women about him "perfectly reasonable creatures…emancipated from instinct" and has fled into the healing solitude of the countryside, Wells does an extraordinary thing. Under no narrative or structural necessity to restate the particulars of his character's symptoms, he rears up and detonates his anodyne reassurance with a passionate, vividly detailed outburst which blows open the doors:

> When I lived in London the horror was wellnigh insupportable…I would go out into the streets to fight with my delusion, and prowling women would mew after me, furtive craving men glance jealously at me, weary pale workers go coughing by me, with tired eyes and eager paces like wounded deer dripping blood, old people, bent and dull, pass murmuring to themselves, and all unheeding a ragged tail of gibing children. Then I would turn into some chapel, and even there, such was my disturbance, it seemed that the preacher gibbered Big Thinks even as the Ape Man had done; or into some library, and there the intent faces over the books seemed but patient creatures waiting for prey. Particularly nauseous were the blank expressionless faces of people in trains and omnibuses; they seemed no more my fellow-creatures than dead bodies would be…And even it seemed that I, too, was not a reasonable creature, but only an animal tormented with some strange

> disorder in its brain, that sent it to wander alone, like a sheep stricken with the gid.

The mute, enervated condition of the outcast poor and the laboring class from which Wells had vertiginously rescued himself, the spectacle of a city thronging with men and women so brutalized and deadened as to resemble beasts, shames and threatens his narrator. These dumb animals, wounded, hungry, unappeasable, are what he secretly knows himself to be. This abhorrent, unacceptable knowledge is the source of the recurring sense of the uncanny which haunts Prendick's every step on Moreau's island, for the uncanny is what reminds us of what we wish not to know. His magnificent outburst concluded, Wells instantly backpedals to grasp sustenance from Moreau's domain, the technology of science. The irony, though crushing, remains resolutely unconscious. "I spend many of the clear nights in the study of astronomy. There is, *though I do not know how there is or why there is,* a sense of infinite peace and protection in the glittering hosts of heaven." (My italics.) A final appeal to the eternal laws of matter suggests that the consolation Wells trusts us to find in his tale is located only in yet another mysterious and hidden text.

Dracula
Introduction

Eighteen years after Bram Stoker's death, his widow, Florence, ensured both the comfort of her seventh decade and her husband's literary survival by taking advantage of an emerging technology and committing an act that would have been unthinkable (because impossible) during his lifetime, selling the film rights to *Dracula* to Universal Pictures for $40,000. In its startling linkage between the era of the hansom cab and that of the taxicab, Florence Stoker's coup encapsulates the peculiar unlikeliness surrounding the circumstances, past and present, of her husband's most famous novel. We see the book from the distinction-blurring perspective of an added hundred years, but to a great portion of its original readership, *Dracula* must have had the reassuringly nostalgic flavor that a contemporary replication of a traditional country house murder mystery in the style of Margery Allingham or Agatha Christie would have for us. Yet despite the creakiness of its methods, *Dracula* had something of the effect on late-Victorian England that Thomas Harris's *Silence of the Lambs* had on late-twentieth-century America. Hollywood did not create *Dracula*'s audience, but it did create the conditions that permitted the novel to stay in print for more than a century.

Left to her own devices during much of her marriage, Florence Stoker appears to have been indifferent to her husband's fiction until after his death, when her position as executor obliged her to oversee his literary affairs. In that capacity, she spent years trying to assure the incineration of Friedrich Wilhelm Murnau's *Nosferatu*, which had done more than any other adaptation to maintain *Dracula*'s popularity. Universal's canny largesse won her over, and Tod Browning's film played a large role in the creation of the horror movie as a genre, spawning sequels, imitations, updates, and revisions. If it is true that most people will think first of Browning's movie and Bela Lugosi when they hear the word "Dracula," it is also true that Browning and Lugosi rescued Stoker's novel from literary oblivion. The only other case I can think of in which a faithful film adaptation of a worthy novel brought success to both, with no damage to either party, is Brian De Palma's *Carrie*, which led to Stephen King's first great commercial breakthrough. Those who wish to argue the merits of Merchant Ivory-style productions would have to convince me of two dubious propositions: (1) that films like *Howard's End* and *Washington Square* are faithful adaptations of literary works by E. M. Forster and Henry James; and (2) that they brought about significant increases in sales of their underlying sources.

For both *Dracula* and *Carrie*, the film adaptation honored the fiction, and the strengths of the fiction became those of the adaptation; then the adaptation repaid its debt by winning a considerably greater degree of popular attention for the novel on which it was based. Stoker's novel is more accomplished than *Carrie*, but in its readability, narrative technique, structural command, and accumulation of tension over a series of carefully timed climaxes, it has much in common with King's more mature novels. In fact, it is precisely these elements that make Stoker's sixth novel more satisfying than both King's first and all the rest of Stoker's own.

From the very first pages, *Dracula* grabs us by the lapels and compels our attention: once begun, it is one of those books that demand to be read all the way through to the end. You *can't* drop out and walk away, it's too exciting. The epistolary nature of the book—that it is narrated piecemeal, in letters and journal entries—permits Stoker to establish suspense and heighten it by the simple but infallible method, later to become one of Alfred Hitchcock's favorite devices, of letting the audience in on a crucial fact unknown to the characters whose lives are imperiled by it. The longer the characters remain in ignorance, the greater the danger to their lives, and the tension becomes more and more unbearable. In a Hitchcock movie, the unknown fact might be a live bomb concealed in a suitcase beneath a table where two people linger over coffee, maddeningly discussing a cricket match; in *Dracula*, the unseen threat is in the vampire's nighttime visitations, first to Lucy Westenra, then, even more horrifyingly, to Mina Harker, which smuggle his corruption into his enemies' camp.

One of the things I most admire about *Dracula* has to do with the relationship between the dramatic tension aroused by this unseen threat and the novel's triangular structure. A three-part structure is a sturdy armature for any genre of fiction, and it is especially suited to horror fiction, which tends naturally to divide itself into a first section that sets up the particular nature of the disorder to be faced by the protagonists, a second, exploratory section in which the protagonists cope with the spread of that disorder, and a third section in which order is restored wholly, partially, or not at all. In a novel with a triangular structure, the great climax at the end of part three involves a conscious return to the elements, whether setting, motives, atmosphere, or specific actions, of part one. My novels *Floating Dragon* and *Koko* fall into three basic sections, *Koko* less obviously than *Floating Dragon*, where the part titles are "Entry," "Establishment," and "Dominion." In *Dracula*, the three basic sections might be called "The Count," "The Little Band," and "The Chase." The vampire's depredations that begin in part two with his corruption of Lucy into a figure of hideously seductive evil, and the sweaty, sexually charged horror of her postmortem murder, which takes place on what would have been her wedding night, raise the ante when the reader sees the more responsible Mina, a figure of impeccable orderliness and common sense, succumbing to the same corruption in part three.

Stoker manages his effects here as well as any writer could, mixing in various complexities (the hunt for Dracula's bolt-holes, the discovery of Mina's hastening peril, the division of the little band of heroes into smaller units, and a wealth of travel arrangements) and one powerful countermovement (Mina's psychic contact with the foe) with the confidence of a real master. The authority of his narrative technique makes even his occasional moments of fussiness, such as the long pause for stock-taking at the beginning of part three, seem vibrant, for they come as welcome breaks in the steadily intensifying tension. We can lie down, apply cold washcloths to our foreheads, and breathe deeply for a few pages before rushing off to Transylvania. When we do set out with the little band on the last, long chase across Europe, the tension surges back into the narrative with renewed force.

Many of Stephen King's best works of horror fiction share this triangular structure with *Dracula*, including three of my own favorite King novels, *Salem's Lot*, *The Shining*, and *It*. Others, such as *The Tommyknockers*, *Rose Madder*, and *Desperation*, also divide themselves into the three-part structure described above. Unlike King, no such list of commercial and artistic successes can be cited for Stoker: if asked about other works by the author of *Dracula*, a number of readers would be able to name *The Lair of the White Worm*, in most cases because of Ken Russell's 1989 film version, a wildly unfaithful treatment of a wildly incoherent narrative. A few readers might know *The Jewel of Seven Stars*, which occasionally turns up in antiquarian bookshops. His fifteen other novels, which include halfhearted gestures titled *Miss Betty*, *The Mystery of the Sea*, and *The Lady of the Shroud*, were quickly forgotten. Stoker never duplicated or built on his first success, and the reasons for his inability to do so merit consideration.

The uniqueness of *Dracula* in Stoker's output must have been as clear to its author as it has been to later generations. Certainly, it is the book that most engaged and challenged him, and the one that demanded the greatest imaginative investment. For nearly all of his adult life, Stoker worked as theatrical manager for the legendary actor Henry Irving. Irving, his acting company, and their theater, the Lyceum, kept him extraordinarily busy. Contemporary memoirs and news clippings consistently depict him in perpetual motion—he was like a foreman with a clipboard and a whistle, always moving from task to task, pointing at work left undone, issuing commands, keeping order, maintaining the schedule. Fiction was secondary to his real occupation, and had to be squeezed in at odd moments. Nonetheless, Stoker wrote most of his novels in a few short months, usually while on breaks from his theatrical duties. This is the timetable of the desperate, overworked inhabitants of Grub Street, who had to rattle off three or four books a year to keep their heads above water. To name just one example, the career of James Hadley Chase demonstrates that the work produced under such conditions, essentially no more than rewritten first drafts, rarely rises above the level of hackwork. I wonder how many contemporary readers who, like me, got a cheap thrill out of *No Orchids Miss Blandish*'s lurid sadism, ever felt the need to hunt down *Twelve Chinks and a Woman*, or any of Chase's other eight-plus efforts.

Dracula is altogether another matter. In utter contrast to his usual methods, Stoker devoted six years to its creation. He made notes; he did research in the British Library and the Whitby Library; he created a lengthy outline; he wrote with unusual care, revising, rewriting, and editing continuously. Along the way, something unprecedented happened to him: he gave himself to his book. Stoker opened his internal doors and allowed sexual fears, fantasies, and obsession he ordinarily kept out of sight to find expression on the page, encoded into the receptive language of vampiric seductions and penetration. (The child-Stoker had loved codes and ciphers. At the end of his childhood, he encoded his given name, Abraham, into Bram, and used it for the rest of his life.)

Stoker never stopped wanting to be a literary man as well as a man of the theater, but when Henry Irving and the Lyceum Theatre faded from existence, thereby releasing him to write full time and produce, he hoped, a novel a year, he failed to match the success of his masterpiece. Nothing ever gripped him as *Dracula* had, but another factor also contributed, just as significantly, to his failure. This factor is centered in the aspect of Stoker's aesthetic that made his masterpiece something of an anachronism for the time in which it was published.

Although *Dracula* was published in 1897, only four years before the death of Queen Victoria, its sole acknowledgment of the contemporary world is in the gadgetry that permits its many documents to be distributed amongst its characters. Dr. John Seward speaks his diary entries into a device that records them onto a wax cylinder, and Mina Harker knows how to use a typewriter. Stoker's own grasp of typewriter technique was less firm than his character's: Mina copies and transcribes several hundred pages of text in a single night! In every other regard, the novel looks determinedly backward to the high noon of the Victorian novel, in particular that subset of Gothic Fiction known as the Novel of Sensation, which dealt with implausible events and guilty secrets. It is this literature from which *Dracula* takes its manner, tone, and narrative values. Wilkie Collins, Stoker's primary literary inspiration, died in 1889, his best work long behind him. *The Moonstone* had been published in 1868, and *The Woman in White* in 1860, nearly forty years before *Dracula*'s appearance. The other two landmarks of the Novel of Sensation, Mrs. Henry Wood's *East Lynn* and M. E. Braddon's *Lady Audley's Secret*, came out in 1861 and 1862.

By the end of the nineteenth century, the idea of the novel form was already moving toward Modernism, and in 1897, evidence of a new, transforming wind lay close at hand: Conrad had published *An Outcast of the Islands* (1896) and *The Nigger of the Narcissus* (1897), Henry James had just published *The Spoils of Poynton* (1897) and H. G. Wells had charged onto the scene with *The Time Machine* (1895), *The Island of Dr. Moreau* (1896), and *The Invisible Man* (1897). Stoker could never have seen how quickly the novel of gas light and hansom cabs was to go out of date.

The same adherence to a fading model shaped his career in the theater. Stoker, a Protestant Ascendancy Irishman, escaped the drudgery of a civil service clerkship in Dublin Castle by ingratiating himself into the entourage surrounding his hero, the actor Henry Irving; the hero responded by offering him a job that demanded near-total self-effacement. Star-struck, Stoker happily accepted the conditions of his employment in exchange for constant proximity to his beloved master. For twenty years, he filled the role of sycophant, admirer, manager, troubleshooter, and professional companion to the most famous actor of his day, who greedily absorbed more and more of his life. Irving was his Dracula, and he was Irving's Renfield. Stoker undoubtedly knew precisely what psychic battery he drew on in the creation of his most famous character—the parallel is too striking for it to be otherwise—and Irving must have intuited something of the same, for at a time when he was desperately in need of new material, he refused to consider staging *Dracula*.

Stoker may seem to have been ruthlessly exploited by the domineering star, but we must remember that he welcomed his position and flourished in it. He should not be pitied for his long association with Irving. Stoker loved his job and was very good at managing its unending challenges. He took care of the theater, organized the meals and travel arrangements, managed the lighting, scouted new material, oversaw rehearsals, cared for the props, massaged the press, wrote Irving's letters and served as his listening post and dogsbody. The foreman with the clipboard—in this case, the tall, bearded, formally dressed Irishman with a starchy public demeanor—became a reasonably well-known figure in London life, "the ubiquitous Stoker," in Irving's phrase.

However, that *Dracula* was old-fashioned from the day of its publication in no way detracts from its intrinsic merits. This is a thriller that actually thrills, a horror novel that actually induces horror. Unlike other kinds of fiction, horror finds its successes and achieves its end—the creation in the reader of the emotion that gives the genre its name—most often by pushing one or another of a specific culture's hot buttons. At any one time, a significant number of the citizens in any particular society are going to be afraid of the same few things. From decade to decade, the hot button of a single culture might be unemployment and poverty, a suddenly intransigent youth culture, or some other fresh redefinition of "the Other"; at all times, however, depictions of sexuality can be counted on to arouse a degree of uneasiness. The effectiveness of most horror novels depends on the power of their set-piece subclimaxes, which deliver the emotional goods while preparing the way for the great fireworks displays at their conclusions, and *Dracula* is no exception. *Dracula*'s effectiveness is as much a product of the splendid, in fact truly riveting subclimaxes at the end of part two and at midpoint in part three as of its tidy structure, and what gives these two passages their extraordinary power has everything to do with the way Stoker infuses his ongoing imagery of horror with an even more horrific sexuality.

Unfortunately, by applying a debased, parlor version of Freudian analysis to the novel, several generations of readers and critics have rendered the sexuality in *Dracula* completely banal. By now, everyone thinks they understand that the book portrays a conflict between Victorian repression and anarchic eroticism, and that the slaying of the vampire at its conclusion represents the triumph of repression. In this drastic misreading, the vampire embodies the erotic, which threatens the orderly societal fabric woven from premarital chastity, well-supervised courtships, lengthy engagements and sensible marriages, so the vampire must be destroyed. *Finis*.

I want to be clear unto transparency on this point: horror, at least good horror, horror worthy of the name, *never* works to such a reductive template. We expect more from a reasonably sophisticated children's book, why not then from a genre that has given us Shirley Jackson's *The Haunting of Hill House*? Or, for that matter, gave us Mary Shelley, Edgar Allan Poe, and Stephen King? An influential and otherwise intelligent science fiction editor once said to me, "All category horror is about good versus evil, and that's that." Right, and that's why it's weightless and disposable—it's no more than a formula. The conventional view of *Dracula* is not merely reductive, it ignores precisely those psychic distress signals and linguistic giveaways that represent Stoker's willingness to surrender to his own text, in other words, the very passages that elevate *Dracula* above even the most skillful examples of "category" horror.

In this novel, the eroticized vampire certainly does threaten the civilizing social patterns of gender identification and courtship, but first it threatens the self. The nature of that threat lies in its sheer enormity of scale, the depth of its seductiveness regardless of gender, and its presence throughout the natural but extra-human world. These qualities locate the erotic within the realm of the supernatural. When the erotic and the supernatural share a common territory beyond the control of human beings, the erotic cannot be a simple referent for evil. Instead, sex and horror merge in a way that joins ecstasy with revulsion, a combination too powerful for the self to handle. Seen through the lens of horror, sex becomes risky, savage, overloaded with destructive energy: submission invites destruction; fluids spurt with elemental avidity; orgasms strike with volcanic force.

It is a lot more comfortable to see the vampire as an emblem of the forbidden and repressed, a two-dimensional icon, dazzlingly handsome and glamorous as all get-out. He's beautiful, he's conflicted, he's a neat guy to hang with. The ever-more-numerous fictions by writers like Anne Rice describing the adventures of contemporary vampires, which adopt the repression vs. sexual anarchy template by inverting it to make the vampire heroic (Repression, boo! Go, you sexy immortal!), are almost always utterly enjoyable, but they are "goth" rather than Gothic: less grand, less inward, and stabilized around a less inclusive vision of human nature. The supernatural has been externalized, therefore tamed, and what we are left with are empowerment fantasies disguised as "transgression." Stoker's vampires are Gothic, and the transgressive, while immensely seductive, is about as glamorous as a wound.

Doubleness and duality ripely inform the Gothic, which abounds in lost twins, doppelgangers, secret sharers, and mirrored images. Wilkie Collins built his career on this theme, and the first of *Dracula*'s references to it occurs on the morning after Jonathan Harker's arrival at the castle, when he is approached from behind by the Count while shaving and discovers that his host is not reflected in the shaving glass. To overcome the hard-nosed reader's objections to this impossibility, Stoker has Harker hammer the point home by repeating it twice more:

"But there was no reflection of him in the mirror! The whole room behind me was displayed; but there was no sign of a man in it, except myself."

This is akin to the dog that did not bark in the night, an absence that defines a presence. The doppelganger, the most psychologically loaded version of duality, is the figure that has stepped out of the mirror to roam the world, a split-off or denied part of the self allowed to run rampant by reason of having been defined as the Other. (And the Other is always that aspect of ourselves we least wish to see in the mirror.)

The book begins and ends with the same gesture, movement from Bistritz through the Borgo Pass and toward the castle. Within the triangular space defined by these two moments, multiple dualities declare themselves: Lucy and Mina, Dracula's targets; Dracula and Renfield, original and inferior copy; Van Helsing and Dracula, paired foes; the castle and Carfax Abbey, the vampire's paired residences; Carfax Abbey and Dr. Seward's sanatorium, the Bad Place and the Good Place, side by side and linked by a common wall. Each pair of dualities is linked in the same fashion. Near the end of the book's first half, Lucy becomes a vampire and is murdered; near the end of the second half, Mina almost *becomes* Dracula and begs to be murdered if the process becomes irreversible. Lucy's fate nearly overtakes Mina, and Mina begins to see the contents of Dracula's mind. Each half of a duality shares a deep connection with its partner, and the only case in which the connection is benign is the last and least of them. On the final page, Quincey Morris, the adventurous American, dies; in the Note that follows, we learn that on the anniversary of Morris's death, Mina gave birth to her son Quincey, in whom she detects "some of our brave friend's spirit."

The first term of the first of these dualities, the movement through the mountains to the castle, occurs in the shortest of the book's three sections. Stoker consciously casts Jonathan Harker's account of his travels as a journey into the exotic and unknowable—the territory of the Other. "The impression I had was that we were leaving the West and entering the East." That is, we are leaving the world of rationality, science, and common sense cherished by men such as Harker and Dr. Seward, and venturing into the insecure, treacherous, fablelike realm ruled by superstition, which is the science of the irrational. Harker writes, "I read that every known superstition in the world is gathered into the horse-shoe of the Carpathians, as if it were the centre of some sort of imaginative whirlpool." Here, ordinary English reality unravels before the assault of the unstable and dreamlike and becomes its own twin, a superstition like any other. To interpret a universe in which a nobleman may be a monstrous four-hundred-year-old leech, Englishmen need Dr. Van Helsing, who does not appear for another hundred and twenty pages and who is a battle-hardened veteran of assaults on rationality. In Van Helsing's absence, Harker ignores every warning signal and misreads all the evidence. As blithely ignorant as Nigel Bruce's Watson to Basil Rathbone's Holmes, he disregards the reader's admonishments and goes his merry, though increasingly puzzled, way until the walls close in around him.

Here is the Count as Harker first sees him:

His face was a strong—a very strong—acquiline, with high bridge of the thin nose and peculiarly arched nostrils; with lofty domed forehead, and hair growing scantily round the temples but profusely elsewhere. His eyebrows were very massive, almost meeting over the nose, and with bushy hair that seemed to curl in its own profusion. The mouth, so far as I could see it under the heavy moustache, was fixed and rather cruel-looking, with peculiarly sharp, white teeth; these protruded over the lips, whose remarkable ruddiness showed astonishing vitality in a man of his years.... The general effect was one of extraordinary pallor.... I could not but notice that [his hands] were rather coarse—broad, with squat fingers. Strange to say, there were hairs in the center of the palm. The nails were long and fine, and cut to a sharp point.

And here is Van Helsing, as described by Mina:

...a man of medium weight, strongly built, with shoulders set back over a broad, deep chest and a neck well balanced on the trunk as the head is on the neck. The poise of the head strikes one at once as indicative of thought and power; the head is noble, well-sized, broad, and large behind the ears. The face, clean-shaven, shows a hard, square chin, a large, resolute, mobile mouth, a good-sized nose, rather straight, but with quick, sensitive nostrils.... The forehead is broad and fine, rising at first almost straight and then sloping back above two bumps or ridges wide apart.... Big, dark blue eyes are set widely apart, and are quick and tender or stern with the man's moods.

All of this is taken in while Van Helsing enters the room and walks toward her! Clearly, we are meant to align the two portraits and note the contrast between "eastern" animality, which incorporates a strong whiff of "peculiar," perverse sexuality, and bluff yet sensitive "western" heroism.

Count Dracula's perversity extends to his three handmaidens, who ensure that Harker realizes he has left the familiar world behind by awakening in him a form of desire that in its passivity seems more feminine than masculine. "There was something about them that made me uneasy, some longing and at the same time some deadly fear. I felt in my heart a wicked, burning desire that they would kiss me with those red lips." What burns is wicked, and when one of the women bends over him, the moral dilemma heats up. "There was a deliberate voluptuousness which was both thrilling and repulsive, and as she arched her neck she actually licked her lips like an animal…." I like that "actually," which turns an unexceptional gesture into a sensuous threat. We get to the heart of the matter with these two sentences: "I could feel the soft, shivering touch of the lips on the super-sensitive skin of my [*of my what? Oh, it's just*] throat, and the hard dents of two sharp teeth, just touching and pausing there. I closed my eyes in a langourous ecstasy and waited—waited with beating heart." The passive male's ecstasy flirts with penetration, and penetration reads as a version of castration. Harker is fighting, none too successfully, for his manhood. Release from these women and the primal fears they evoke is purchased at the cost of an even greater peril, for when the enraged Count barrels in, he stops them with a dire stage whisper: "Back, I tell you all! This man belongs to me!"

Harker's language emphasizes the nature of the threat he wishes to escape: "At least God's mercy is better than that of these monsters, and the precipice is steep and high. At its foot a man may sleep—as a man."

The second section of the novel runs from Chapter V to Chapter XVII and is primarily centered on Mina Murray (Harker-to-be) and Lucy Westenra. It begins with a complete reversal of tone in the light-hearted epistolary dialogue, much of it about fickle Lucy's suitors, between the two young women; it ends in the orgasmic bloodbath of the book's true climax, which is occasioned by the depredations of Lucy's most successful suitor.

It is vastly to Stoker's credit, and to the power of the novel, that he does not make explicit the causal linkages between the events reported by Lucy and Mina. By declining to connect the dots, Stoker permits the reader to do it for him, and the deeper engagement for the reader produced by this strategy makes the individual scenes and actions at once more mysterious and vivid. The reader must associate the wrecked *Demeter* with the boxes Harker saw being taken from the castle; the disappearances reported in the captain's log with Dracula's presence on board; the "great dog" that leaped from the ruined vessel and ran uphill into Whitby with the wolves seen in Transylvania, therefore with Dracula; Renfield's mood swings with his master's approach; Lucy's weakness with submission to the vampire; and, most breathtakingly, the enigmatic "bloofer lady" with the dead Lucy. (For readers who may have missed the point, Stoker does finally make this connection, but only in a throwaway line spoken twenty pages later.) Much of the effectiveness of the novel's second movement, which is its most powerful section, comes from Stoker's silence.

Only a few contemporary horror writers trust their readers to this extent. I've never understood why that should be, apart from our general cultural tendency to simplify and streamline narrative into a cartoon. Modern horror, alas, is chockablock with cartoons. Since many of the cartoonists are friends of mine, I will refrain from listing a representative sample of their names, on the grounds that they are doing exactly what they think they are supposed to do, and there is no need to embarrass them. Besides, a lot of readers, also a good number of reviewers, prefer having everything spelled out for them. What I prefer are writers like Robert Aickman, Thomas Tessier, John Crowley, and Jonathan Carroll, who are after larger game. (My own efforts at deliberate indirection have led to indictments on several counts of Unnecessary Obfuscation, Aggravated Slowness, Assault With Intent to Stupefy, Irresponsible Neglect of Reader, and so on, all cases currently under appeal.) In any case, Stoker consciously chose not to explain the connections between the events remarked by Lucy and Mina, in my view to great effect; another kind of silence speaks even more powerfully through a consistent set of associations Stoker establishes in the novel's second part, consciously or not. These associations, which have to do with Dracula's invasive appearance upon the stage, build upon Harker's shameful thrill at his near-rape by the Count's lascivious female attendants.

Whenever a writer of fiction places two elements in close proximity several times in the course of a single work, those elements are being associated with each other, indelibly: no matter how disparate they may seem, they have an intimate relationship, and the qualities of one will inform the other. Throughout the whole of the second part of *Dracula*, Stoker aligns descriptions of ravishing sunsets with revelations of the vampire's otherwise unheralded presence. After the explosive climax to this section, the point of this association or linkage has been—we might as well say—driven home, and it vanishes from the text. The relationship of sunsets to vampire enters with the newspaper clipping about the wreck of the *Demeter* that Mina pastes into her journal. An unnamed "Correspondent" writes of "splendidly-coloured clouds…clouds of every sunset-colour—flame, purple, pink, green, violet, and all the tints of gold; with here and there masses not large, but of absolute blackness that preceded the tremendous storm, when the whole aspect of nature at once became convulsed…the lately glassy sea was like a roaring and devouring monster….”

The prelude to Dracula’s long-plotted invasion of England incorporates a staggering natural beauty. Ruled by sunrise and sunset, the Count partakes of these transformative times of day, but the connection is far more than a harmless metaphor. While innocently describing her friend’s corruption at the hands of the Count, Mina remarks “brilliant moonlight, and the soft effect of the light over the sea and sky—merged together in one great, silent mystery—was beautiful beyond words. Between me and the moonlight flitted a great bat, coming and going in great circles.” Dracula emerges directly from the “great, silent” moonlit scene, for he has created this magnificence out of his own substance. Stoker’s sense of the vampire’s grandeur compels him to use the word “great” three times in a sentence and a half.

When the Count moves unnoticed onto a nearby bench on Whitby’s East Cliff, “The setting sun, low down in the sky, was just drooping over the East Cliff and the old abbey, and seemed to bathe everything in a beautiful rosy glow.” This stunning, seemingly ironic overflow of natural beauty *is* the Count in the sense that it would not be present if the bat had flown on, and it expresses the incalculable range of his powers. What is supernatural holds dominion over conventional nature, which becomes its silent voice—Stoker is reaching out into a realm almost expressionistic in the violence of its transformations. Menace and evil saturate the transformed landscape, painted in heightened colors by the vampire’s presence.

Dr. Seward provides the most telling of these associative linkages. On his way home from visiting a temporarily improving Lucy, he pauses to look at the sunset. “It was a shock to me to turn from the wonderful smoky beauty of a sunset over London, with its lurid lights and inky shadows and all the marvellous tints that come on foul clouds even as on foul water, and to realise all the grim sternness of my own cold stone building, with all its weight of breathing misery...."

Marvelous tints color foul clouds, and lurid lights cast inky shadows: a suffused eroticism has been displaced into the esthetic, where it takes on a mysteriously sinister aspect. Against the literally ravishing backdrop from which the vampire comes toward us—and which is no more than the reflection of his erotic appeal *as defined by Stoker*—the rational world is grim, stern, cold, and made of stone, miserable because it has been drained of the erotic energy felt to be so threateningly powerful that it had to be displaced. Compared to Dracula, Van Helsing is made of stone, and maybe he's miserable because he suspects that whenever he encounters a sexually attractive woman, he will have to cut her head off and ram a stake into her heart.

Dracula's second section foregrounds Van Helsing's attempt to cure Lucy of an illness only he can diagnose. When he fails to save the living Lucy, he must save her after her death. His first task is to reveal the most immediately pressing aspect of his secret, that it is the deceased Lucy who has been attacking children on Hampstead Heath. Dr. Seward does not believe him; when their turn comes, Quincey and Godalming react with dismissive outrage. Van Helsing's second task, then, is to present the little band with the evidence that will destroy their innocence.

The Lucy we find in her coffin has been transformed into one of the wanton creatures that tormented Harker. Van Helsing's obscene theory is true after all. "She seemed like a nightmare of Lucy as she lay there; the pointed teeth, the bloodstained, voluptuous mouth—which it made one shudder to see—the whole carnal and unspiritual appearance, seeming like a devilish mockery of Lucy's sweet purity."

What is frightening here, we should ask; Lucy's alteration into a sexually inviting supernatural monstrosity, or the absorption of sexuality into the monstrous?

Arthur Godalming, Lucy's intended bridegroom, drives the stake into her heart. Penetrated, Lucy

> shook and quivered and twisted in wild contortions; the sharp white teeth champed together till the lips were cut, and the mouth was smeared with a crimson foam.... Arthur never faltered. He looked like a figure of Thor as his untrembling arm rose and fell, driving deeper and deeper the mercy-bearing stake.... And then the writhing and quivering of the body became less, and the teeth seemed to champ, and the face to quiver. Finally it lay still.... The hammer fell from Arthur's hand.... The great drops of sweat sprang from his forehead, and his breath came in broken gasps.

The Victorian era was one of the great ages for pornographers and collectors of pornography, and no Victorian, except perhaps for Queen Victoria herself, could have read this parody of a wedding night as anything but ripely sexual. The point is not that repressive male insecurity cannot tolerate the spectacle of unfettered female sexuality and must put it to death to restore the fantasy of female purity. Godalming is an equal partner in this bloody celebration, and he drives deeper and deeper until the deed is done, leaving him sweaty and gasping. The real impact of this extraordinary scene, which is the book's high point, literally its central moment, depends upon *Dracula*'s status as a Gothic novel of supernatural horror. Here the natural beauty-vampire association comes home to roost where it began, in the realm of the erotic—in a gesture of absolute trust in his genre, Stoker turns the conventional paradigm upside down and locates sexuality as an aspect of the supernatural. Thus located, sexual power and sexual fantasy become terrifying, capable of animating the dead and coloring the natural landscape.

The third and longest section of *Dracula* runs from Chapter XVII through Chapter XXVVII and covers the last half of the book. Renfield's usefulness as a prototype of his master is erased by the Count's immanent departure from England, and he has only one more function to perform before he is subtracted from the story, that of pointing out the countermovement to the search for Dracula's resting places undertaken by the little band. Because we are privy to Mina's latest journal entries, we know that the Count has turned his attentions to her as he did to Lucy, but the members of the little band, including Mina, do not. With his dying words, Renfield gives the game away. "When Mrs. Harker came in to see me this afternoon she wasn't the same; it was like tea after the teapot has been watered.... I don't care for the pale people; I like them with lots of blood in them, and hers had all seemed to have run out.... It made me mad to know that He had been taking the life out of her." While Dr. Seward, Quincey Morris, Harker, and Lord Godalming, the males of the band, went out to seek the monster, he was breaking in to corrupt Mina. By protecting her—they kept her ignorant of their actions—they have endangered the member of their group they most wish to protect.

On the spot, the three men who have heard Renfield's jealous swan song break into Mina's room and come upon the novel's second great scene of horrific Gothic sexuality. It is more perverse than the orgiastic wedding night and less powerful only because it does not end in slaughter. (It cannot, for both parties are off the hook. Mina is still a human being, and the heightened circumstances of this novel forcefully prohibit male-to-male penetration. The withheld slaughter finally occurs when Van Helsing, his "very instincts of man" aroused by "voluptuous" female charms, dispatches one of the handmaidens in an act of what he calls "butcher-work.") The invading party finds Harker unconscious and his wife kneeling on the bed before Dracula.

> With his left hand he held both Mrs. Harker's hands, keeping them away with her arms at full tension; his right hand gripped her by the back of the neck, forcing her face down on his bosom. Her white nightdress was smeared with blood, and a thin stream trickled down the man's bare breast.... The attitude of the two had a terrible resemblance to a child forcing a kitten's nose into a saucer of milk to compel it to drink.

The allusion to fellatio could scarcely be more direct, but Stoker reinforces it with Mina's horrified description of what has been done to her. The entire scene is replayed, this time from her point of view:

> ...he pulled open his shirt, and with his long sharp nails opened a vein in his breast. When the blood began to spurt out, he took my hands in one of his, holding them tight, and with the other seized my neck and pressed my mouth to the wound, so that I must either suffocate or swallow some of the—Oh my God! my God!

Here, we could say, sexuality has been so completely absorbed into the supernatural that there is no longer any significant distinction between the two.

At this point, the plot obligingly goes into overdrive. What had been the search for the Count's bolt-holes turns into the thriller's defining trope, the chase. Brilliantly, Stoker compounds the tension by dividing his band into three parties of two and sending each on a different route to the end of the chase and the final confrontation. The novel's last three chapters, amounting to some fifty pages, rattle irresistibly to the moment when the three parties converge, minutes before sunset, on the gypsy cart bearing the Count's coffin back to his castle. The five men battle with the gypsies, Quincey Morris receives a fatal wound, the gypsies scatter, and a moment before the sun slips beneath the mountains, the dying Morris stabs the Count with his Bowie knife while Jonathan Harker takes his revenge by slitting the vampire's throat. Count Dracula turns to dust and vanishes for good.

We get a brief description of the sun setting against the castle. Morris breathes his last, expressing his gratification at having served a worthy cause, and the book ends in praise of his gallantry. It is all perfectly satisfying, up to a point. The problem, of course, is that we have been cheated of the great moment in which Dracula meets a cinematic demise like Lucy's, only on an appropriately larger scale. Fifty pages of rising tension culminate in two short paragraphs consisting of seventy-five words. In contrast, the scene of the vampire-Lucy's destruction occupies an expansive three pages and 4,500 words. Stoker's reasoning for avoiding such a scene seems clear to me: no matter how well he wrote it, the scene would never be more than a weak imitation of the first one. Even in Van Helsing's slaying of the female vampire, Stoker wisely declines to go into details.

Any writer accomplished enough to have conceived of *Dracula*'s magnificent structure would have seen the weakness of its final climax; the man who did set its structure in place understood exactly what was missing, and after the brief description of Dracula's death, Stoker immediately invokes sublime nature to supply the requisite grandeur. In the revised, finished text, Dracula's death is followed by this one-sentence paragraph:

"The Castle of Dracula now stood out against the red sky, and every stone of its broken battlements was articulated against the light of the setting sun."

In the original manuscript this was followed with six long sentences Stoker later crossed out.

> As we looked there came a terrible convulsion of the earth so that we seemed to rock to and fro and fell to our knees. At the same moment with a roar which seemed to shake the very heavens the whole castle and the rock and even the hill on which it stood seemed to rise into the air and scatter in fragments while a mighty cloud of black and yellow smoke volume on volume in rolling grandeur was shot upwards with inconceivable rapidity. Then there was a stillness in nature as the echoes of that thunderous report seemed to come as with the hollow book of a thunder clap—the long reverberating roll which seems as though the floors of heaven shook. Then down in a mighty ruin falling whence they rose came the fragments that had been tossed skyward in the cataclysm. From where we stood it seemed as though the one fierce volcano burst had satisfied the need of nature and that the castle and the structure of the hill had sunk again into the void. We were so appalled with the suddenness and the grandeur that we forgot to think of ourselves.

All the sexual imagery throughout the book informs this passage and culminates in it. Eroticized by a displaced sexual urgency that has been subsumed into the supernatural, nature "satisfies the need" to expel all traces of the vampire in a massive erection and ejaculation, which are followed by a relieved "detumescence." Stoker was so insistent on the "grandeur" of the spectacle that he used the word twice.

And then, before the manuscript went to the typesetter, Stoker deleted everything after the first sentence. His biographer, Barbara Belford, suggests two possible reasons for the deletion: his publishers may have wanted to leave open the option of a sequel; and Stoker might have been troubled by the resemblance of this scene to the ending of *The Fall of the House of Usher*. It seems likelier that the scene was cut for more personal reasons. Either Stoker or his publisher could have found it too much, too graphic, thus unacceptable; and Stoker could have had second thoughts about having this grandly phallic moment recorded by the pen of Mina Harker, in whose final journal entry it appears. The Victorians may have been much more like us than we wish to admit, but on the evidence of *Dracula*, they differed in at least one significant way—they took sex and horror far more seriously than we do.

100 Best Books of Horror
Introduction

Ever savvy, also incredibly well informed, Stephen Jones and Kim Newman have chosen to bring out this companion volume to their 1988 collection *Horror: 100 Best Books*, at what seems to me exactly the right time, which is to say the moment at which a sophisticated contemporary reader might well come to the startling recognition that the one hundred most significant, most interesting books in the sprawling, multiform, definition-shedding field of horror might well be substantially different from any such list compiled nearly twenty years ago. Things have changed, in my opinion radically and entirely for the better.

That horror now should be a different kind of animal than it was in, say, 1975, to pick the year of *'Salem's Lot* and my substantially less successful first effort at writing a horror novel, *Julia*, might seem inevitable. Over the past thirty years, general fiction itself mutated and evolved, as the generation dominated by Bellow, Roth, and Updike gradually gave way to writers such as Jonathan Lethem and Michael Chabon. The culture changed, and so did tastes in literature, a matter already in evidence by the late 1980s. But it's an odd and telling fact that while general literature shifted away from the 1970s Bellow-Updike axis to a Thomas Pynchon-influenced model, then yet again around the time of the new millennium, horror writing pretty much stuck to its guns from the mid 1970s to the late '90s, which is the reason it began to seem pretty tired. Witches, vampires, haunted houses, and serial killers chased each other round and round the tree until they met the fate of the tigers in *Little Black Sambo*—they turned to butterfat. It was as though everyone noticed except the writers—especially, alas, those who, while replicating the old formulas in largely self-published chapbooks, supposed themselves to be innovators. (Douglas Winter got so fed up with this lazy spiral that in a speech at the World Horror Convention in 1994, he told everyone that horror didn't actually exist, at least not in the way they thought of it. Using a phrase particular to the demolition industry, he recommended that the assembled conventioneers "make some sky.")

As the contributors to this book demonstrate, sky has been made, in abundance. During the late 1990s, this wonderful thing happened—it became clear that a number of emerging writers had figured out how to extend, ignore, or transform horror's (and dark fantasy's) supposed boundaries. By doing so, they were treating it as what at its best it had aspired to be all along, a kind of literature distinguished from other kinds chiefly by an angle of vision that, while resisting most culturally determined forms of denial, celebrated the grotesque, the eccentric, the marginal, and the magical. This point of view respected the hard facts of loss, pain, emotional extremity, and grief; mainly, I think, it honored the capacity of vivid, liberated imagination to discover unexpected and often unsettling truths. Among these writers—most of whom are included here—were Poppy Z. Brite, Dan Chaon, Peter Crowther, Terry Dowling, Tananarive Due, Jeffrey Ford, Christopher Fowler, Elizabeth Hand, Glenn Hirshberg, Graham

Joyce, Caitlin R. Kiernan, Tim Lebbon, Thomas Ligotti, Kelly Link, Christopher Rowe, Michael Marshall Smith, Rosalind Palermo Stevenson, Jeff VanderMeer, and Conrad Williams. The non-fiction writers Stefan Dziemianowicz and Bill Shcchan, both of whom appear in this volume, provided intelligent and supportive commentary on the exciting developments, as did almost everyone who contributed reviews and luxuriantly thoughtful journal *Necrofile* (1991-98, RIP).

Readers of a conservative bent—inherent conservatism being one of the qualities critics reflexively attribute to horror—generally respond with a shudder of distaste to my concept of the genre (or nongenre) as the essentially boundaryless product of a particular interpretive stance, but here I was tutored by my own experience, and I want to explain how it happened. Between 1988 and 1994 I published three novels that concentrated on childhood trauma, the profound shadow of the Vietnam war, emotional extremity, grief, buried crimes, and buried feelings. There was nothing supernatural in these books; and although they dealt with multiple murders, they did not actually feel like mystery novels—they were more like what I thought mystery novels *should* be. If asked to categorize them, I would have called them thrillers, with the unspoken proviso that these thrillers (1) were not housebroken and (2) read better if read twice. Initially to my dismay, later to my satisfaction, just about every reviewer of these books used his or her first sentence to describe them as horror novels.

Then, as if to prove the point, came "The Specialist's Hat" (Link), *The Tooth Fairy* (Joyce), *Mortal Love* (Hand), "Notes on the Writing of Horror: A Story" (Ligotti), and a host of other, startlingly original fictions that seemed to emerge from an utterly free and unconfined imaginative space. If I were one of the people in this book, I'd have a lot of trouble trying to make my selection. It's wonderful, this sense of amplitude, of a rich bounty.

Quietly Now
Not So Quiet, Maybe
An Appreciation

Charlie Grant was one of the first writers I met after moving from London to the New York area, and he was a revelation. Worlds within worlds existed, none of them known to me until I accepted an invitation to Necon and discovered a very lively scene, centered, it seemed to me, around the extremely engaging figure of Grant, this writer from New Jersey whose work was completely unknown to me. Until the moment when I walked into a cinderblock dormitory in Warwick, Rhode Island, and found myself under the intermittent scrutiny of a slender, active-looking pirate with long-ish, Breck girl-like hair, a dark beard, and the face of a comedian, I had been under the illusion that besides myself, there were—in my generation—basically only three other horror writers worth reading, Thomas Tessier, Ramsey Campbell, and Stephen King, and all of them were friends of mine.

Of course there were others, but writers like Frank deFellita and Ken Eulo didn't seem to have what it took to produce interesting fiction over the long haul. According to me, they couldn't produce interesting fiction over the short haul, either. Even in 1980, most mass market horror fiction stank of formula and dim-witted greed. (What came later made stuff like *Audrey Rose* and *The Brownstone* look pretty good.) In effect, I had been living in a sort of artificial bubble, and most of what I thought I knew about horror and horror writers was untrue. By the simple act of being who he was and saying the things that went through his head, the piratical-looking guy with the face of a comedian clued me in to what was really going on. Charlie let me know that the world I had fondly imagined myself and a few talented friends to be making up already existed, and was larger, brighter, and more various than I (perhaps we) could ever have imagined.

First of all, Charlie Grant was one of the funniest men I'd ever met. Almost everything he said struck me as hilarious, and when he stood up in front of a crowd, as he often did during that Necon weekend, he more or less turned himself into a raucous, rip-roaring standup comic. I remember him MC-ing one of those gatherings and thinking, *Jeez, these guys set the bar pretty high.* A few years later, I saw Charlie take the podium at a World Fantasy Convention where he was once again Master of Ceremonies. He let his eyes wander over the crowd, drew his papers from a jacket pocket, and said, "Four years ago, when we first entered these halls and gazed in wonder at…" He stopped talking and stared at the papers in his hand. With beautiful timing, his face fell. "Shit," he said, loudly. "This is my high school graduation speech." I thought every bit of that was brilliant.

Charlie always seemed to be having a good time, always in motion. Other Necon attendees trailed him around the campus of Roger Williams College, through the halls and lounges of its dorms, up the hill to the dining room and the bar. Clearly, they adored him and looked up to him. (A lot of them also probably hoped one day to be published in the *Shadows* series of anthologies.) It took Charlie only a little while to size me up and in effect welcome me, who really knew nothing, into the group. And it took me only a little while to become very fond of him.

Not only was he an excellent, enlivening character to know, he also gave me one of the best reviews of my life, in a copy of the now long-defunct *Fantasy*. What made it so good was that he understood precisely what I was trying to do in *Shadowland*, and the reason he did is that he read it with a generous heart and mind. The same qualities speak, with utter clarity, through his fiction. I think *The Pet* and *Raven* are among the absolute best horror novels of the past twenty years and represent much of what is most valuable and most significant in our genre. That is because they are novels first and genre novels only secondarily, by dint of their subject matter. I've always felt that this is the right, the most dedicated and writerly, approach, and as a servant to the well-nigh impossible task of creating fiction that is both literature and horror, Charlie Grant, at his best, really cannot be bettered. It was of this ambition that he was speaking when he wrote, "Those who ask for what I like are told I want contemporary horror, with an emphasis on *people* and their problems. I want quiet horror."

Shadowland
Preface

In the early nineteen-seventies there came to me the idea, along with several others I possessed nothing like the knowledge or the expertise to execute, of writing a novel about an American Vietnam veteran expatriated in London and involved with magic and the fraudulent end of the antique business. This error never progressed beyond the note book stage. Another such notion, *Hot Country*, a hypothetical account of the life after the death of his lover of a sixty-five year old gay American male who owned a hotel on the Costa del Sol, wasted about five or six months and perhaps a hundred pages before coming up against its author's limitations: he knew nothing about hotel management, Spain, gay life, or what it was like to be sixty-five. Both of these stillborn novels were in imitation of the magisterial John Hawkes, specifically *The Lime Twig* and *The Blood Oranges.*

After finding my feet with two supernatural novels (I'm still gamely trying to play John Hawkes' idiosyncratic keyboard in the second one), I resurrected my hotelkeeper, turned him into a charming and sexually conventional old rogue, and installed him in *Ghost Story's* Chowder Society, where the other members all thought he was a bit, as we used to say, slow.

In those days my wife and I were living in the first house we'd ever owned, 79 Hillfield Avenue, three red-brick stories in a Crouch End terrace, the entire middle floor and office equipped with so many records played so continuously that the amiable workmen who moved in with us for six or seven months ultimately decided that I must have been a jazz critic. Our first child, a son, was born in the middle of *Ghost Story*—August, 1977. He may have thought that I was a jazz critic, too. I completed the book about the Chowder Society and went fishing for new ideas in the usual misguided way. I'd been reading Frances Yates on Giordano Bruno, I was just beginning to get interested in Gnostic writing, and my notions of the meaning of magic had developed. I had no idea why this should be important to me, but magic, real magic, which could be expressed in stage magic but was not confined to it, was connected by the internal resources of the magician to the unseen, subtle, powerful internal structures of the world itself. (Now that I think about it, the dead lover of *Hot Country's* innkeeper was a *brujo*. The secrets hidden behind other secrets, now literalized, now not, keep knocking at the door.) The world was a gnostic structure, and so was the self. Writing, a form of magic performed daily, led into revelation. I had just experienced success as measured by both the most grossly and finely tuned of instruments: my agent and accountant were delighted by those worldly effects brought about by the other effects which delighted, more satisfyingly, my internal auditor. The agent, the accountant, and my publishers desired a sort of replication of *Ghost Story*; in charge of the fiction-machine, the internal auditor gleefully grabbed the wheel, mashed the accelerator, and went where he wanted to go.

Where he wanted to go was where he'd always wanted to go, backward. Ever since I had struggled half-way out from under my influences, the stories I had been telling myself had to do with the way, everywhere, urgently and immediately, the past lay beneath the surface of the present, shaping events and responses to events with a propagandist's dictatorial command of form. As in actual life, the past of a story determined the story. Most of what you thought you knew throbbed upward, like the bass line in a song, from the history of the occasion, as did all of what you couldn't even guess. In 1978, an English Professor from Milwaukee to whom I had described the disruptions preceding the departure for his farm in Perigord of a mutual friend from my house in Crouch End, said, "You can never understand what's happening to people until you find out what happened just before." We were both, for different reasons, satisfied. He because he had discovered why our friend had behaved so strangely. I because he had uttered that wonderful sentence. I wanted to write a kind of *Bildungsroman* in which the present literally developed out of the past, so I went back to my own experiences in a Milwaukee boy's school, and gave them, in retouched, heightened form, to Tom Flanagan. Insofar as I had a general scheme, mine was to have everything happen twice—what took place at the school would be repeated, in a more dreamlike and dramatic, therefore more unreliable, fashion, at the magician's Vermont estate, Shadowland. Realism, perhaps even the idea of reality itself, would dissolve into a hallucinatory field of possibility. (The origins of this idea, which seemed pretty good at the time and now and again still nudges me in the ribs, were certain passages in *Ghost Story* in which it seemed to me that I was doing something fresh and personal—writing scenes approximate to my own experience—for the first time.) From the resulting ambiguity, cloaked in an eerie, dreamlike emotive state close to the classic definition of "the uncanny," there might emerge a more accurate truth, a gnostic truth.

That this untruthful but accurate truth could emerge directly from the process of storytelling occurred to me because my son had in the meantime become old enough to comprehend the words spoken to him, and therefore was old enough, at least in a general way, to listen to stories. And that was when *Shadowland* really found itself.

I worked at home; I spent a lot of time with my child. He was alert, endearing, intelligent, and like all infants trying so hard to turn into toddlers that they're actually toddling, he absorbed endless quantities of his parents' attention. It was clear that I'd never coach his Little League team, go on fishing trips, or, as my father had, sign up with the Boy Scouts and become a scoutmaster. I was pretty sure I'd never spend crisp fall afternoons playing touch football. H. Rap Brown, or was it O. J. Simpson, said, "When I hear the word culture, I reach for my gun," but I say, "When I hear John Madden. I reach for my remote control." However, there was at least one skill, narrative, I knew I could share with my son. *Kid, dear boy, beloved,* I thought, *now you're going to find out about stories. We're going to have some fun together.*

I read him stories and made up a lot more of them. This must have been along toward the end of 1978. I had finished with Milburn, the Chowder Society, and the snowstorms early that year, then taken six months off for the customary herbal wraps, seaweed immersions, Tarot readings, aura massages, and the like—well, actually, for the aimless downtime drift which happens along like *El Niño* whenever a novel manages to get out of my hands. Toward the end of that year my son was a year and a bit, and I was about to start re-inventing my old school and echoing whatever happened there in a mysterious Vermont estate owned by a Gnostic magician. Nights, when I came downstairs from puzzling about the school and the magician, my son crawled into my lap. I'd say something like, "Did I ever tell you about the old, old eagle who lived at the top of a mountain at the edge of the deepest, darkest forest?" "Uh uh," he'd say, and I was off.

Stories poured out me. I had no idea where they were going when I started them, but along the way they always turned into *real* stories, with beginnings, middles, and ends, complete with hesitations, digressions, puzzles, and climaxes. This was thrilling. My little boy was entranced, and I felt as though I had tapped into the pure, ancient well, the source of narrative, the springwater which nourished me and everyone else like me. After I had uncorked maybe twenty of these home-made fairy tales, it occurred to me that I should write some of them down. Now I wish that I'd written down every single one. I made up stories for years, and the only ones I tried to put on paper are in *Shadowland*—the best one is about why frogs leap and croak. Many of these stories concerned that ancient eagle at the edge of the deepest, darkest forest and an acquaintance of his, a bear with firm opinions and a moral streak. A minor character in *Floating Dragon* is called upon to illustrate a children's book called *The Eagle-Bear Stories*, a ghost-book, spoken but unwritten.

Traditional fairy tales, which I began to investigate soon after I started making up my own, pervade *Shadowland.* The beautiful story called "The King of the Cats" is the novel in miniature. Rose Armstrong is Hans Christian Anderson's Little Mermaid who accepts human form and even after walks across nails and razor blades. Tom Flanagan and Del Nightingale step in and out of the skins of the lost, wandering children inhabiting the Brothers Grimm's compilations of folk tales, and the Brothers Grimm inhabit Coleman Collins' mansion, as they do the imaginations of many people who do not remember reading or hearing the stories they collected.

Fairy tales, especially those assembled by the Grimms, offer a paradox to any writer not in the business of compiling folk tales. Powerful, made of nothing but metaphor, they move with the speaking simplicity of tapestries, epics, and cartoons, but are also startlingly raw. Their experiential truth, also often raw, is sometimes contained in vessels so randomly constructed as to undercut, mock, or question their power. They seem as irrational as dreams, as fanciful as the inventions of a four year old trying to explain away a broken vase. This inconsequentiality, this sense of the inorganic, could come from the way certain particular tales emerge from a history of melding, marrying, parts of similar but unrelated stories over time: in the end, you have a story as smooth as a stone from a river. It coheres because it's been polished by elemental handling.

Earlier that year, I had been moved by John Fowles' novel, *The Magus*, which suggested a way to unite the powerful strangeness resulting from the oral tradition with more conventional narrative satisfactions. No one familiar with *The Magus* who reads *Shadowland* can fail to notice Fowles' influence on me, which was profound and pervasive; but this influence was above all liberating, not enslaving. Fowles demonstrated how the seductive uncertainty implicit in theatrical illusion and, even more importantly, the emotional effects of this uncertainty, could find expression in a narrative which itself moved through successive layers of surprise, doubt, suspicion, and discovery.

A being of overwhelming psychological penetration tells a series of stories. The stories unfold, they exercise an increasingly gravitational power, seeming to speak to the inner life of the listener. Together, put end to end, they form a single, unreliable construct, a house filled with hidden passages and trap doors, also an entire wing sometimes but not always entered by a certain flight of stairs.

Two nights ago, you found that wing. In one chamber, your father thundered a dire warning; in another a loved one awaited; in yet another, someone lay bleeding to death. Tonight, you cannot even find the stairs. When you found them last night, they led to a blank wall. You must heed the warning, you desire the beloved, your own life depends upon saving the life of the afflicted one, but if you cannot find the stairs, or if the stairs, when found, lead to a blank wall, where do you begin? You require another story, one which resolves your separate concerns within a larger and unsuspected conclusion, not by answering any of them, but by arranging them in a different order before you, as across a grassy, distant field. This final story, as dubious and unreliable as the others, will be both a beginning and an ending.

• • •

The English novelist Pamela Haines, a dear friend, read an early draft of *Shadowland* and, with merciful tact, made available a great deal of necessary information about World War One, especially information concerning medical officers; Pam also told me much about English popular culture during and immediately after the first World War, the world of the music hall, and gave me a photograph of the Wood Green Empire, the site of Coleman Collins' ultimate performance.

Other memories, of old teachers and friends, found their way into the Carson School section of *Shadowland*, so much so that this part of the book is a kind of *roman á clef.* My friend Morris Holbrook, now a Professor at the Business School of Columbia University and an eminence in marketing theory, provided Morris Fielding. Robert Schuster, another old friend, now a lawyer and entrepreneur in Los Angeles, appears as Bob Sherman, who in the yellow boots and splendid office of his period as partner in Albert Grossman's world-altering management firm (they represented Bob Dylan, the Band, Blood, Sweat and Tears, many other bands) tells our narrator a story about Lake the Snake and his Doberman. Chip Hogan is a wildly insufficient version of my fellow 1961 Country Day scholarship student, the brilliant William Ulick "Chip" Burke, Bobby Hollingsworth an even less adequate representation of Robert Mahnke. Within Tom Pinfold, the sweet Tom Churchill, now a lawyer in Milwaukee, can scarcely be glimpsed. (Tom Pinfold's bank scandal is grafted onto him from another boy, one not from our school.) The ironic English instructor Mr. Fitz-Hallan is an affectionate depiction of Sandy McCallum, once my teacher and now a valued friend; Mr. Thorpe, Harvey Ramaker, who ruled over Latin with an almost sadistic ferocity; Chester Ridpath, our History teacher and football coach, Ken Laird, kindlier by far than his fictional stand-in; Mr. Whipple, an engaging extrovert named Forrest McQuitty; Laker Broome, Lake the Snake, resembles our own Headmaster, Warren Seifert, only in his physiognomy and taste in shirts. Dave Brick, Marcus Reilly, Skeleton Ridpath, and Tom and Del have no counterparts in the other, exterior, life, although the saxophonist who enlivens Morris Fielding and our narrator at a school dance is based on a good local tenor player named Ronnie Wirth, whose habit of stuffing his instrument case with bottles of codeine later attracted the unhappy attentions of the authorities.

Shadowland was written, so to speak, on the run, the first third in London, the remainder in Westport, Connecticut, after the same English accountants who had not long ago been so pleased with me banished me from the United Kingdom. I wrote the middle third in the room which would be the dedicatee's bedroom as soon as my office on the floor above was finished, the final section put there, in the best workplace I've ever had or will have. I was still writing by hand in big journals, by pencil, then laboriously typing up what I'd written, revising it, typing it all over again. In mid-December, 1979, when I began the final third, my publishers, Coward, McCann & Geoghegan, demanded a finished manuscript in two months—they'd already bought the front page of *Publishers Weekly* to advertise the book as an October publication. Somehow, I wish I could remember how, I found Barbara Bouchard, a wonderful woman in my neighborhood married to an official at the U.N. and willing to do typing. Every couple of days, after finishing another stretch of pages I walked over my lawn down to Beachside Avenue and over the little stone bridge at the entrance of Burying Hill Beach to Barbara Bouchard's pretty white house, where Barbara took me to a room on the second floor, settled herself down before her trusty Underwood, me in another chair behind her, and, medium-like, flawlessly, typed every word I read aloud to her from my journal. Together, we sailed along to the end of the novel. The immense satisfaction of this process can be explained in a phrase—it was exactly like telling a story.

Two Essays and a Frivolity

The Fantasy of Everyday Life

He practically *said* he was Elvis, so you should not be surprised by his behavior. That was there right from the beginning. On the "Charlie Rose Show," he looked straight at the camera and sang "Don't Be Cruel." And that blond woman standing next to him is the celebrated Scottish socialite, Lady Macbeth. Lady Macbeth knew what she was doing when she consented to become Mrs. Elvis, and she is doing her best to put up with all that rocking and rolling. They came from the Arkansas Highlands in a pink Cadillac, and they left a trail of corpses in their wake.[1] Now that they live in that handsome building on Pennsylvania Avenue, the one with the iron fence around it, corpses tumble out of broom closets, what used to be the Nixon Helipad looks like the last act of *Hamlet*,[2] and the Earl of South Africa and Tiffany, his new girlfriend, are coming for a State Dinner. "Don't Be Cruel" is played before every press conference.[3] They have been shot at only once, and they weren't even there at the time.[4] Every night after the cannon smoke has been dispersed by the staff as yet unsubpeonaed, they get together and plot.

I like these people. They are creatures of the purest fantasy, and they prove over and over that this world, ours, is an alternate universe. No authentic universe would act this way for a second. You might have some giddiness now and again, and the occasional extravaganza, but giddy extravaganzas such as bodies discovered in the trunks of pink Cadillacs, never. I know what an authentic universe is like, and so do you. We share a dim, ancestral, memory-like illusion. It's like a dream-fragment, of a world that began with the pastoral and darkened over time into an industrial society that was flawed, maybe even terrible in some ways, especially in those precincts dominated by dark satanic mills, but at least theoretically open to improvement.[5] This world had rules. It had inexorable causes and immutable results. I believe the authentic universe was largely English, though it did have a French Quarter.[6] Either George Eliot grew up there, or he imagined it in ravishing detail.[7] Among other things, the authentic universe paid attention to the kind of rationality evolved from common sense, to logical connections, to humane values and nuanced judgments, and, since we are talking about writing, to the realistic tradition.

By "the realistic tradition," I mean the assumptions about the contract between reader and author and the representational techniques found, speaking very generally now, in the novels of Jane Austen, Anthony Trollope, Arnold Bennett, and John Galsworthy; in Balzac, Zola, and some of Flaubert; in Tolstoy and Turgenev; in Howells, Dreiser, and James T. Farrell.[8] What does not emerge directly from the nineteenth century is rooted in it. Harold Robbins started as a disciple of Farrell's, but speedily ascended into the altogether elsewhere.[9] In the late 1970s, I thought that people like Robbins and Judith Krantz represented the sole, comically degraded, survival of the nineteenth-century novel. It seemed as though all of that imaginative treasure had dwindled into verbal cartoons, because only readers satisfied with cartoons could still buy into narratives about a protagonist's struggle with, or progress through, definitive social contexts. The sort of fiction considered serious, both honorable mainstream-middlebrow[10] and avant-garde[11] had long ago abandoned this strategy. Nobody cared about tribal customs and rituals, unless they were held up for ridicule, and not, as in *Main Street*, against exterior standards, but by a caustic, self-involved, deracinated insider. (I'm thinking of *Goodbye Columbus*, *Portnoy's Complaint*, and Richard Yates's *Revolutionary Road*.) No one was going to write *Sister Carrie* or *The House of Mirth*, although special dispensation was always granted to Louis Auchincloss.[12]

I also thought that one of the unacknowledged capacities of what I was doing, horror fiction, was that, along with a great deal else and in a way no one would ever really notice, it readily adapted itself to the disregarded strengths of the Victorian novel. In spite of everything I felt to the contrary, nineteenth-century English novels seemed the foundation, the essential ground base, of the fictional enterprise. The best of those novels could never be equaled, because never again would it be possible to experience the conjunction of an expanding popular audience hungry for narrative and the development of the form most capable of satisfying this hunger into a supple, discursive, passionately expressive vehicle. They wanted Charlotte Bronte, Thackeray, and Dickens, and we want our MTV.

Clueless people who suppose they have a handle on the nature of the process, people who don't know anything about the nature of novel-writing, like to say that if Dickens were living now, he would be working in Hollywood—film directors and screenwriters say that, mainly. They can't help themselves.[13] This concept seems sensible to them. They think in visuals, in camera movements, narratives whittled down to their least novelistic elements, and because they know Dickens was a great storyteller who enjoyed, therefore desired, enormous popular success, they automatically assume that the narrative medium is irrelevant. If you are a great storyteller in a time when movies reach a far greater audience than fiction, of course you'll tell those great stories of yours on film. Well, no, resoundingly, especially if you are Charles Dickens, a person so organized as to require the process of putting words on paper for the sake of survival. If that is what you need, you need it. And movies will really not do. Movies can come later. Directors and screenwriters think this way because they are in the alternate universe along with the rest of us. It's a good thing that science-fiction writers invented that trope, or we'd be reeling through the streets clutching our hands to our heads, muttering, "What do they call this place? Isn't there some phrase that means everything is upside down, inside out and backward?"

Just in case you harbor some doubts concerning this alternate universe business let me remove them. In 1997, a certain television talk show hostess did a week at the Rainbow and Stars, alongside the Rainbow Room at the top of the RCA building in Rockefeller Center, where they don't even look embarrassed at charging you $10 for a drink, where the average dinner for two costs $300, and where you will undoubtedly be seated at a table near the Hudson River, or even in New Jersey unless you have the foresight to slip an extra $20 into the palm of an amused-looking fellow named Bismark. The talk show hostess was Kathy Lee Gifford, and the place was packed.

Last month, I read in *New York* magazine that an editor at Random House, my very own publisher, came up with a brilliant idea at an editorial meeting. He suggested that for the next three years, Random declare a moratorium on publishing fiction. They were doing too many novels. Their more important books, like the biographies of Kathy Lee Gifford and Bob Barker, were far more profitable despite their $6 million advances, and besides, the only novels anybody read any more were technical manuals about weapons systems with a few characters thrown in for the sake of tension. This idea was rejected, but I wouldn't be surprised if a few of those present speculated about a moratorium on works of fiction not yet sold to film studios. That makes a lot more sense. You can have a lot of fun in an alternate universe, especially if you think about Mrs. Gifford yodeling into the mike at the Rainbow and Stars, but I am not overjoyed about novels turning into "pre-films," like prequels only worse, filmscripts with a lot of boring descriptions[14] and tedious bits in which people do nothing but talk to each for page after page without blowing anything up.

On Internet discussion groups devoted to writers, subscribers intervalically cease their mutual flirtations to daydream about which actors should be cast in the movies made of their author's books. The subscribers take this activity seriously. They think they are doing something real, something significant, even helpful. In their heart of hearts, they are convinced that their author lurks in the aether, taking notes. It must be as clear to the author as it is to them that the ultimate form of narrative is filmic, and they have taken time out from their imaginary assignations because they want him or her to get it right.

On the Internet and, though less frequently, in non-aetheric life, one comes across people who feel entirely qualified to discuss the merits of a particular novel on the basis of having seen the movie version. Think about what that means.

Here's another one: my agent informed me the other day that my publisher's enthusiasm for the book I have just completed would be in direct proportion to how short it was. That is exactly how he said it. The next time I lunge out of the paddock and begin to charge around the course, I think I'll tell myself I'm digging my heels into a kind of longish short story, a virtual haiku, and whip it across the finish line after 250 pages. It will take three months to write. Everybody will like it a lot.

Here's a great one: Princess Di. No, forget I said that. The Earl of South Africa arrives at Presley's public housing unit tonight, and he's very, very touchy.

All right, here is another sure-fire indication. Before he and his new girlfriend, the well-bred and delightful Tiffany, left the armed compound in Johannesburg to board his private jet and fly to Ronald Reagan International Airport in Washington for tonight's State Dinner honoring the cast of "Friends," the Earl of South Africa, speaking to me from the sacred hush of his armaments room, divulged that many a savvy publisher goes straight to the source, in an alternately universed manner of speaking, and submits to the marketing experts at Barnes & Noble books still in the infantile or soggy diaper stage of the process. The Barnes & Noble experts graciously respond with recommendations as to cover design, number of copies printed, how high the price per copy must be to keep the discounted price at a happy level, and so forth. The Earl, who isn't half so terrible as everybody claimed he was about ten minutes after they all finished adoring him, trusted that it would not be long before collaborative synergy evolved to its inevitable ultimate form in which the experts counseled editor and writer in aid of creating the most acceptable product possible. Let us make every book most like the version of that book most people would want to read, then let them fight it out on the shelves at Barnes & Noble. Film studios poll viewers at test screenings and reshape their entertainments according to the results, because film studios are run by grown-ups perfectly adapted to a changing world.

Do you remember "Family Feud"? It was an anti-quiz show. There were no correct answers except for those decided by majority opinion. I can't tell you how strange I thought that was.

Before we came to the digression concerning the hypothetical present-day Dickens telling those great, great stories given him to tell on account of his being a great, great storyteller in movies, a proposition that must be right because 75 percent of those polled agree with it, I was saying that twenty years ago my little corner of the fantastic seemed to me inherently receptive to the confident, easy-breathing manner of nineteenth-century fiction. I nearly, though not quite, implied, which of course means that I did imply, that I had something like that in mind. I apologize to you. I was lying through my teeth. I'm sorry, but not really. Like everyone who has stood here before me, I tell lies for a living; purposefully, with an absolute disregard for the sorts of ideational structures generally thought of as truth.[15] If you do that long enough, you come to the opinion that a deeply imagined lie contains…no, finish that sentence for yourselves. I don't have to tell you everything and I'm not supposed to talk about that subject anyhow. I think our by-laws specifically forbid it.

Twenty years ago, I had not yet observed that I lived in an upside-down alternate universe invented by a science-fiction writer with a violent sense of irony. However, I did know there was more to life than Victorian novels.

It seemed to me then, and still does now, that there exists something that can be called the fictional space.[16] The fictional space is necessarily, essentially unlocated. It hovers a little distance off the ground.[17] It bears a resemblance to that moment when one awakens from a compelling dream just disappearing from memory. As it whisks, coat-tails flying, out of sight around the corner, it leaves behind charged feeling-traces that no longer precisely refer to objects and actions. You are suspended between two equally authoritative realms. Half a second later, a mixture of bad conscience, anticipatory dread, and brute reality remind you that today you have to buy a birthday present for someone you no longer like all that much, take the car in for an oil change, and deal with that other issue, the one you don't even want to think about, and you are nowhere but back in bed.

What I'm calling the fictional space has more endurance, though sometimes it can be just as difficult to recapture. Its authority derives from its uncertainty, because the uncertainty keeps it what we might as well call moral. Within the fictional space, certainty of any kind speaks of what is unexamined, unfelt, improperly imagined—it is the space between the received and the as yet unknown that will never really be known, except as it is glimpsed there.[18] Judgments and opinions, especially the opinion that you knew what you were doing when you walked in, vanish into sets of possibilities arrayed beside other, contradictory, equally valid possibilities, some of them entirely unexpected but filled with mysterious promise. In fact, anything like conclusions, answers, and finalities no longer exist, because in the fictional space these blunt conditions instructively dissolve before their own rigidity. A kind of generous, exploratory receptiveness allows for inconclusiveness, ambiguity, and a general, accommodating recognition that in this particular alternate universe no valid position can be final.

Let me read a couple of passages to you. The first one isn't from a novel. It isn't even prose, and it may seem entirely tangential to our mutual concerns, especially once you hear what it is. But I want to read it to you for two reasons. It is very beautiful, as long as you're willing to suspend the expectation that each syntactical unit will relate to the preceding one and lead to the next in the usual fashion. The second reason is that although they do not quite do that, the unmistakable authority of this passage makes the conventional set of expectations seem reflexive and sentimental. This is the final, six-line stanza of a double sestina embedded within John Ashbery's book-length poem, *Flow Chart*. Because we are concluding a double sestina, each of the words at the end of the six individual lines has ended eleven previous lines over as many stanzas, according to a predetermined pattern:

> The story that she told me simmers in me still,
> though she is dead these several months, lying as
> on a bed. The things we used to do, I to thee,
> thou to me, matter still, but the sun points the
> way inexorably to death,
> though it be but his, not our way. Funny the way
> the sun can bring you around to her. And as you
> pause for breath, remember it, now that it is
> done, and seeds flare in the sunflower.[19]

"[S]eeds flare in the sunflower." "The story that she told me simmers in me still." After all the formal rigor and spontaneous inventiveness of the eleven preceding stanzas, not to mention the 186 preceding pages, we get to these amazing verbs. When *Flow Chart* is filmed, I recommend that the role of "Simmers" be played by Louise Brooks, circa 1929, and "Flare" by the present-day Tommy Lee Jones.

The next passage is an imaginative ascension near the end of Raymond Chandler's *The Long Goodbye*. Chandler was sixty-five, and he knew he was writing the book of his life.[20] Everything he thought about the emotional depth available within the genre of crime fiction blossomed under his hand. It was the last good book he would ever write, and it was his best, his richest and most fully achieved. Cissy, his wife, who was much older than he, had begun irrevocably to weaken, and after a long period of abstinence, he had started drinking again. Cissy would be dead in a year, Chandler in six.

Peter Straub

In this paragraph, an exhausted Philip Marlowe is standing late at night at the window of his apartment, listening to the traffic on Laurel Canyon Boulevard and looking at the glare of what he calls the "big angry city." The moment adds nothing to the plot. It tells us nothing about Marlowe that we do not already know. There is no need for it at all, and that's why it is so moving. It's just Chandler soaring off into the fictional space.

> Far off the banshee wail of police or fire sirens rose and fell, never for very long completely silent. Twenty-four hours a day somebody is running, somebody else is trying to catch him. Out there in the night of a thousand crimes people were dying, being maimed, cut by flying glass, crushed against steering wheels or under heavy tires. People were being beaten, robbed, strangled, raped and murdered. People were hungry, sick, bored, desperate with loneliness or remorse or fear, angry, cruel, feverish, shaken by sobs. A city rich and vigorous and full of pride, a city lost and beaten and full of emptiness.[21]

This is a kind of aria, a kind of solo. That it might offer a consolation never enters its mind. This little solo is too wise for that. Without being in any way conspicuous about its methodology, it links together three perfectly cadenced lists that ascend from means of death through specific crimes to their emotional consequences and floats them into port with a grandly summarizing, grandly balanced conclusion. Only an alternate universe can provide moments like this, and I am grateful to be living in ours.

NOTES

1. Mr. Foster, the most publicized of their victims, was scarcely an anomaly. For weeks, chambermaids and cleaning staff at Comfort Inns and Motel Six franchises were discovering corpses underneath beds, concealed behind shower curtains, secreted within hollowed-out air-conditioning units and tucked into every conceivable nook and cranny. Some of these people required long-term therapies of several kinds, but their medical expenses were invariably paid by a donor who chose to remain anonymous. The most severely afflicted, a Mrs. Violetta Puce of Charleston, South Carolina, who displayed the classic symptoms of post-traumatic stress disorder after opening an abandoned cooler containing the origamic remains of an entire Boy Scout troop and endured six applications of electro-shock therapy, annually receives a black velvet Christmas card embossed with a golden crown.

2. A tragedy written by William Shakespeare as a "showcase" for the talents of Mr. Mel Gibson.

3. A minute of compulsory silence, intended as an opportunity for meditation upon the universality of human sorrow, follows the performance.

4. At the time, a misguided perhaps, even deranged, gentleman from a tropical Protectorate fired one round through a gap in the gate-posts, the royal couple were cheerfully strolling hand in hand along the wide and decorous avenues of some picturesque foreign city, I forget which one, maybe Toulouse.

5. Think of Vergil's *Eclogues*. Think of Spenser's *Shepheardes Calender*, "Tintern Abbey," even. Compare

and contrast with Charlotte Bronte's *Shirley* and the "Tom-All-Alones" passage of *Bleak House*. Remember the stout, bearded figure of Karl Marx on its daily plunge from the grim lodging house to the Reading Room of the great British Library.

6. Briefly.

7. These possibilities are in no way mutually exclusive.

8. A ridiculously inclusive list, I know. Jane Austen and Theodore Dreiser? Not a marriage fated for even a tiny quantity of success, a marriage doomed to shipwreck the moment the door to the Bridal Suite slammed shut behind the coarse, ungainly groom. In Jane Austen's imaginative world, Dreiser is very faintly admissible as a hideous, shudder-inducing curate of such spectacular awfulness that he must be shuffled off stage moments after his arrival and even after kept in mind as a monstrous threat to the civilized sensibility; in Dreiser's world, Jane Austen appears in the second chapter as an elderly butterfly soon to be crushed beneath the wheels of a milk-wagon.

9. A novelist friend of mine once lived in the same small city in Provence where Harold Robbins had established a luxurious exile. Their mutual dentist suggested a *tête-à-tête*. My friend's initial refusal wavered before a succession of cold rainy days and nights, and he expressed his willingness to enjoy the pleasures of his fellow-author's hospitality. A launch picked up my friend and his wife and whisked them to a lovely villa, where they were met by a tall, youthful blond woman of the type once described as "statuesque." This was the latest Mrs. Robbins. She explained that her husband was at the moment involved in trans-Atlantic business dealings and offered to show them through the villa. Room after spacious room opened before

the novelist and his wife. At last, the latest Mrs. Robbins admitted them to a spacious chamber furnished only with an enormous desk bare but for a Dictaphone positioned in front of a magnificent leather chair. "And this," said the latest but not the last Mrs. Robbins, "is Harold's study, where he composes his novels."

10. It seems like an oxymoron, I know, and many will think it is, but these are the fictions always most celebrated and honored by the culture as a whole. Myself, I see no essential contradiction between "honorable" and "mainstream." For a long time, John Updike's tireless production kept its sensitive nose to the ground, in the process unearthing an endless series of truffles. The truffle is not to be despised, no matter who you think you are.

11. For example, Gilbert Sorrentino, William Gaddis, John Hawkes, Robert Coover, John Barth, Ronald Sukenic, Thomas Pynchon, and William Gaddis. Also Coleman Dowell, Guy Davenport, Joseph McElroy, Water Abish, Toby Olson, Paul Metcalf, and Harry Mathews, dazzling writers one and all, and to a man as gutsy as the last survivor of a Polish cavalry unit charging uphill toward a ridge mounted with enemy machine-guns.

12. Please forgive this cheap joke.

13. Of course they can't. These people avoid actual novels like the plague. They read nothing but "treatments," drastic condensations prepared for them by their minions, who are paid so little that it is assumed that they cannot object to the toil of wading through that kind of thing.

14. Any descriptive passage unrelated to the motivations of a specific character.

15. The day after this address was given, Brian Aldiss took me to task on this point, although he had not remembered, precisely, that it was the present author who had made it. Mr. Aldiss enquired in his typically forthright manner if I did not agree with him that a writer of fictions endeavors in those fictions to speak the truth. I agreed on the spot. Mr. Aldiss was absolutely right. Once the captive reader begins to observe the seams in the backdrop or the instability of the principal actor's moustache, the moment he detects a flickering artificiality in the dialogue, he bolts for the nearest door.

16. A phrase given me by my dear friend, the poet Ann Lauterbach, whose books include *Many Times, But Then* (1979), *Clamor* (1991), *And for Example* (1994) and *On A Stair* (1997).

17. Somewhere between three and six-and-a-half feet mostly.

18. I may have been five years of age, I may have been six. I cannot quite pin it down. As I barreled, the latest issue of the *Blackhawk* comic book gripped in my sweaty hand, through the portals of the neighborhood drugstore, a gentleman whom even then I recognized as of the utmost unreliability interposed himself between myself and the sidewalk ahead, compelling me to come to an abrupt halt. The gentleman bent down and bared his snowy-white teeth in what was intended as a smile. I could smell camphor and Barbasol. "Kiddo," he said, "I can see you just wasted a hard earned dime on that comic book, and I have a question for you."

I recall experiencing an urgent need to urinate. "What question?" I asked him.

His brilliant smile widened until the corners of his mouth seemed to brush his earlobes. "Don't you know that you'd be better off taking a walk through the park, playing catch with your little buddies, setting fire to a tree-stump, anything along those lines, than ruining your eyesight on junk like *Superman*?"

"*Superman* doesn't come in until Wednesday," I said, and executed an end-run around the nosy old jerk.

19. John Ashbery. *Flow Chart* New York: Knopf, 1991, 193.

20. This is what I said at the conference, but memory gilded the facts. It was his best book, the book of his life, but he never felt more than a decidedly shaky confidence in it. On 27 October 1951 Chandler wrote to his agent Carl Brandt, "I am having a hard time with the book...I just didn't know where I was going and when I got there I saw that I had come to the wrong place. That's the hell of being the kind of writer who cannot plan anything, but has to make it up as he goes along and then try to make sense out of it."

On 11 June 1952, after revising the novel upon hearing from Brandt that Marlowe had become too "Christlike," Chandler wrote back, "I was trying to write the book the way I wanted to write it and not the way somebody else thinks I ought to write it."

By 29 October 1952, he had recovered sufficiently to tell an English critic called Leonard Russell, "To me it seems in some vague way one of the best things I have ever written, but an author is a very poor judge of his stuff." *Selected Letters of Raymond Chandler*, Frank MacShane, ed. New York: Columbia UP, 1981, 295-96, 318, 321.

21. Raymond Chandler, *The Long Goodbye*, in Raymond Chandler, *Later Novels and Other Writings*. New York: The Library of America, 1995, 645.

Mom

My mother, Elvena, the third of five children, four of them daughters, born to Julius and Clara Nilsestuen, was raised on the family farm in what is called the "coulee country" of western Wisconsin. Halfway down the length of a country road, across a wide plain, and up a winding stretch over a steep, mountainous hill from a small town named Arcadia, not far from the bustling metropolis of LaCrosse, my grandparents' farm consisted of a hundred and fifty acres embedded within a context so comprehensively populated by the descendants of Norwegian immigrants that it was called "Norway Valley." Obviously in another time, that of the twentieth century's second decade, it might also have been in another country.

My mother's parents, grandparents, aunts, uncles, and all of the adults she encountered spoke Norwegian as well as English, and she and her siblings learned Norwegian side by side with English. My mother retained the traces of a Norwegian accent all her life. Her family's values, diet, and mores were those of mid-nineteenth century, rural Norway. (The name Nilsestuen means "Nils's little house," so deeply back-country that modern Norwegians grin when they hear it.) In winter, they traveled by horse-drawn sleigh, complete with sleigh bells. Christmas began with a monumental housecleaning and universal baths on Christmas eve, an hour of bell-tolling from the Lutheran church down the valley, the arrival of relatives in chiming sleighs, gift-giving and a reading from a Norwegian translation of Luke, then a Norwegian-language service the next day, and it continued until New Year's. They ate lutefisk, fried pork with cream gravy, bread with sour cream and sorghum, and, as a special treat, lefse, a flat, circular, pancake-like bread concocted on a wood-burning stove, then smeared with butter, sprinkled with sugar, and rolled up. (Lefse was meltingly delicious, I remember from childhood visits to the farm, but unless it is made on a wood-burning stove, forget it, it's not the real thing; you might as well be eating cardboard.)

Despite the evocative bell-tolling, the religion passed along to my mother and her siblings was merciless, unforgiving, and apocalyptic. My Uncle Gerhard, generally known as "Swede," wrote in his contribution to a collection of family reminiscences that "The Norwegian Lutheran God was not exactly a God of Love as I remember it." Sermons tended to focus on the Last Times, always terrifyingly close at hand. Swede felt that his Sunday school teacher, one Rönhovde, a forbidding character otherwise called "the Klökker," relished describing the horrors consequent upon the end of the world because he had intuited his pupil's fear before the prospect of the event. My mother now and again dreamed of a great fire spreading across the sky, and she knew these dreams originated in the sermons she had heard in her childhood. (Nightly, her brother used to pray for the arrival of dawn. She probably did, too.)

I allude to this background because every part of it was crucial to my relationship with my mother. Rural and small-town Midwestern Lutherans of Norwegian descent tend to share traits as distinctive, in their own way as piquant, as those of second- and third-generation Italians raised in lower Manhattan or Brooklyn, but no Norwegian-American counterpart of Francis Ford Coppola or Martin Scorsese ever came along to dramatize those traits. Instead, Garrison Keillor began to deliver lengthy, improvised-seeming monologues, funny, rhapsodic, and surreal in about equal measure, during weekly radio broadcasts of his own devise called "A Prairie Home Companion." Keillor's extended riffs depict Norwegian-American Lutherans under the unsparing but affectionate lens of close observation, and the ripe comedy of his reports is a direct product of their accuracy. "A Prairie Home Companion" demonstrates at least two great principles every time it is aired: that responsive human beings are capable of feeling tenderness and hostility for the same object at the same time; and that comedy is rooted in anger.

Like the residents of Lake Woebegon, nonfictional Lutheran Norwegian-Americans avoid complaint, lamentation, rebellion, and displays of sullenness in favor of steady, ongoing acceptance, because they do not believe anyone but a fool ever imagined that life was supposed to be easy. They avoid introspection and self-analysis because they believe that kind of thing can only make you feel worse instead of better. They do not believe that anyone should ever suppose himself or herself superior to anyone else, because sooner or later someone else is going to notice, and then you'll look stuck-up. They believe conversation to be a tricky business riddled with booby traps and other opportunities to make yourself look foolish, and therefore should be confined to the weather, gossip, stoic accounts of recent ailments, tales of the grandchildren. They distrust any display of emotion. You know how you feel, so the last thing you ought to do is talk about it or, even worse, act like you're a big deal and put it on display. Act nice, be a good neighbor, do your job without grousing about it, don't expect too much, be grateful for whatever you have. Remember that the world doesn't owe you a living, that God barely knows you exist, that life is a grim struggle from beginning to end, and you'll be all right.

This point of view sounds far worse than it turns out to be in practice and, in fact, embodies a great deal of common sense. I don't see why people shouldn't be polite to each other, do what they are supposed to do without grousing, and know enough to avoid putting on airs. Snobs and whiners really are second-rate human beings, unless of course they possess enough wit to irradiate their snobbishness with brilliant self-awareness and whine with gorgeous, luxuriant eloquence. No matter what your job is, composing minimalist string quartets, fielding grounders and making the throw to first, putting on an eye patch and singing Wotan in *Ring* cycles, winning stock-car races, delivering one-liners in comedy clubs, or delivering *pizzas*, the values taken for granted by the average Norwegian-Lutheran farmer would tend to elevate your standards of performance. One thing I learned from my mother was that if you didn't work hard enough to do your job better than you thought you could, you had already failed.

Nothing I have said negates the presence of ordinary happiness. The collection of family reminiscences I mentioned earlier refers again and again to the pleasures and satisfactions my mother and her siblings experienced during their childhoods. (Being Norwegian-Americans, one and all they eventually mutter something like, "it had its bad side, too, if you know what I mean, but I won't go into that.") They lived intensely, out there on that farm. They formed internecine alliances, ran through the woods, told stories, sang, played games and endless pranks, climbed trees, skied down a homemade ski jump, and marveled at the stiff collars and dress shirts of relatives visiting from LaCrosse. (Ruth, the baby of the family, wrote, "I could never understand why Shevlin liked coming to the farm so much. To me it seemed that anyone would surely rather be in a glamorous city with stores and sidewalks and ice cream parlors." Ruth eventually took off for Seattle.) My mother emerges from the family memoirs as an active, even adventurous child, the sort of girl that used to be called, as she was, a "tomboy." She loved riding and was in "seventh heaven" when a neighbor asked her and her brother, to whom she was devoted, to halter break a number of Shetland ponies. Later on, she and Swede saved up enough money to order McLelland saddles from the Montgomery Ward catalog. My mother liked to remember the wild fun of dashing around bareback on an unbroken pony, also the different kind of pleasure afforded by saddling one of the farm horses, climbing aboard, and coaxing the enormous animal into a gallop.

Another time, she described the transcendent moment when, running, she felt the gears mesh as never before and realized that she had just learned really how to *run*. My brother John inherited this capacity from her—John could run like an antelope. Me, I hated running, and instead of transcendent moments, I got stitches in my side, but I did eventually learn to walk without falling down or holding on to the furniture. After I discovered jazz and began spending every cent I had on records, my mother confided that at roughly my current age, thirteen, she, too, had been intensely interested in music: though she could not quite explain how it happened, she had decided to become an opera singer, like Jenny Lind or Nellie Melba. This ambition must have come from some source other than the strictly musical, because her family did not own a Victrola, and although Atwater-Kent radios had appeared in neighboring farmhouses, her father refused to buy one on the grounds that he couldn't stand all the racket. Undaunted by never having heard a single aria, my mother invented her own and sang them to the receptive cows and horses until some more demanding listener, probably one of her sisters, informed her that she couldn't carry a tune and had a voice like a crow. It was the truth, and she knew it—her operatic career evaporated on the spot.

John may have inherited running, but I am proud to say that my mother's musical talent came down to me in undiminished form. In grade school, our music teacher told me to move my lips along with the other kids, but not to make any actual noise.

I stumbled into an appreciation of Benjamin Britten and Peter Pears while working in a record store during my last two years of college, but began filling the air with Wagner, Richard Strauss, Verdi, *Lulu, Béatrice et Bénédict, A Village Romeo and Juliet, Pélleas et Mélissande,* and *Cleofide* only after I turned forty, by which time my mother had entered into the vanishing act that was the last stage of her life and endured, becoming more and more horrific as it went along, until 1990. One Sunday afternoon in 1993, my wife and I went to a recital by the great mezzo-soprano Christa Ludwig at Alice Tully Hall. Although I had loved Christa Ludwig's singing for years, I had not consciously taken in her resemblance to my mother until she strode smiling onstage, halted three feet north of James Levine's keyboard, opened her mouth, and floated, in plangent voice, into her first song.

"Does she remind you of anybody?" Susie whispered, but I was already in tears. There she was, doing what she had wished to do, gloriously.

• • •

For her last two years of high school, my mother moved into an apartment in Arcadia with Swede and Ruth. She began nurse's training at Lutheran Hospital in LaCrosse. Then she summoned all her courage and took the train to Milwaukee to earn a degree from Mount Sinai Hospital. In Milwaukee, a fellow student named Kathleen Marie Straub introduced Elvena, by then known as "Nels," to her brother

Gordon, a good-looking athlete unlike anyone she had ever known, and after that everything changed.

• • •

Nels and Gordon, "Gordy," a Catholic from the all-but-surreal hamlet of Lone Rock and a creature imbued with more passion, fantasy, and recklessness than anyone from Norway Valley had ever imagined possible, flirted, dated, fell in love, married. They became Gordy and Nels, a lifelong couple. Gordy roistered, dreamed, and ranted, translating every inch of life into his own point of view. Nels earned her R.N. and went to work. Spinning fantasies at every step, Gordy worked at this and that, tried and failed to enlist in the Army (varicose veins), became a salesman, a "manufacturer's rep," a job for which he was ideally suited. Nels starched her nurse's cap, ironed her uniform, and reported for eight-hour shifts at Mount Sinai. After meandering from one shabby apartment to another, they moved into the ground floor of a duplex on North Forty-fourth Street near Sherman Boulevard on Milwaukee's west side, then a Jewish neighborhood. According to my father, they never wasted any time thinking about children, but children came along anyhow, three of them, all boys, the first of them me.

Nels never stopped working, and Gordy never stopped being himself. Neither one of them had any choice. My father hatched schemes, moved from job to job, and roistered; my mother held things together. Caroline and Rhoda, younger cousins of hers happy to escape the family farms, moved into the house on Forty-fourth Street to baby-sit while she was on duty at the hospital. I loved Caroline and Rhoda, they seemed like unusually playful adults to the three-year-old, four-year-old me. Both of them adored my parents, in their eyes as sophisticated as William Powell and Myrna Loy. Never less than charming to younger women, my father dazzled Caroline and Rhoda. Now and then, I hope, he took the girls out and showed them off to his friends. He brought me with him a couple of times, and I remember the laughter, the bobbing faces, the haze of cigarette smoke above my perch on the bar. My father had no problem including his children in situations where he knew he was going to have a good time. Gordon Straub, that remarkable piece of work, is not the focus here, but he cannot be ignored, because his combination of impulsivity, loyalty, sentimentality, wild outbursts of anger, outright irrationality, emotional violence, and whimsical invention played so large a role in my relationship with my mother.

• • •

The children of nurses grow up in an atmosphere responsive to illness but not especially sympathetic to it, and they learn not to expect much slack. Sniffles, headaches, low-grade fevers, minor aches and pains mean nothing. You go to school anyhow. When your fever reaches 101, you can stay home, but your mother won't be there, because she has a job to do. Measles, chicken pox, whooping cough, influenza, diseases that leave you limp as a dishrag, soaked with sweat, and prone to hallucinations, she has seen a thousand times before, in versions a thousand times worse than yours, so lie down, drink lots of fluids, and enjoy your day off, because tomorrow you're going back to school. Experience has taught nurses to regard most doctors with a cold, cold eye, so their children spend little time in pediatrician's offices. There were periods during my childhood when I nearly wished I were in the hospital, so I could receive the attentive care my mother bestowed upon her patients. However, because I was not in the hospital, I could listen to her tales of what went on there when she got home to change out of her uniform, pour a drink, drop into a chair, and light up a Kent. These tales were both comic and irate.

She was one kind of person at work, another kind at home. The tomboy, the breaker of ponies and builder of ski jumps, had disappeared. My mother sailed through her workday with professional expertise, and when she came home turned into a nervous wreck. Life had stranded her with three sons, a demanding occupation, and a colorful husband whose mother had taken care of every sort of household obligation and expected her to do the same. The sons charged squalling around the house, the husband was liable to come home late, come home in a raging sulk caused by something he had overheard or imagined overhearing, come home blasted along with a couple of friends who were also blasted, and in the meantime she had to make dinner and do the laundry. She was a resentful cook, and her meals showed it, a matter my father never quite took in. As long as it was food, it was fine with him. His mind was entirely elsewhere, generally off in contemplation of that topic of unfailing satisfaction, his own splendor.

It is true that when my father was not tormented by self-doubt or undergoing one of his spells of illumination, he really did like to contemplate his all-round splendor, but I must add here that my mother loved him. Gordon Straub astonished her in a thousand ways. He made life funny, heartbreaking, dramatic. Boredom was not a problem. My mother learned how to deal with his multiple vagaries; he kept her on her toes, alert for the next wave of fantasy, ire, or ambition. What undermined her was the sheer, hard, unrecognized labor of holding down a job and doing all the housework for a family of four inconsiderate males. Also, she had been raised with three sisters, and she missed the company of women. My mother always regretted that she never had a daughter. We were nothing but a noisy bunch of boys, my father included, and none of us understood anything, we were not at all like girls. In the familial chaos, my mother represented the single voice of reason, groundedness, useful common sense. Besides that, she was often the voice of pure grievance. During the nineteen-fifties, suburban wives and mothers, even those with full-time jobs, were unpaid domestic servants, except for the slovens among them. My mother was not a sloven, she was a Norwegian. She did all the cleaning, dusting, and vacuuming, all the laundry, the bed-making, the straightening and picking up, and 95 percent of the shopping. My father's excursions through the grocery store tended to result in a great many bags crammed with peanut brittle, cookies, cocktail olives, doughnuts, and buttermilk. About once a week, he decided to give her a break and wash up after dinner, and once a month or so it occurred to him that my brothers and I were tall enough to reach into the sink. When ordered, we washed the dishes, but with sullen lack of grace. It wasn't *our* job, after all.

The voice of grievance was the sound of my mother talking to herself, *sotto voce*, as she hauled bundles of laundry back and forth from the basement, mopped the kitchen floor, or pushed the vacuum cleaner around the house. In a stage whisper, she talked to herself nonstop, unreeling her complaints in an endless sentence devoid of punctuation or even breaks between the individual words.

WhatdotheythinkIamtheirservantwellI'mnottheirse rvantandIamsickandtiredofbeingtreatedlikeoneit'shight imeTHEYdidsomeofthisworkoronedayI'mwalkingoutandn evercomingback...

You could hear it from two rooms away. You could practically hear it from the other side of the house. Even when you couldn't hear it, you knew it was going on, that endless, steaming sentence, looping around the house and trailing up and down the basement stairs, following my mother's resentful progress like a great ribbon. Her bitterness was too much for us, too scary. We didn't know how to cope with it, so we turned to stone and hoped it would pass. The stage-whisper monologue frightened us less than her rare outbursts, when she went over the edge and railed at us face-to-face. *I am sick and tired of being treated like your SERVANT! All I do is go around cleaning up your MESSES! Listen to me, I've had it up to HERE!* Certain stock phrases emerged over and over again: "one iota," as in, "I never get one iota of help from you ungrateful little shits," and, a great favorite, "twenty-seven times," as in, "Peter, I've told you twenty-seven times to hang up your shirts instead of throwing them on the floor, but do you pay one iota of attention?" I heard that so often that I began paying at least half a dozen iotas of attention, and now I hang up my shirts and trousers before going to bed even on nights when I'm operating on remote control. Once when we were all fairly small, therefore particularly nauseating, she actually did make good on her threat and tossed some clothes into a suitcase, tore out of the house, and drove off. *(You can take care of yourselves from now on, because I am SICK AND TIRED of doing it for you!)* Stunned, we crawled into various corners and pretended to be statues for an hour or two, after which she returned. For the next couple of days, we barely opened our mouths. Then we reverted to being ungrateful little shits, our natural condition.

The voice of reason, groundedness, and useful common sense was both more pervasive and more personal. My father's volatility and self-absorption, not to mention his unshakable assumption that disagreement equaled defiance, made our relationship difficult, but I always felt that my mother understood me, valued me for myself, and took pride in my accomplishments. There were times when she seemed able nearly to read my mind, which was enormously reassuring. In the dynamic of family life, she was my ally. Without an ally, I would have been lost. My father had been an athlete, and like most former athletes saw participation in sports as a crucial element in the development of character. He had played football and basketball in high school, been a football player in college, and played semi-professionally afterward. That he had always loved reading and had an instinctive gift for narrative, qualities I undoubtedly inherited from him, was merely personal, of no significance in his value-world. Reading and story-telling were essential to him but weightless when measured against sports. Somewhere inside him, I am sure, within a chamber he entered as seldom as possible, he imagined that these activities were tainted, suspect…effeminate.

• • •

Right from the start, from the moment I opened my eyes and took in the presence of billboards, road signs, labels, and headlines, I hungered for the written word. One of my clearest memories from early childhood is of an overwhelming desire to understand print. I taught myself to read by memorizing comic books and "reading" them to other kids until the words locked into place, and after that I was off, I was insatiable. After an encounter with a moving automobile in my seventh year led to a couple of operations and a year out of school, I turned to reading even more intensely. Because my father had been addicted to Tom Swift and Edgar Rice Burroughs in his boyhood, he was happy to drive me weekly to the local libraries and let me check out the maximum number of books, six. I was a terrific student, and he liked that; it reflected well on him, it gave him something to brag about. Yet he did not think it was enough, especially for a son destined to play for the Green Bay Packers. In summers, I was supposed to charge outside and play games, not just sit around and read novels. He didn't get it. I was missing the boat, and I didn't seem to care.

My father feared that there was something wrong with me, some characterological flaw that would lead me deeply astray, if not ruin my life. My mother worried, too, but she always trusted me to work things out in the end. Unlike my father, she knew that my encounter with the automobile and its lengthy aftermath had contributed an extra degree of darkness, of suppressed anger and unacknowledged fear, to my personality, and at my worst moments she suspended judgment and, as thoroughly as she could, mutely shared my suffering, which was also mute.

For Norwegian Lutherans of her generation, as for her parents' generation, physical demonstrations of love took place in private, behind a closed door. After my brothers and I advanced out of babyhood, we were never hugged or kissed, except for the brief period when our father used to kiss us good night. (He told me later that kissing boys made him feel creepy.) The only times I remember being hugged by my mother took place when I had alarmed her by doing something extraordinarily stupid. She was stiff, awkward, uncomfortable, twig-like. It was like being hugged by a maiden aunt who on the whole would rather not, like being hugged by a frightened bird. My father sizzled away in the background, waiting to get rid of me.

The grounded, sane, never less than necessary voice of reasonable common sense emerged on those rare occasions when no one else was in the room. She had been saving up some comment or bit of advice, and she looked you in the eye and got it off her chest. At those moments, the things she said could put to rest a dozen different worries, problems, and fears. She was giving you the real deal, and you knew it. This happened over and over, and I hardly remember anything my mother said at those times. What I do remember is the sense of becoming acquainted again with the real world, in which people's motives led to actual consequences. A haze of illusion and conjecture had been blown away. When I was fourteen or fifteen, she said to me, "Even if you don't like most of the people you meet, you should pretend you do, because after a while you will, and your whole life will be better." She was right—I started acting as though I liked other people, quickly discovered that I really did, and my life improved. She worked the same earth-mother magic on my brothers. John once told me that at nine or ten he had begun to imagine that he was a Martian and everyone knew but him, and when he mentioned this to our mother, she instantly dispelled his fears by saying, "No, John, that's crazy."

The things about me that infuriated my father—my total disinterest in business; my sense that literature, music, and art were essential to a civilized life; my adolescent intellectual pretensions; my assumption that somewhere there existed a world beyond Milwaukee and my father's circle of concerns, and that this larger, more generous world was not only of tremendous interest to me, but also necessary to my psychic survival—appealed to my mother as much or more than they aroused her concern. Long after I had found my place in the world, my father, on a visit to New York, sat down in my living room, where he was surrounded by paintings, and said, "You know, I hate art. I don't know why, I just hate it." (I know why, though—because he didn't know anything about art, he thought it diminished him.) My mother would have said, "I don't know much about art, but Peter knows what he likes." She believed that what was important to me would eventually let me find my path; she trusted me to find the *way out* that was also the *way in*.

• • •

In 1977, when Susie and I were coming to the end of our long residence in London, my father's letters began to report disturbing news. My mother was having peculiar medical problems her doctors could not diagnose. One night after dinner, she had collapsed outside a restaurant. There were periods when she seemed unable to remember what she had been doing or saying. My father put an optimistic gloss on these matters. He could not disguise his worry, but he assumed everything would turn out fine in the end.

That summer, my parents spent a week at our house on Hillfield Avenue, N8, and for the most part my mother did appear to be fine. She rejoiced in Susie's pregnancy, she planted a ring of pansies around the rose bush in our small front yard, she regarded her husband's occasional flights into outer space with her by then customary mixture of wariness and amusement. After serving for more than a decade as alderman in Brookfield, our suburb, my father had run for mayor and lost, a failure which led him to brood about taking a powder somewhere not populated by knaves. We drove through the Sussex countryside and lingered in pubs. My father teetered around the house on his troublesome knees and bare feet, sometimes getting confused about which floor the living room was on—"I'm looking for that room with the big, square furniture," he said—now and then letting a freshly made drink drop from his hand to detonate on the tiles of the ground-floor hall. He seemed more disturbed than my mother.

One night when she and I sat up late in the kitchen, she said, "I'll never forget the first time I was sent out to spend a night in a patient's house. I was fresh out of nursing school, and the patient was an old woman who had been released from the hospital that day. She had a box of chocolates in her refrigerator." During the night, the old woman died. My mother was told to do nothing until morning. Unable to sleep, she ate all the chocolates. It was an interesting story. Five minutes later, my mother smiled and said, "I'll never forget the first time I was sent out to spend a night in a patient's house," and told me the whole story all over again. She perspired more than I had ever seen her do before. By early afternoon, a flushed red band crossed her face from cheek to cheek. There were times when she forgot what she had been talking about and fell silent. I had no idea what to make of these lapses, or even if they were lapses. They became significant only in retrospect.

The following summer, Susie and I paid a visit to Wisconsin with our infant son, Benjamin, and the damage could no longer be dismissed as a temporary aberration. Whatever was happening to my mother had accelerated to the point where its outward manifestations presented a persistent state of confusion and anxiety. The mother I remembered surfaced only intermittently.

My father had abandoned traitorous Brookfield to relocate himself and his wife in a small, "contemporary" house on Lake Halley, northwest of Milwaukee and close to Eau Claire. In the coulee country, Eau Claire was home to Rhoda and her sister Germaine, both of whom came for dinner on the second night of our visit to Lake Halley. Before we got there, I didn't know what to expect: my parents' letters had described a placid existence enlivened chiefly by the sightings of exotic waterfowl. According to them, their new life was working out perfectly well. It might have looked that way, too, if you were an expert in the psychological mechanism known as denial. Surrounded by trees, the little house was attractive, clean, functional, a sort of combination of a hunting lodge and a "hospitality suite" in a modern hotel. The backyard led to the water's edge and a short, sturdy pier where my parents liked to sit in the evenings.

Yet my mother seemed to exist in a mild but unassuagable panic without specific referent. Sitting down, she jittered, preoccupied with her own unease. Something had been left undone, an essential domestic task had been neglected, and the world was under the threat of ever-increasing disorder until the neglected task had been answered. Finally, her sense of responsibility pulled her from her chair and sent her pacing through the house in search of the overlooked duty, the thing undone, the forgotten. The kitchen offered a wrinkled dishcloth and a couple of used napkins, the bedroom a single pair of socks my father had dropped into a hamper an hour before. My mother gathered up these few objects and, intent on taking care of business, hurried washing machine-wards. By our second day in the new house, I understood that she did this all the time. She trotted from one room to another, collected socks and dishcloths, and washed them in the washing machine, usually one by one. It was like watching a dog in a dog run.

At other times the compulsion to re-enact the rituals which once had evoked the voice of grievance abated, leaving a vaguer, more distracted but recognizable version of her old self. Infant Ben delighted her—everything he did gave her pleasure. I will never cease to be grateful for that. During our stay, my mother prepared meals, conversed, joked, described her adaptation to Lake Halley. She knew why Gordy had sold up and moved out, and that they had landed near most of her relatives eased the grief of having lost the house in Brookfield.

The grief was real, and the loss was profound. My mother may have filled that house with her endless sentences, but she had lived there for better than two decades, and she both loved and missed it. My brothers and I, along with our wives, spent about a year attributing Nels's problems to the shock of having been abruptly torn from her familiar surroundings: clearly, she would have preferred to remain in Brookfield and, but for her husband's wounded narcissism, would have done so for the rest of her life. Instead, she had been uprooted, drastically. In the absence of any other explanation, this one looked pretty good.

Rhoda and Germaine, my mother's younger cousins, arrived for dinner on the second night of our visit and yakked away in a manner I found wonderfully familiar, spinning off jokes and pungent comments on everything in sight. They were Gilbertsons, from my grandmother's side of the family, women blessed with a raucous wit, a lively capacity for enjoyment, unflagging warmth, and a sturdy sense of loyalty. Both of my parents meant a great deal to them, and before and after dinner, they took in their cousin's lapses into vagueness, her deposits of single dish towels into the washing machine, without breaking stride. During a private moment later on in the evening, Rhoda and Germaine expressed their concern for my mother, whose deterioration they, too, supposed a product of the almost brutally abrupt removal from Brookfield. This, of course, was not an opinion that could be aired in Gordy's presence. No one had any idea of what was actually going on. In any case, my father had chosen to ignore all signs to the contrary and act as though nothing, at least nothing of any significance, was wrong with his wife. He would maintain this position, which I am tempted to call a façade, for years to come. He surrendered to reality only when the inexorable progress of my mother's disease gave him no other choice.

• • •

Susie, baby Ben, and I went back to London and began the process of disentangling ourselves from England. My father wrote that disagreements with a neighbor had soured him on Lake Halley, too bad but nothing serious, he and my mother were moving to a townhouse development in the village of Hartland, closer to Milwaukee. (The "disagreements," I learned later, had been the product of Gordy's response to the neighbor's observation that Nels seemed to be losing her marbles.) In June of 1979, Susie and I swanned back to the United States on the QE2, for some reason rented a house in Westport, Connecticut, and, in step even deeper into delusion, bought a big, lovely Victorian, just up from Burying Hill Beach on Beachside Avenue, known locally as "the Gold Coast." (Should you be wondering about the use of the word "delusion" in the previous sentence, a reading of *Floating Dragon*, a book I wrote on the third floor of that house, will clear things up.) My parents came through Westport twice, and both times my father's capacity for denial had expanded to meet the increasing challenge to it posed by his wife.

That they were traveling at all, much less covering hundreds of miles every day on their journey from point to point, was remarkable in light of my mother's condition. She no longer knew quite what to do with silverware, so he cut up her food and brought it to her mouth with his own knife and fork. Because she was incapable of selecting her wardrobe for the day, he chose it for her, which meant that she wore sweatshirts and sweatpants, as he did. She conversed in fragments, and the fragments usually drifted off into benign silence. Startling, unexpected obscenities peppered her speech: in the old days, she had called us "ungrateful little shits" only when pushed over the border of propriety by stress and frustration; by the early nineteen-eighties, the border no longer existed, and she cut loose whenever she felt like it. However, being in my house made her happy. Her grandchildren, now including our daughter, Emma, born in 1980, thrilled her. She still had a grasp of who she was and what her life had been like, and if now and then she felt impelled to say, "Gordon, I don't give a shit about changing my goddamned socks," "Gordon, to hell with you, I want to sit out here a while longer," or something earthier, the worst part of what was happening to her seemed to be a relentless withdrawal into a distracted but essentially passive remoteness.

The withdrawal was baffling, disturbing, painful, horrible to behold. It was like seeing her being subjected, inch by inch, to an inexorable erasure. Medical professionals still had not identified the causes for the erasure, but it progressed. My father's sister, a former professor of nursing at Catholic University and long since metamorphosed from Kathleen Marie Straub to Dr. K. Mary Straub, diagnosed the central pathology as the failure of sufficient oxygen to reach the brain and recommended an operation. Unable to admit the gravity of the problem, her brother went on as before. I think he *couldn't* admit it, I think any such recognition would have blasted his world to pieces. Going on as before, whatever the emotional cost, was all he knew how to do.

He also knew that the retreat from the external world, the core of his wife's symptoms, brought with it others that were far from passive. Her obscenities emerged from a helpless rage that erupted only in private. A few years later, after bitter reality had claimed us all, my father told me that my mother had often stormed inconsolable and furious through their apartment, railing. She wanted *out*. To keep her from escaping, he piled furniture in front of the front door, and when she tried to toss it aside, they battled. One night while they were "vacationing" in Florida and my father was asleep, my mother managed to unlock the door of their motel room and vanish into the streets, to be found only after hours of desperate search in the rented car. Her incontinence had almost driven him crazy. The stress became unbearable. My parents drove to Rochester, Minnesota, and there, at least seven years after its onset, my mother's illness was finally given a name in the Mayo Clinic.

Most readers of this memoir were probably able to identify the illness the moment my mother repeated her story of the dead patient and the chocolate box, but in 1983 Alzheimer's disease had not yet come into anything like general public awareness. I'd never heard of it before I learned of my mother's diagnosis at Mayo, and neither had anyone else I knew. Until I saw the name in print, I thought it was spelled "Aylzheimer's."

For the following eight years, Alzheimer's disease greedily devoured the remains of my mother's life, character, and self, turning brain cells into tangles of filament and swallowing trace after trace of humanity until the body it at last murdered had been reduced to a withered, fetal husk. These years were enormously, cruelly, even—I want to say—exquisitely painful for all of us. My father soldiered on until, realizing that he was about to snap, he placed Nels in the nursing home, or "elder care," wing of an old hospital in Trempeleau County, where the staff's unfamiliarity with Alzheimer's resulted in inadequate, sometimes ignorant treatment. The one time I visited my mother there, a shrunken, stick-like wraith on the verge of death came shuffling down a gloomy corridor, looked at me with red eyes instantly blazing forth love and recognition, and my heart folded in half with shock. My father quickly transferred her to a far more modern and humane facility in tiny West Salem, just outside LaCrosse, and moved into an apartment down the street. For the rest of her life, he visited her twice every day, gabbed at her for hours on end, joked, washed her hair, cut her nails, escorted her on walks, fed her, insured that she was getting the best possible care. Under his ministrations, she put on weight and, to the extent this was possible, flourished. My father prolonged her life for many years, lovingly and selflessly. Attending to my mother amounted to an extended repayment for decades of what he perceived as less than stellar treatment, the years in which he had been, as he announced in a West Salem bar on a night when both of us had too much to drink, "a son of a bitch bastard."

I felt like one myself, because the combination of misery, terror, and sheer horror aroused in me by my mother's Alzheimer's made it extremely difficult for me to visit her. The shuffling, red-eyed wraith had all but paralyzed me, and although I knew that she had come a long way back from the lip of the grave, I feared to stand in her presence. My mother's deterioration surrounded me like an invisible, toxic atmosphere; since what she was enduring was truly unthinkable, I thought of it constantly, at one level beneath consciousness. It was as though I were gazing into the absolute darkness gathering about her, and the idea of that darkness unstrung me. I often wished that I could face the darkness in her place, take it on for her and set her free. Mistakenly, I imagined that death must be preferable to that cruel imprisonment—I mean, that I would experience her death as a release. Susie and I flew to LaCrosse once or twice a year, and every time we drove to West Salem, picked up my father, went the next eighth of a mile down Garland Street, and turned into the drive leading to the nursing home, my anxiety doubled and redoubled, increasing exponentially. By the time we pulled up before the entrance, I half expected to be killed by my own emotions a second after we walked inside.

What kept me from returning to West Salem more than once or twice a year was grief of such power and magnitude that my existence as a working, rational being seemed to depend on keeping it at arm's length. Like most great emotional misjudgments, this feeling was entirely unconscious. Though I was doing nothing of the kind, if anyone had asked I would have said that I was dealing with my sorrow about as well as I could. Inevitably, the unconscious took its revenge: shortly after Valentine's Day, 1990, my father called to say that my mother was fading fast; the next day, a few hours after her death-in-life had slipped into straightforward death, we arrived in Wisconsin and joined the extended family of Straubs and Nilsestuens in a cycle of funeral parlor visitations, reunions, meals, marathon conversations, reminiscences and condolences which culminated in a memorial service in the same Tamarack Lutheran Church where Rönhovde, "the Klökker," had sown terror; we flew back to New York—and my accumulated grief and sorrow, no longer to be held at bay, swarmed up, blew the hinges off the gate, and flattened me. For that, too, I shall always be grateful.

After the gate flew open, I learned the most important lessons of my life. I learned that grief is precisely equivalent to love, and that the terrible grief felt after the loss of a person one has loved deeply is a necessary consequence of that love and represents its survival in another form. However bitterly, grief is an honor. I learned that grief universally saturates and enriches our world, for sooner or later loss of an almost unimaginable order transforms everyone. Parents die, spouses and siblings die, even children die, and these deaths create irreparable wounds that shrink over time but never heal. They are not supposed to heal. On all sides, tears lay just beneath the surface. The emotion that gives rise to those tears is a connective tissue extending far, far down into our common humanity and our individual beings, and in those depths it becomes indistinguishable from joy.

Why Electricman Lives in New York

Two weeks after his fortieth birthday, Electricman still feels cheerful on the surface, dark and edgy underneath. Things seem to be going all right in both halves of his odd life, but he knows that "seem" is the only accurate verb for that sentence: if things really were all right, he would not experience these odd waves of panic and despair that boil up, unpredictably, from some hidden source felt to be more or less infinite. He knows of course that he is undergoing a mid-life crisis, a common, if not ritual, passage for men of his age. Upon entering their fourth decade, males, at least American males, tend go into mourning for what is suddenly perceived as their (cruelly) vanished youth and exhibit their (largely unconscious) grief by reverting to the patterns of adolescence: increased indulgence in drugs and alcohol, and frantic skirt-chasing. Many of the afflicted neglect their jobs and suffer the shock of abrupt unemployment.

Electricman has not yet reached this pass, in either half of his life. As Arthur Groom, he continues to fulfill, however grudgingly, his duties as author of "Don't Ask Arthur," an advice column published in an alternative weekly located in the East Village and syndicated in hundreds of journals throughout the country. That he can produce his advice column from his apartment on West End Avenue greatly facilitates that side of his life in which he is obliged to shuck his clothing, slip into a hooded, skintight outfit of black Spandex emblazoned front and back with a yellow lightning-bolt, dive into the nearest electrical outlet, fly through an immense network of wires to pop out of a wall or a transformer convenient to a crime scene, and make hay with the perps, thereby rescuing the grateful victim. The obligation to become Electricman descended upon Arthur at the age of nineteen, when during a rain-drenched family picnic on the outskirts of his home town of Ladysmith, Wisconsin, he wandered disaffected beneath a giant oak to guzzle Gatorade he had previously spiked with Daddy Groom's Smirnoff Platinum. A lightning bolt made smoke dribble from his ears and turned his eyes buttercup yellow. When taken home, he slept for three days straight and on the fourth day discovered, neatly folded beneath his pillow, the Spandex cat-suit he has worn ever since.

"Don't Ask Arthur," frankly, has become a bore. Once, getting paid for telling young men that their girlfriends sounded much too good to abandon and young women that their boyfriends sounded like manipulative creeps had satisfied something within Arthur, perhaps the same desire for order expressed more physically in his Electricman work. Whupping the malefactors and accepting the embraces of rescued damsels could never really lose its appeal, but of late it has become tediously repetitious, almost as much so as his column. When information of a crime in progress leaks from a nearby electrical outlet and awakens his Electricman-senses, he sighs, "Oh, hell, not again—mug, mug, mug, but at least it's better than advising Larchmont Tiffany to dump two-timing Scarsdale Harry."

In his unhappiness, Electricman has taken to wearing his superhero outfit throughout most of the day, even when he goes over to Broadway to buy a salami-and-swiss on a Kaiser roll, or to wander through a museum. It makes him feel better, it bucks him up—besides that, girls, even those who loiter in the galleries of the Metropolitan Museum of Art, like a man in uniform.

"So you can sort of pick the crimes you want to foil?" asks Janet Hale, a very pretty example of the sort of young woman to be found loitering in the Met's galleries. She and Electricman are having tea in the lobby of the Carlyle Hotel, a place where Electricman can relax, uninterrupted by autograph-seekers.

"Oh, for sure," says Electricman. "Otherwise, my life would be a nightmare. You have no idea what comes down through the wires. Hour after hour, day by day. Rapes, burglaries, hold-ups, arson. Assaults with Intent. Jury tampering. Mail Fraud. Coupon forgery. It never stops, not for a second."

Now Janet Hale looks stricken by the sheer quantity of wickedness going on in New York. "Maybe you should think about moving somewhere smaller. You'd still be able to fight crime, there just wouldn't be so much of it."

Electricman sips his Darjeeling and appears to consider her suggestion. "Just out of curiosity, what do you like to read?"

"Lots of stuff, I guess." She glanced up at the ceiling. "Don DeLillo and Donald Westlake. I read John Ashbery and Ann Lauterbach and Louise Gluck. Umm, who else? Well…Joyce Carol Oates, Henry James, Raymond Chandler, Charles Dickens, George Pelecanos, Fernando Pessoa, Iris Murdoch."

"If you don't mind my asking, where are you from?" he asks her.

"Grand Rapids. Michigan. I moved here five years ago, right after I graduated from Ann Arbor."

"Because you had to live here. Didn't you feel that? I do. I think I could only find you, or someone like you, here in New York."

"Ah," says pretty Janet Hale.

"Here's something else. Last week, I went out on two different nights, to two different clubs. Thursday, I went to this place called Smoke, a little jazz club on 106th and Broadway. In Smoke, people don't give a damn if you're a superhero, they're too hip. It might be the best jazz club in New York. I heard a tenor player named Eric Alexander. He has a big, fat sound and great technique—he knows every single thing you can do with a tenor saxophone, and he always makes beautiful, exciting music. It's like listening to a young Sonny Stitt, or a young Dexter Gordon. Then on Saturday night, I went down to the Mercury Lounge, on Houston. The people there thought I was wearing a costume, so they didn't give a damn, either. I went to hear Future Bible Heroes, whose leader is an amazing genius named Stephin Merritt. It's like chamber pop, or something—exquisite songs with weird, quirky rhymes and gorgeous melodies."

"I begin to see the point," says Janet. "Actually, I'm crazy about Eric Alexander and Stephin Merritt, too. But right now, I'm getting into Neil Halstead, Bangs, and that trumpet player, Dave Douglas. Do you know him?"

"Not yet," Electricman says. "But I will, I promise you. Would you do me a favor?"

"What?"

"I'd like you to call me Arthur," he says. "I'm starting to feel a little more integrated than I have been lately." He signaled to a waiter. "How about walking over to the Frick? It isn't far, and we could look at the Bellini St. Francis."

"And that Rembrandt self-portrait," Janet says, wonderfully.

"You know," Electricman says, "I really am beginning to feel much better."

A Proud and Lonely Voice from the Back of the Room:

The Collected Observations of Putney Tyson Ridge, Ph.D.

Putney Tyson Ridge, RIP

The recent demise of renowned literary figure and leader in Popular Culture Studies, Putney Tyson Ridge, Ph.D., occasioned a chorus of grief from all who knew him, as well as from the thousands of scholars and general readers who had been touched and influenced by his work.

Professor Ridge, long the Chairman and sole member of the Department of Popular Culture at Popham College, a small liberal arts institution located in Popham, Ohio, died of causes as yet undetermined on March 3, 2003, the day after the 60th birthday he shared with his lifelong, though frequently thoughtless and inattentive friend, author Peter Straub. Surrounded by hundreds of loose copies of the erotic journals that were the focus of his latest research project, his body was discovered at the foot of the basement stairs in his beautiful former residence on Traipse Lane in the Bluebell, or "faculty," section of his college town. It was there he spent what he once described at "the most satisfying, yet oftimes the most humiliating, years of my life."

That the much-honored and widely-respected Professor Ridge should have been moving out of his beloved residence of nearly thirty years on the day after his 60th birthday was the unhappy product of the humiliations the groundbreaking educator experienced at Popham. Those familiar with Dr. Ridge's work, in particular his "Remarks" on the fiction of his oldest friend, Mr. Straub, will have noticed occasional allusions to the utterly unjustified accusations of sexual misconduct that bedeviled the last decade-and-a-half of his career. Out of the woodwork they swarmed, intervallically, these young women, driven by God knows what combination of envy, malice, soured flirtatiousness, bad faith, and bad politics to charge a none-too-robust elderly scholar of the highest professional standing with conduct entirely foreign to his nature. It was Dr. Ridge's opinion, whispered but to the deepest of intimates, that most if not all of these young women were in the pay of Popham's English Department, especially as chaired by the late Everard Glade Blessing, who from the first viewed his rival's inspiration, the Popular Culture Department, as a threat to his own bailiwick. Even Professor Glade Blessing's supporters cannot deny his increasingly obsessive desire to nullify Popular Culture as a separate discipline and reinstate it as a sub-specialty within his Department.

With the unfailing support of "Bob" Liddy, Popham's thirty-ninth President, Professor Ridge long withstood both the accusations of mercenary female undergraduates and the political machinations of Glade Blessing and his followers. Many an evening, from the depths of adjoining club chairs in the president's handsome library, "Bob" and "Put" whiled away enchanted hours discussing the advancement of Popular Culture in general and the expansive activities of the Popular Culture Association, co-founded by Professor Ridge in 1971, his second year on the faculty. These "sittin' an' spittin'" sessions, in President Liddy's fond term, were of great importance to Professor Ridge, and he missed the camaraderie, support, and advice he gained from them after the president's abrupt 1999 dismissal and eventual imprisonment. (The charges, which shall not be repeated here, remain inexplicable to those who knew "Bob" Liddy as a caring and compassionate gentleman.)

However, with "Bob" Liddy's shocking departure from the graceful confines of Confluence of Wisdoms House, Professor Ridge lost both a friend and the support that would have been essential to him during the following two academic years. When yet another deluded female student came along to confide to Ms. Wilhemina Frost, conductor of the United in One Voice Willo Cathe Wymyn's Choir, a fantasy involving a harmless jest, a locked door, and a misplaced key, Ms. Frost reported the tale to both the Popham Police Department and Popham's Faculty Honor Board.

In the hurricane that followed, Professor Ridge's many accomplishments and distinctions counted as nothing. The court case was mercifully short, the verdict just, but his acquittal on all charges could not spare this eminent scholar the surfacing of other gnat-like, niggling accusations (some dating back decades), physical and mental exhaustion, and his ultimate suspension from the faculty. In December, 2002, the College evicted Dr. Ridge from the comfortable haven on Traipse Lane, a dwelling perfectly suited to his needs, and he moved into what were supposed to be temporary quarters in the notorious Black Flag Motel on Commerce Avenue in nearby Lead City.

It is felt that, when stricken, Professor Ridge was attempting to transport research materials from his still-uninhabited former residence to his room on Commerce Avenue. As a principal ornament to the field he helped bring into being, Professor Ridge acquired many honors. Three times President, for the past six years President Emeritus, of the Popular Culture Association, he was the winner of six prestigious Atwood Awards, its highest accolade. Although despite tireless efforts his work never found publication in book form, over the years he spent at Popham, hundreds of Dr. Ridge's groundbreaking papers appeared in academic journals and periodicals devoted to popular culture.

Peter Straub, Professor Ridge's oldest friend and the recipient of perhaps his most heartfelt criticism, declined to comment on his death. No doubt Mr. Straub has reasons of his own.

—Ernie Tremple, Popham '96

A Brief Biography

Long acknowledged as a crucial, even an essential figure in the field of Popular Studies, Putney Tyson Ridge has also been described as its "maverick" (Jason E. Dent, Ph.D., in *Central Plains Popular Studies Journal)*, its "wild-eyed gonzo cowboy" (F.S.W. Honeyhouse, Ph.D., in *Mid-South Journal of Popular Studies)*, its "official yahoo" (Milton R. Packer, Ph.D., in *Permanent Ephemera: Studies of Recent Developments in Popular Culture)*, its "Delegate from Outer Space" (Hermione Uffnee-Lazarus, in *South-West Nebraska Community College Popular Culture Review)*, and much, much more. Professor Ridge can take whatever they throw at him, these lesser figures. His contributions to his chosen field, which in fact he helped not only to establish as an accepted academic discipline but to bring into being through his own tireless and oft-challenged efforts, have been acknowledged by many awards.

A four-time recipient of The International Popular Culture Society's highest honor, the Elmer J. Atwood Award or "Atwood," Professor Ridge is a Past President of the Society and a popular keynote speaker at its International Congresses. As the first and Permanent Chairman of the

Department of Popular Culture at Popham College, where he was made for years to combat the intransigence of certain short-sighted, blaggardy Deans and academics not at all above stooping to personal attacks of the vilest sort, he has been invited as Guest Lecturer to such notable institutions as Willetsville College of Applied Arts, Southern Ohio University's Extension Division, Cape Cod Business College, LaGrange Louisiana Female Academy for Higher Learning, and many others. He has been awarded more than a dozen Plaques and Citations for his unceasing efforts on behalf of Popular Culture studies, most recently by the North Florida Popular Culture Association, whose Citation reads in part: To one who has never failed to illuminate our Discipline by his controversial, some have said reckless, willingness to examine it through the lens of his own personal experience.

This renowned scholar was born in Milwaukee, Wisconsin, in 1943, where by coincidence his family lived next to the Straub family, who inhabited a rather smaller and less distinguished residence none the less possessing a degree of cozy charm. Family legends report that the infant Professor was introduced to the infant novelist, Peter Straub, when baby Peter's mother lowered him into baby Putney's cradle, whereupon the infant Professor smiled a toothless smile and patted or perhaps thumped the infant novelist on the head. This may be said to have defined the relationship between the two—set, as it were, its tone—for ever after. Side by side, the two friends passed through the era of the sandbox, the age of the tricycle and swingset, the epochs of elementary school, high school at Milwaukee Country Day and college at the University of Wisconsin, and at every stage the budding eminence of Popular Culture freely bestowed upon his creative but excitable, unfocussed, illogical, oft-confused, too-fanciful-by-half, sadly literal-minded, mopery-prone, unrealistic, unworldly, uninformed and sometimes utterly clueless friend the benefits of his cooler, more developed, altogether more authoritative mind. After college, Straub wriggled his way into Columbia University's Graduate School while Ridge declined the insult of placement on its "waiting list" and wisely ensconced himself in the sober, level-headed comforts of Bloomington, Indiana, a locale more suited by far to the study of literature than hectic, faddish Manhattan. Yet despite this separation and his own punishingly demanding schedule, Ridge continued to provide his needy friend with ongoing support, advice and counsel.

That to this day Straub fails publicly to acknowledge his selfless friend's lifelong assistance, much less to pay him the simple tribute of a dedication to one of his many books, is of no consequence to Professor Ridge. Professor Ridge does not require the embarrassment of further accolades. Also, Professor Ridge has long been educated in the harmless, helpless selfishness of authors and their ilk. Mr. Straub has expressed gratitude for his pal's steady presence by requesting Professor Ridge to supply the "jacket copy" for several of his "limited editions," sign enough of his respect for the truth, painful though it may be.

Professor Ridge wishes it known that he offers the following "Observations" on his life-long chum's work and career as a public service only, though he cannot but hope that one day the wayward author might hear of these remarks and, should he have so far overcome his tyrannical ineptitude in the face of any technology more advanced than the electric pencil-sharpener, might learn to employ the devices of point-and-click well enough to summon them to his screen and while yet again absorbing the hard realities his childhood companion is duty-bound to present, find it possible to relish with him the pleasures of revisiting these moments from their shared, their continuing history.

Leeson Park & Belsize Square

That this volume, comically overdressed in a wrapper depicting the interiors of Salisbury (front) and Ely (back) Cathedrals and emblazoned with Gothic lettering in an iridescent red, is perhaps minimally more compelling than, say, *The Collected Early Verse of Mickey Spillane,* is due to its advance re-enactment, its miniature pre-figuration, of this writer's later and more consequential errors.

I shudder from a consideration of the techniques my friend must have used upon the eponymous director of this little publishing firm, Mr. Underwood-Miller, while encouraging this gentleman to bring out a volume of the poetry written in his youth. I also decline to pass judgment on the verses themselves, which I gather are passable, however imitative of those older, more established, more accomplished, in every way better poets Straub happened to be reading at the time. I remember Peter's immersion into poetry, which was total and all-consuming, and therefore I understand his reasons for pressuring poor Mr. Underwood-Miller into publishing this collection.

What I do wish to remark, however, is the curious fact that after beginning with a reasonable version of workmanlike clarity my friend's brief career as a poet steadily, relentlessly declined into murk and pretension. Once he stumbled upon the likes of Mr. Jaques Dupin and Mr. Yves Bonnefoy, who jointly preside over the final sections of this book, Peter was finished, through. His abandonment of poetry can be explained in no other way. One wishes that he had been capable of learning from his own, no doubt bitter, example.

Marriages

Our boy's first, fond, tender fictional shoot! It is hardly unusual that a writer's maiden effort, the record of his baby steps, as it were, the transcription of his initial, endearingly primitive efforts at speech, should be inferior to his later work, but *Marriages* represents a particularly embarrassing example of the general rule that "First is Worst." He had not even the mitigating excuse of extreme youth to justify this aimless, unsavory and influence-ridden absurdity: more determined figures have produced their first novels in their early twenties, but Straub published *Marriages* in his thirtieth year.

I well remember the circumstances, for I visited the Straubs in their dank, unwholesome Dublin flat only a few weeks after Peter began his work on the book. I was in the Ph.D. program at the Indiana University, and Peter was supposedly engaged in the same pursuit at University College, Dublin. Since he had harbored ambitions of writing fiction from youth, I offered him both my encouragement and assistance. From elementary school on, it has ever been my part in our friendship to support frail ego while restraining id's excesses, grandiosity and pretension. To my horror I discovered that my friend had neglected fiction's first, central necessity, the creation of an outline. He had simply "plunged in," depending upon the untested and immature resources of his imagination to see him through. I remonstrated, vainly. He believed, with a nearly fanatic irrationality, that the production of five hundred words a day would somehow magically result in a finished novel. Had I been able to spend more than two weeks in the Straubs' dismal basement flat, I know that I should eventually have prevailed, but both finances and considerations of health conspired toward my departure, and *Marriages* dripped from the heedless and uncaring pen until it had staggered to its enigmatic conclusion.

Briefly: this is an incoherent and adolescent affair about an incoherent and adolescent affair. Never entirely talentless, Peter stumbles upon a number of nicely evocative phrases and manages perhaps a single reasonably effective scene. Otherwise, a trivial bit of juvenilia understandably suppressed very nearly since its publication.

Under Venus

Oh, how Straub romanticized, how he wailed over, this, his so-called "lost book." At least he had sense enough to understand that *Marriages,* despite the fawning compliments of his fellow expatriates, could not stand as anything more than a desperately minor achievement. In the course of a transatlantic conversation after pub closing hours (Peter had discovered a pay telephone somewhere in the bowels of London which, if struck with sufficient force in just the right place, enabled him to dial the United States for the price of a local call) he confessed to me that he had completely rethought his ideas about narrative in the light of certain tactful remarks of mine and wished to make his second novel much stronger, that is, more an actual novel, than his first. Wonder of wonders, he intended it to have a plot!

In practice, this entirely welcome ambition meant that he swapped one set of influences for another. Instead of John Ashbery, Iris Murdoch, F. Scott Fitzgerald and John Hawkes, the guiding spirits of *Marriages*, we find the mingled voices and strategies of John O'Hara, Iris Murdoch, Richard Stern, Saul Bellow, the very early

Virginia Woolf and John Hawkes. No one could control such a circus of influence, and Peter certainly does not, yet in *Under Venus* we can observe a greater maturity of characterization and scene-setting, the beginnings, faint but discernible, of something like narrative technique. Characteristically, my friend overreached himself and obscured what might have been a decent little novella about an expatriated artist's return to his (of course) Philistine hometown beneath yet another tired celebration of adultery and its guilts and, even more fatally, a political sub-plot. These strands do not so much mesh as collide, evidence, if evidence were needed, that Peter's actual gifts, a matter I expressed quite forcefully to him over the length of a ten-page single-spaced letter which cost a veritable fortune in air mail postage, were unsuited to the literary novel.

Entirely apart from this consideration, to which we shall return, my stubborn friend ignored the wise suggestion that if his main character really had to be an artist of some sort—never a good idea—he should be a writer, for the sake of a minimal degree of authenticity. Instead, he persisted with the folly of making this character a musician, and even worse, a composer. I do not know why, but when novelists decide to write about artists, they invariably choose that art which they understand least. At this time, Peter knew even less about classical music than he does at present, and as far as he is concerned, musical composition is, as it were, a closed book. His version of the political process is only slightly less misinformed. The passages about adulterous love are both ridiculous and misguided. Yet touches here and there, a nicely observed detail, a moment of living dialogue, some passages of decent writing, and bits of mysticism imported more or less directly from Iris Murdoch, indicate that definite growth has taken place.

The rejection of this book by publishers on both sides of the Atlantic ultimately proved greatly beneficial, but its immediate effect was to put my friend into a profound slump. Some sort of crisis occurred, the details of which remain mysterious. Unwisely, Peter wasted far too much time rewriting, cutting and pasting, rewriting again. It is at such times that the support of an old pal can be most helpful, and I am pleased to say that the beleaguered author did at last finally take in an essential aspect of my ongoing advice, namely that he set this book aside and turn to a type of fiction far more suited than the mainstream literary novel to his modest gifts—the genre of the gothic. True, he needed to be told the simple rules and traditions of this humble form, but for once open to instruction, he proved a quick study. When he had absorbed an elementary grasp of the gothic from my lessons, he did a minor bit of reading on his own and began to write again. The two novels which emerged from this process, *Julia* and *If You Could See Me Now,* are the best to date of his career and seem likely to remain so.

Julia

After the vapors of *Marriages* and the portentous confusions of *Under Venus,* what an immense improvement is seen herein! And without any undue immodesty whatsoever I may also say, what a tribute to the helpful influence an old friend such as myself can have upon a struggling, indeed flailing, writer like Mr. Straub, so prone to excess of every kind, to ignorance of his own limitations and the consequent inability to distinguish strengths from weaknesses, so unwilling or unable to restrain himself within the confines of his own small but satisfactory talents! I know, I am being quixotic, optimistic, selflessly loyal and generous with my time and insights to a degree others may not think justified, but as old-fashioned as it might seem in this cynical era, I imagine that friendship involves responsibility and shall continue to remind my old companion of the sandbox and swingset of the principles he once embraced under my fond tutelage and which enabled him to produce this book and the one that followed, by any rational standards his finest. Those principles are simplicity, straightforwardness, clarity and submission to the traditions of his chosen genre. The minute you hear of someone "transcending" his genre, you may be sure that he has gone astray.

Here we have an evil ghost, a haunted house, a woman in peril. Peter's compulsion to insert into every narrative a ghastly secret hidden in the past first comes to the surface in this book, but it is kept under control and functions merely as an explanatory aspect of the plot. These time-honored elements are treated with an unintrusive originality—the evil revenant is a child, the house becomes overheated instead of cold, the heroine has repressed the memory of a hideous and terrifying deed—which in no way detracts from their familiarity. Our dutiful author understands that formulaic fiction is formulaic for an excellent reason, that the formula, beloved by its otherwise undemanding readers, is its only justification. My pal has worked out his grisly tale in advance, he sets it down with no more than a few unimportant digressions, he delivers the goods. Not least, the narrative begins at the beginning and travels along a straight line to end at the end. This is a book with which to while away a long flight or an afternoon at the beach. Once read, like all good entertainments, it may be cheerfully forgotten. For an efficient work of genre fiction, no higher praise can be given. Three cheers? No, never, but two heartfelt huzzas are certainly in order, and that also is praise of the highest appropriate measure.

Now, I might nearly regret the instinctive generosity which prompted me to send the author a half-bottle of Bluebell's Bubbles, our finest Ohio champagne and made from grapes grown at the lovely Bluebell vineyard in Chalmersville, only twenty miles from my dear Popham and our campus, for I fear that this gift and the accompanying card reading *B+ is as good as it gets,* encouraged the delusional fantasy of "transcendence" soon to announce its destructive appearance upon the stage. Can it be a coincidence that "Bluebell" so closely resembles "Blue Rose?" (I am nothing if not relieved to have decided against sending this suggestible fellow a half-bottle of Ohio's second-best and significantly less expensive champagne, Dark Vale Vineyard's Black Blossom Brut, made at the other end of the state in Meegersville but available everywhere, even at some 7-11 locations.) However, I remain gratified by Peter's obedience to first principles during the writing of at least one more book, his crowning achievement. That the celebratory demi-boutaille I shipped to his shabby little rented house in College Lane, Kentish Town, North London, helped keep his spirits aloft during the creation of *If You Could See Me Now* is enough to dispel any second thoughts. As is his grateful note of thanks, which I hung on an office wall after paying the framer's extortionate fee: Okay chum, whatever you say. / Here's to blue bells, / yours, /Peter.

If You Could See Me Now

Let me reconstruct a scene from Grub Street.

It is late spring, 1975. Upon completion of my dissertation, *Charles Dickens and Jim Thompson: Hamlet as Decadent Bard,* and subsequent receipt of my Ph.D. from Indiana University, I had at last resigned my position as part-time Instructor of Victorian Literature at the Coast Guard Academy and accepted an Associate Professorship in the English Department of Popham College in beautiful little Popham, Ohio, long known as "the Sewanee of the North," and "Middlebury Writ Small." I chose to celebrate this success with a two-week visit to London, where I could combine exposure to the high and low life of that great metropolis with a selfless, mano a mano, eyeball-to-eyeball survey of my old friend's plight from the perspective of a makeshift bed—in the event, a mattress on the floor—in his office. Two weeks (or, as the English charmingly have it, a fortnight) is a laughably brief time in which to apply a lifetime's knowledge to the disorders of a needy friend while unlocking the secrets of an ancient and subtle city, but I could spare no more than that. Already, I was unobtrusively in the throes of preparing the groundwork for the creation of a Department of Popular Culture, an effort rewarded six years later by my appointment as Full Professor and first Chairman of the new Department. Two weeks were what I could give, and give them I did.

My initial task, I must admit, was to conceal the dismay aroused by the smallness, shabbiness and utter charmlessness of every aspect of the Straubs' situation. From the distance of my Popham redoubt, their address on College Lane in North London's Kentish Town had evoked images of greenswards and elegant Georgian buildings. Foolish me, ever the optimist! The ignorance of the cabdriver who ferried me from Heathrow as to the location of College Lane should have alerted me to the coming disappointments, as should the increasing deterioration of the neighborhoods through which we traveled on our journey Straub-ward. The buildings grew smaller and meaner with every passing mile, the streets filthier, the Londoners likewise smaller, filthier, more furtive, more and more attired in the rags of the welfare-state poor. At last, the cabbie deposited me at a bleak, anonymous corner with the instruction that according to his "A to Zed," a mysterious reference soon explained when Peter loaned me his own tattered copy of this comprehensive map of London's streets in book form, I should find the street in question by proceeding into an unsavory alley-way and taking the first left-hand turn. College Lane, it seemed, was too narrow to permit vehicular traffic. My tip, nothing, reflected my opinion of this treatment.

I cannot now imagine how this unathletic scholar, a creature of the library rather than the gymnasium, managed the feat of transporting into the dingy alley, thence down the cheerless length of the so-called "Lane" itself, four heavy suitcases, a Mark Cross briefcase, a cardboard box filled with books, and a paper bag containing my belated housewarming present to the Straubs, a half-pound of cardamom-and-cilantro seasoned peanuts I had secured for a staggering sum from a vendor at New York's Kennedy airport and to which I had resorted only under the pressure of stewardess-induced starvation. I believe I adopted the mountaineer's strategy of establishing a series of base camps from which further forays are conducted. While reeling between the heaps of luggage and sweating from every pore, I could not but take in the sordid character of this "lane," in fact a concrete footpath between a row of workmen's cottages and a railway embankment. The Straubs' residence, a narrow two-story hovel like its neighbors, lay at the far end of the midden.

We are speaking of a time long before Peter entered upon the ostentatious and financially ruinous practice of living like a grandee, a matter as to which I offer continuous, oft-alarmed counsel, yet never would I have dreamed that his circumstances should have progressed so little beyond the dank cellar in Dublin where four years earlier I had risked the health of my respiratory system. This was brighter, but almost anything is brighter than an Irish basement; this was larger, in the sense that a small room enlarges when the closet door is thrown open; in every way, this was scant improvement over the forthright poverty from which *Marriages* had emerged. The narrow, fretful staircase which led from the living room or "parlor" to Peter's office and the Straub bedroom represented the principle sign of upward progress.

The glimpses afforded a tactful guest suggested that the bedroom was adequate, but the office! Peter's office! That shoebox, that doll's house, that oubliette in which every night for nearly two weeks I was made to thrust open the grimy window and semaphore my arms to dispel the miasmic fog of my host's cigarettes before pushing his chair beneath his cheap plank desk, trundling the room's only other chair against the back wall, then lowering the skimpy mattress from its position against the fireplace to the floor, thus affording a scant eight to ten inches of unused space in front of the pathetic bricks-and-boards bookshelves pilfered from nearby construction sites! And each morning, after waiting with a full bladder and an empty stomach in this architectural straight-jacket for my host and hostess individually to make their way downstairs into the bathroom, complete their morning rituals and wander back upstairs, it was MY duty to flip the mattress back up over the fireplace, restore the chairs to their former positions and otherwise eliminate any traces of my presence. Only then could I scurry to the bathroom in hopes of enjoying the last remaining trickle of hot water. The difficulties of the process were multiplied by the Straubs having distributed my luggage randomly about the dwelling, so that although the day's trousers could be found within the suitcase conveniently placed at the top of the stairs, the required socks and underwear might well have been lodged behind the living room sofa.

Some hosts and hostesses make life a misery through a mean-spirited lack of generosity, others through simple ignorance of the ordinary considerations due their guests, and the Straubs, emphatically, should be numbered amongst the latter. It is to this ignorance that I ascribe what those less familiar than myself with Peter and Susan might describe as their withdrawal, their apparent indifference, their even rudeness, toward the end of my visit. On the fifth night of my stay Peter abandoned the living room for an evening's "work session" mid-way through my lively deconstruction of Benny Hill's antics. By Tuesday of the following week, no sooner had we politely dispatched Susan's functional meal than the old night owl began yawning and finding excuses to go to bed at nine. That Friday, three days in advance of my return flight, Susan's forceful request that I depart the Straub household obliged this thoughtful guest to find lodgings in an extortionately expensive hostelry in the Swiss Cottage area. One and all, these behavioral quirks were rooted in (if not, to more sophisticated sensibilities, truly justified by) a discussion between Peter and myself shortly after Sunday opening hours in the seedy public house located at the southern, more remote end of his "lane." Our dialogue precipitated a crucial sea-change in my friend's imaginative life. The Butcher's Blood, I believe, perhaps The Heifer's Corpse, was the name of the smoky, derelict-infested oasis to which Peter repaired at frequent daily intervals during this period. I recall his apocalyptic anxiety over arriving at the pub door exactly at noon, lest, he said, we be deprived of seats at his favorite table in the "garden." At 11:56, still adjusting the knot in his necktie (even then, he took pains to dress as well as he could, one of the endearing signs of my old pal's eternal insecurity), he charged down the lane before me, hurtled into the alley-way and arrived at the entrance of the saloon-bar at the instant the bolt slid back. Gripping pints of bitter and packets of salt-and-vinegar crisps, we fled into the sad little "garden" behind the pub. Peter collapsed into a chair at a rust-stained white table spotted with bird dung, evidently his favorite. Then he proceeded to explain the true source of his anxiety.

After weeks spent vacillating between two ideas for his next novel, he was still unable to decide between them. For good or ill, the choice would affect the rest of his career, and the importance of the decision magnified its difficulty. Due to the inability of most ordinary citizens, even those in editorial positions, to make recommendations on artistic matters, no one had been able to assist him. He could do no more than make notes for both projects while knowing that it was time to begin actual work. Which book should he write? The weak sun picked out the flecks of salt-and-vinegar crisps adhering to the sides of his mouth as he guzzled beer from the pint glass, dribbling only slightly as he rapped the glass back on the table. Conspicuously, like a true friend, I made a show of wiping nonexistent residue from my own mouth, but he failed to take the hint.

"I'm getting scared, Put," he said, using my childhood nickname. "Maybe I'm all washed up. Maybe this is it."

"Nonsense," I told him. "You've just begun to do the decent little tales, the modest but satisfactory little things you were meant to do all along. Describe these two ideas of yours, and I'll tell you in an instant which is the right one for you." The relief which crossed his face as he took another pull on his beer informed me that he had been waiting for this opportunity since even before my arrival. Speaking hesitantly, stuttering only occasionally, pausing for mouthfuls of crisps and warm beer, he unfolded his two stories. The first involved an American family who move to an English village dominated by an aristocratic vampire; the second, a failed scholar—rather like himself—who returns to his grandparents' farm in the Midwest—as he continues to do to this day—there to meet the ghost of a beloved cousin. "You must choose the second story," I said. "There will be much more of you in it. And it must be in the first person." I saw him take it in, I saw him ponder it as he polished off his first pint and downed three more, and while I helped him back up the lane toward his hovel, I understood that his slurred, unintelligible utterances were expressions of thanks. Susan Straub's flinty backward glare as she half-led, half-pulled her husband upstairs and her distinct iciness during the remainder of the day was long ago forgotten on her part, forgiven on mine.

The book for which I feel a greater than usual measure of responsibility is his finest achievement. Small in scale, scope and ambition, *If You Could see Me Now* demonstrates the modest but persuasive charm to be found within the gothic genre. It is quite nicely written, and rises to several piquant and atmospheric moments of scene-painting. The alert reader may find the book's one reference to jazz music, a brief allusion to Gerry Mulligan and Chet Baker, a dire warning of things to come. In his next, unfortunately over-praised work of fiction, self-indulgence of this sort gets entirely out of hand. But coy, smirking references to jazz musicians are hardly the worst of *Ghost Story*'s exhibitionist failings.

Ghost Story

How I wish that a crisis at Popham had not made the years 1977 and 1978 a living hell for me, sapping my energies and demanding all the concentration not already claimed by the preparation of lectures, research for and writing of papers, the demands of students, appearances at Popular Culture symposia and the relentless tedium of academic committees. On the one occasion during those desperate years when I did get to London (I had the honor of giving the keynote address to our International Congress), my twice-daily telephone calls to the Straubs' new and apparently quite attractive house in the Crouch End area met, when answered at all, with rushed, harried-sounding excuses concerning previous engagements, visiting relatives and the like. As ever innocently self-absorbed, Peter and Susan failed to grasp my simple need for a roof over my head, thereby compelling me to waste a fortune on a room in the conference hotel, where a cup of coffee cost the equivalent of three dollars! (On our gathering's second day, a Sussex University attendee let me sleep on his floor.) Had it not been for a treacherous attempt to dismantle my Department and reassign me to literature survey courses on the part of an Assistant Dean named Hartley Smoot acting in concert with two convention-bound members of Popham's English department, and if by evil coincidence I had not been forced at the same time to deal with the false, hysterical allegations made by an erotomaniac female student, I should have steered my old friend back onto the responsible, reasonable path of the honest artisan. Under normal circumstances, I would never have permitted him to plunge into those errors which have since deformed and undermined his work. I would have snatched the manuscript of this misguided, destructive book from his hands and waded through its tangled pages with a machete. Here is what most causes me pain: at the very time Peter was most urgently in need of my help, I was fighting for my career and my reputation—fighting for my life—and could not give him any more than what I could express in two or three letters written with an unquiet mind late at night.

Let us overlook the plot, which, as one reviewer pointed out, might have been drawn from an episode of *Wonder Woman*. In books like this, the plot is of no importance. How it is handled is what matters. Mortals encounter supernatural being, arouse its ire, being returns with blood in its eye. This elementary structure could handily support a brisk little tale of some two hundred pages, but any more weight will cause it to sag. Straub begins with an enigmatic prologue in the style of Joyce Carol Oates, then resorts to the ancient cliché of old fogeys swapping stories in an atmosphere redolent of a men's club, complete with tuxedos, cognac and leather furniture. All would not have been lost had not my feverish old pal imagined it his duty to bestow literary seriousness upon his project—and by extension, the genre it soon betrays—by cribbing the story we are told from Henry James.

I saw the cart begin to jolt off the path when Peter wrote me that he was adapting "The Turn of the Screw" for a Chowder Society tale and intended to follow it with rewritten versions of stories by Poe and Hawthorne. The reader may offer silent thanks that I found it possible to set aside my hideous problems long enough to warn him, in the most unambiguous tones, against the folly of his scheme. I reminded him of the genre writer's Fourth Commandment: Thou shalt not commit a literary allusion. Had I failed in my duty as a friend and mentor, this book would be bloated yet further with plagiaristic homages.

As if this pretentiousness were not bad enough, Peter had by this time fallen under the sway of Stephen King, not in itself a display of poor judgment, since King could have taught him the value of the straightforward narrative single-mindedly depicting the battle between good and evil. Instead, what Peter absorbed was King's one besetting sin, that of garrulousness. The man is quite simply incapable of brevity, concision is anathema to him, he is in love with the sound of his own voice (and a squeaky, womanish, high-pitched thing is, too.) Once my dazzled friend had internalized King's, shall we say, regal defiance of legitimate boundaries, his fictions succumbed to rampant elephantiasis, and even his so-called "short stories" mumbled on for fifty, sixty, a hundred-odd pages. Yet Kingish verbosity is hardly *Ghost Story*'s greatest flaw.

Here the nudging, irrelevant references to jazz music and musicians run amok. Nearly every minor character bears the last name of one of Peter's darlings, and a stereotypical, blatantly racist caricature of an African American musician for some reason named "Dr. Rabbitfoot" pops in from time to time, to no discernable point. I tried to persuade the heedless author to delete this material, but he wouldn't listen. A more significant error in judgment is the inclusion of diaries and invented books within the *bergeschichte,* a device which serves only to break up the narrative. Intertexuality is fundamentally unsuited to the gothic, and has no place in genre fiction in general. In later works, this grandiose and exhibitionistic gimmick becomes so uncontrolled that it ultimately overwhelms the text altogether—see *The Hellfire Club.* Even worse, it is in *Ghost Story* that my friend accidentally tripped over a theme he mistakenly embraced as a revelation and went on, ruinously, to explore and expand in his next two books. The theme, familiar from vapid, drug-influenced novels and films from the Sixties, is of the indeterminacy of reality: what we see with our own eyes in a waking state is merely partial, visions and dreams represent a higher, better form of truth, the mind altered by chemical substances or extremes of stress is capable of superior perceptions, and so on, ad infinitum.

One of my friend's most defining traits is literal-mindedness. A literal-minded person in the grip of mystic fancies can only press them to the dubious conclusion that reality itself is a variety of fiction. *Ghost Story* avoids this ripely decadent notion, but only barely—it lurks beneath the text, inhabiting scene after scene in which one character or another suffers hallucinations. That the reading public responded positively to this balderdash is.... I don't know what it is, but it's extremely discouraging to a responsible educator like myself. The reliable Elmore "Dutch" Leonard knew what was up. His review of the book contained the clear-sighted sentence, "This isn't fiction, it is hype." The novel does contain some excellent descriptions of snow.

Shadowland

A close friend for what may at times seem all too many years, a buddy since the days of the sandbox and the playground, as the undersigned is to Mr. Straub, has the privilege, in fact the responsibility, of speaking unwelcome truths. Those who have attained even the faintest degree of prominence are forever in danger, as they increasingly surrender themselves to illusion, of wandering from those simple principles responsible for their initial success. Self-indulgence takes root, with fatal effect. My old chum Mr. Straub, a once-passable writer of limited but effective powers dwindled into a pathetic but virtuoso case of self-indulgence, has long been an extreme instance of this unhappy process, and the Fifteenth Anniversary edition of *Shadowland* offers his faithful friend a welcome opportunity to set things straight.

Let us be frank. My misguided former playmate, he whom I protected from bullies in high school and allowed to glimpse, at some personal risk, my answers in college science examination finals, stuck to the basics in two books only, *Julia* and *If You Could see Me Now*. With *Ghost Story*, so wrongly praised, the rot set in. *Shadowland* shows him well on the way to the disasters he has since perpetrated. Here we have what should have been a simple tale. A boy encounters a great magician (yawn), endures a series of tests (descent of the eyelids), and emerges from his trials an even greater magician than his opponent (actual slumber). This harmless tale of supersession, familiar to all who have read Homer, Shakespeare, or at least Mr. John Fowles, is here corrupted by the flaws of hyperbole, irrelevance, pretension, and pointless complication to which our boy thoroughly succumbed in his later "novels." Where we expect a rousing story, we are baffled by the intrusions of a dozen internal narratives, a lamentable archness of style, above all a refusal to get to the point. We hear the shuffle of note cards, the rattle of the typewriter, the sighs of deluded self-satisfaction. My old friend has launched himself into the willful obscurity which has all but destroyed what might have been a decent career as a dependable genre writer.

The reader of this laborious farrago may take comfort in my determination to return my foolish pal to first principles: begin at the beginning, end at the ending, and no nonsense in between. Unless forced to see that he began seriously to go astray with this book, he will be lost, and this companion of his late hours, this faithful representative of the sensible reader, shall not neglect his duty. One night soon, as our wayward author interrupts the guzzling of yet another libation to reach for the peanuts on the bar, I intend to speak these words: tell your story and get out.

• • •

To my comments reproduced from the jacket copy of the Gauntlet Publications limited edition of *Shadowland* I wish only to add these few remarks. This may be the most self-indulgent work of fiction since *Tristram Shandy,* shamelessly stealing from John Fowles, pointlessly throwing off mean-spirited, vindictive caricatures of our hardworking and dedicated masters at Country Day School, rocketing backwards and forwards in time and so thoroughly muddling the distinction between what is real and what is not that lengthy passages mean nothing at all. A swamp, a noxious vapor, a will-o-the-wisp. The cruelty, even sadism of some passages render the book unsuitable for the younger readers who might otherwise have found it palatable. It includes one passable fairy tale originally invented for the entertainment of the author's son. On the whole, the wise reader will avoid this book as if it were a contagious disease. Some of the cadences of its final pages are nicely turned.

Floating Dragon

Within this crazed, hyperbolic, fatally excessive monstrosity, a horror novel which proved too much even for horror's undemanding and star-struck readership, there exists the teasing little ghost of a tale about the intersection of an industrial accident and an accursed village. The hints one has while reading *Floating Dragon* of this unrealized story, glimpses of what the book might have been, justify a brief account of the circumstances under which it was written, even as they cast a colder, harsher light on what it finally became. The sense of what *Floating Dragon* might have been, i.e. a swift, intriguing yarn in a post-Lovecraftian manner, makes its failure to locate narrative containment of any sort all the more offensive, but the perspective granted by "inside" knowledge of the author's situation at the time may at least provide some explanation of the catastrophe.

The inexplicable chilliness which had affected my relationship with the Straubs—he my oldest friend, she his deeply valued daily support and buffer against the world's intrusions (I must say, Peter is perhaps the most deeply defended person I've ever known)—toward the end of their long residence in London dissipated altogether upon their return to the United States in 1979. At this time, they would have been well advised to return to their native Midwest, as I took pains at every opportunity to point out. The purchase of a modest but accommodating house in Milwaukee would not only have saved them a vast, in fact an actually almost unimaginable sum in real estate costs, home repairs, taxes and so forth, at a stroke eliminating my stressed-out friend's continuous financial anxieties, it would also have reconciled him to his humble but sturdy roots, thereby freeing him from the neurotic fixation on his birthplace which deforms the next stage of his work. Failing that, I could have found them a perfectly adequate residence right here in Popham, and it would have been no problem for me to arrange a non-tenure-track appointment for the returning author in our English Department, involving minimal teaching duties, a bi-annual reading, and all the accompanying benefits. This generous offer fell upon deaf ears, four of them. Instead, Peter chose to purchase a crumbling mansion located in Connecticut's "Gold Coast," Fairfield County. Specifically, in the town of Westport. Nothing less congenial could be imagined.

I visited the Straubs on two occasions during their residence in Westport, early and late, that is, in 1980, during the first flush of my old friend's success, and in 1983, his fortieth year, by which time his loathing of his adopted town had so undone him that he spent his weary days, to judge by those he spent with me, in piloting his yacht-like Mercedes from one bar to another. Alarmed by his behavior, which incorporated an inordinate degree of churlishness toward this long-time friend and confidant, I staged a one-man, personal intervention and convinced him to change his ways, whereupon he embarked upon *Koko*. But that is another story, to be addressed in its own time.

We are concerned now with my first visit to 1, Beachside Common, Westport, the ruins of a formerly grand house still in the throes of restoration when I appeared for a weekend's visit which extended for another five happy days upon the conclusion of the 1980 Conference on Popular Culture in New York, at which I had been gratified by the presentation of that year's Elmer J. Atwood Award For Superior Achievement in the Field of Popular Culture Studies. The "Atwood," as we call it, is a handsome little cast-iron sculpture in the form of a 1951 Motorola television set, and it so weighted the largest of my suitcases as I trudged toward Peter and Susan's new residence from the Greens Farms train station, following a none-too-accurate map hand-drawn on what appeared to be a cocktail napkin by my old friend, that I had sweated through my undershirt, shirt and suit jacket by the time I had managed to get myself and my complement of luggage up onto their porch. Various muscular workmen under the command of a white-bearded giant (a gentleman later to be affectionately drawn as "Ben Roehm" in both *Floating Dragon* and *Koko)* observed this entire process without offering any assistance whatsoever. Susan Straub opened the door with the infant Emma in her arms and three-year-old Benjamin Straub beside her. Little Ben's face illuminated with a smile, Susan's, alas, fell. I attribute this less-than-hospitable response to the sight of my many bags and the thought that she might have to assist me with them. In any case, she doubtless remembered the invitation to drop in any time I was in the vicinity her husband had given me a scant three weeks before at the end of a telephone conversation, recovered her politesse and invited me in. Little Benjamin instantly darted forward and kicked me smartly in my right ankle, resulting in a nasty dark discoloration which persists to this day.

After the installation of my various bags in the guest room, a space scarcely large enough to accommodate the requirements of the usual traveler, and a hasty sponge-bath, I was escorted upstairs to my friend's newest office, which occupied the entire third floor of the spacious manse. I had been informed that months of work had resulted in a space Peter found "very nice," even "good for work." These mild words in no way prepared me for the sybaritic grandeur the once-impoverished author now deemed appropriate to his station in life. A parquet floor, an immense Oriental rug, an Italian sofa of butter-soft leather some ten feet long and two matching chairs like leather thrones, huge glass-and-marble coffee tables with marble ashtrays weighing at least fifteen pounds apiece, hand-made bookshelves, massive speakers on clever revolving stands, graphics by an internationally well-known artist, a state-of-the-art set of stereo or "hi-fi" components in a handsome wooden case, many subtle, even cunning, lights, a half-mile of records near the expansive desk, two skylights, hand-fashioned wooden platforms beneath the dormer windows, all of it elegantly disposed within a space the size of a bowling alley. I believe the only reason I did not faint away altogether before the attack of light-headedness which this display of lunatic expenditure brought on was that on the desk itself I observed an open journal and a jar filled with pencils—Peter was, at least, still writing his books by hand, he had not completely lost his mind. For a dread moment, I had feared to see a "computer's" or "word processor's" hideous shape there.

Those who have become parents to small children tend to forget that adult guests and visitors do not share their obsession with the offspring, grow weary of the perpetual demands made by the little dears, not to mention the tears, screams, howls and other unpleasant noises emanating from the adored, and wish for conversation on subjects other than the children's accomplishments, in fact heartily desire that the precious wee ones might be sent off to a distant room for lengthy periods, especially when one of them imagines it a comic treat to deliver sharp little kicks to the adult guest's tender ankles. So it was with my hosts, and it was with a magnificent display of good-humored tact that I marveled at little Benjamin's messy performance with a bowl of spaghetti and little Emma's hunger for the maternal breast. (There are spectacles a guest really ought be spared.) I do not believe that the besotted parents ever quite comprehended the honor bestowed up me by the "Atwood," and their failure to give adequate attention to the fine points of the speech I delivered at the Conference during any one of the half-dozen opportunities I granted them would have disappointed me deeply had I not known of their hunger for any sort of intellectual discourse, even if it had to be repeated to be grasped. In fact, the few occasions for anything like serious discussion over the course of this week-long visit presented themselves either late at night in Peter's office, when Susan and the children were safely tucked in bed, or in his automobile as I accompanied him on his frequent journeys to Waldbaum's supermarket in search of diapers and the like. What I gleaned of his current project during these conversations filled me with a familiar unease.

My hapless old chum, he who would never have escaped Professor Military's Philosophy 101 course with a passing grade much less his eventual A without my thrice-weekly tutorials, was now resolved to devote a lengthy novel to the problem of the indeterminacy of reality, a theme well beyond his intellectual abilities. Even worse, he intended to clothe this theme in horror's gaudiest and most self-referential motley, to court excess and its concomitant shapelessness deliberately, abandon all restraint as a matter of principle, and indulge himself by exploiting every cliché of situation and imagery known to horror, or at least those that should come into his mind, not to invoke their pulp-magazine capacity to entertain, but to exemplify and summarize the genre of horror itself, to objectify it within the context of indeterminacy, to simultaneously undermine and celebrate the very genre from which it detached itself by this objectification! He did not use these words, he was barely conscious of his own intentions, but this is what he meant. Even more fatally, as well as employing diaries, invented histories, etc., in another misguided attempt at intertextuality, the book would finally reveal itself as the work of one its own characters! His final delusion was that this grotesquery, at once arid and overblown, would be met with overwhelming approval by the fans, aficionados and connoisseurs of horror.

The actual reception of this farrago by those for it was most intended was best epitomized by the review written by Thomas M. Disch for *Twilight Zone.* Sensible Mr. Disch eviscerated the book, pointing out with an appalled amusement its sloppiness, verbosity, slap-dash construction and sophomoric errors of style. Other, less intelligent genre reviewers expressed their disappointment at what they took to be a reckless imitation of Stephen King, their favorite writer. Influenced more by its author's reputation than the book itself, the British Fantasy Society bestowed upon it their Best Novel Award for 1983, a matter which cooler heads amongst that august organization must still find embarrassing. Of course, the general reading public gobbled it up. The careers of Tom Clancy, John Grisham, Robert Ludlum, Anne Rice and many others demonstrate that the public at large will read anything at all, providing it is bad enough.

Floating Dragon does offer some tender pages toward the end, if you have the stomach to read that far. I must say that I was horrified but not at all surprised to learn that Peter had virtually committed artistic suicide half-way through the book—he purchased a "word processor." Thenceforth, he processed words instead of writing them.

The Talisman

I have never met Stephen King, but I believe the man must be a saint. No amount of posturing on his collaborator's part about efforts to achieve a "common style" can persuade me that King did not single-handedly and entirely unaided write the vast majority of the pages contained within this overlong book. Now and then, at intervals of hundreds of pages, one stumbles over a slow-moving passage bearing the Straubian thumb-prints of piled-up dependant clauses, pompous diction, a self-conscious and nearly ironic use of slang quite different from King's command of demotic language, and the pointless elaboration of unnecessary details, as if the fellow imagined that distinguishing the exact shade of grey on the underside of a leaf observed for a moment by his hero could bring the scene to life. I suppose it must have been he who inserted the names of the jazz saxophonists Zoot Sims and Dexter Gordon, but King's allusions to rock groups are far more suited to the text. I happen to know that after a brief infatuation with the work of J.R.R. Tolkien, Straub lost all interest in fantasy fiction. That King continues to pretend that Peter played a significant role in the creation of this novel is testimony to his loyalty and generosity, to say nothing of his compassion.

Koko

Misguided in every aspect of its intention, design and execution, actually misguided at its core, this resolute display of narrative perversity now and again nearly succeeds, quite mysteriously, in its far-too-evident ambition to surpass the time-honored conventions of genre fiction. Before I describe my own vital but unacknowledged contributions to the achievement, simple modesty requires that I point out that *Koko*, for all its flaws, deserves a greater degree of consideration than would ordinarily be granted to a desperately played-out horror writer's attempt at producing an international thriller in the manner of Robert Ludlum or David Morrell, while in the midst of a classic mid-life crisis. My own role in its creation was crucial merely in its timeliness.

Near the end of August, 1983, not long after the completion, so to speak, of my friend's minimal "role" in the writing of the Stephen King novel, *The Talisman,* I arrived unannounced at his Westport palace with the idea of "filling in the gaps" of our recent histories during the five days between my return from the Conference on Popular Culture on the lovely isle of Corfu (at which I had been awarded my second prestigious "Atwood" while enjoying the hospitality of the Earl of Macclesfield's charming villa, "The Antlers") and my return flight, delayed by reason of my airline's intransigent notions concerning the allocation of frequent flier miles, to the humbler comforts of Popham. The only economical means of managing the journey from Kennedy airport to Westport, Connecticut is by a van or bus under the management of the sadly misnamed Connecticut Limousine Company, which deposits the weary traveler in the parking lot of a Westport motel. I called my former companion of the sandbox from a pay telephone in the lobby of this establishment and was gratified by his willingness to appear upon the moment and deliver myself and the usual luggage to his abode. Unusually for one lately so absorbed by his own concerns, he seemed cheered by the prospect of my visit.

Within minutes a new Mercedes, even longer and more splendid than its predecessor, spun into the motel parking lot, driven by a deeply, in fact almost alarmingly, sun-tanned Peter. The fellow had virtually grilled himself to the color of a well-baked Gingerbread Boy. Not only that, in place of his usual garb he wore a short-sleeved polo shirt, khaki shorts and loafers without socks! His language had undergone a similar transformation, incorporating many casual obscenities previously unheard in his speech and frequent usage of the meaningless interjection, "man," as in the startling phrase with which he greeted this long-lost friend, "Put, man, shit, it's really good to see you, man, you know, fuck, man!" I believe I concealed my shock at this coarsening of speech and manner even as I worked out its most likely causes during our wild ride back to Straub Manor, a journey which included lay-overs at two favored drinking establishments. My friend, evidently, was in no hurry to rejoin the domestic scene.

The first of these establishments, a mediocre restaurant located a short distance down the Post Road and named something like Mahler's, or perhaps Schoenberg's, was remarkable only for a barren, wholly suburban ugliness epitomized by the bar to which Peter urged me, a comfortless and irregularly shaped slab of marble fitted with spindly metal stools. The youth behind this modernist, in fact all but Cubist structure greeted my friend with a wide grin and a cabalistic handshake. Any doubts that the sun-blackened author had attained the status of "regular" at this dubious and even slightly sinister place were dispelled by the incomprehensible conversation chiefly, in so far as I could follow it, about the comings and goings of mutual acquaintances which began the instant this fellow placed Peter's brimming glass upon the bar and rather grudgingly, I felt, filled my own order for a Lime Rickey diluted with a splash of Coca-Cola. (No prude, I enjoy a cocktail as well as the next fellow, but three in the afternoon seemed too early for a genuine Rickey, much less for whatever filled my friend's glass, a potion I judged by its odor to be gasohol.) During the hour we spent at this inexplicable place, so involved was Peter in conversation with the bartending youth, as well as with the waitresses arriving for their evening shift, each of whom greeted him with a glad cry and a fond embrace, also with two smooth thugs with slick-backed hair I understood to be the owners, that he and I exchanged but a few sentences. This left me sufficient time to interpret the event in the following way: if after some three years in this affluent and self-consciously artsy community his chosen companions were bartenders and waitresses, Peter and Westport were a bad match indeed.

Our next stop, an even unhappier establishment known as the Black Mutt and located within an ancient houseboat berthed at a riverbank, deepened this impression. Here the attractions were what my deluded friend described as the "ambiance," meaning the general gloom, the listing stools, the battered old bar lined with sots, and above all the prematurely aged, decidedly common bawd serving up drinks, whose faded good looks Peter found attractive. Like all her cynical breed, the floozy knew to keep her distance while returning his flirtatious sallies, thereby compelling my friend to turn his conversational efforts toward myself. These had mainly to do with jazz musicians whom he had succeeded in befriending or at least to some small degree attaching himself, their various approaches to improvisation, yawn, I mean, really, the disquisitions of the musically illiterate upon such things are helplessly infantile, the habits and quirks of these obscure folk and the many hours their devoted fan had spent in company with them. Sadly, he was trying to impress me with the familiarity he enjoyed with these gentlemen, whose names, I confess, I failed one and all to recognize. It was they, of course, who had so affected my friend's speech patterns. My poor old friend had so lost his way that he aped the hipster language of his jazz musicians and consorted with waitresses and bartenders—Westport had provoked him into a ruinous second adolescence, and while we swilled our fifth or perhaps sixth drinks of the day I vowed to do my utmost to bring about his return to the safety of his native Midwest.

During our jet-propelled, careening drive to his palatial house, he confirmed my observations by singing along, more or less, with the jazz solos on the tapes he fed into the car's sound system. "Get hip to this, man," he told me while blasting through a four-way stop, "I don't know why it took me so long to realize, that I'm an artist, not a bourgeois square, I mean, man, damn, I blow like Bird, man, you dig, except Bird blew through his horn, and I blow with words, you dig?" In response to this pathetic utterance, I could but answer, "I dig, man, you can be assured of that," and wondered what sight would greet me upon arrival at 1 Beachside Common. I imagined Susan puffing on a "reefer" and attired in black tights, skirt, sweater and beret while the children wandered in foul diapers through a landscape of record sleeves and empty bottles. The scene which greeted our arrival was of a deeply reassuring normality. Evidently accustomed to her spouse's new incarnation, Susan joined us in the manse's handsome library for another round of drinks while my friend discoursed upon the fine points of several "solos," then disappeared to prepare the evening's entirely adequate repast while the children squalled and screamed in the manner of ordinary tots, those not under the sway of imitation jazz musicians. To my surprise, Susan never betrayed even the slightest displeasure at my unheralded arrival, my characteristic mountain of bags or the declaration that I should be joining the household for a few days. She even took the time to admire my second "Atwood" and attend to my descriptions of the dear old Earl's residence high upon the curving streets of Corfu. By that time, I imagine, she had become accustomed to just about everything.

Over the next few days, we settled into a routine. As of old ensconced in his office, now within a bed prepared on one of the dormer platforms, I arose at seven and joined the rest of the family downstairs so that Peter might spend a couple of hours writing, or thinking about writing, or whatever he did while playing the endless records which penetrated all the rest of the house. In practice, this meant that I was left to my own devices while Susan ferried the children hither and yon. At noon there was some sort of hasty lunch. From one to three o'clock, my old friend and I occupied adjacent lawn chairs and read books while Peter, clad only in his khaki shorts, soaked up yet more damaging ultra-violet rays and several bottles of St. Pauli Girl beer. After that he threw on a polo shirt, gestured me toward his Mercedes and sped off to one or both of the bars we had visited on my first day, there to drink gasohol until six or seven, when we rocketed homeward for the evening meal. At nine, when the children had been dispatched to their beds, he and I returned to his office, where he drank single-malt Scotch whiskey, now and then permitting me a miserly dram. During these hours, which often extended into the wee hours, he frequently repaired to his desk to conduct lengthy telephone conversations rendered inaudible to me by the incessant moaning of saxophones and pounding of drums emanating from the gigantic speakers installed on every side, front and back, and even overhead.

During these late hours, he at last confessed to me that his latest project was a sort of thriller involving Vietnam veterans and with no discernible supernatural element whatsoever. So daunting did he find this basic material—a plot even he knew to be better suited to a half-hour of television than a novel-length work of fiction—that he had been unable to write any more than a kind of introductory but unrelated short story, which he declined to offer for my inspection. He had spent months writing no more than increasingly irrelevant notes. "Put, baby," he said while pouring another twenty dollars of malt whiskey into his glass, "I don't know if I can still blow my horn any more, you dig? Can't hear the changes, man, can't get into the groove like I did when I was a young cat, sometimes it's like my talent went Splitsville, man, this is some crazy shit, dig?"

I couldn't help myself—I let him have it straight between the eyes with both barrels. What I said to my despairing old buddy must remain forever confidential, but from that day to this he has at least managed to conduct himself like a responsible citizen and not a blear-eyed denizen of sordid late-night haunts. Neither does he sprinkle his conversation with filth. I wish only that I had succeeded in deterring him from writing the tediously long thriller on which he had embarked and in persuading him to return to his native soil. Even the imprecations of a devoted friend can only go so far, it seems. At least he changed his ways and did a decent job of writing *Koko.*

Koko

Despite its irresolute conclusion and frequent lapses into inconsequentiality, this book manages to keep its head above water most of the time. The sour, vindictive chapters set in Milwaukee should have been edited out of the book altogether. No one who did not serve in Vietnam is capable of writing about that experience. That accepted, Peter's effort to do the undoable contains at least a poignant tone which renders several passages of this muddled but oddly effective tome very nearly…what shall I say? Moving? No, but "affecting" will do well enough.

Mystery

Mystery, indeed. This dozy genuflection to crime and detective fiction, the genre least intrinsically suited to the arrogant breed of writers who, like Peter, disdain outlines, asks the reader to endure a hundred page introduction concerning irrelevant events of its protagonist's (and, shamelessly, its author's) childhood before settling down into a tale in which a gifted youth encounters an aged master detective and helps him solve both an ancient and a contemporary crime. One of the Hardy Boys meets Sherlock Holmes, that is the essential matter of *Mystery.* Again, our native city of Milwaukee is subjected to willful and mean-spirited distortions, here taken to the extremity of its transformation into an anomaly-ridden Caribbean island. So incapacitating is the author's laziness that he names his great detective, the "amateur of crime" standing in for Sherlock Holmes, "Lamont von Heilitz" and dares call him "the Shadow," thereby invoking those halcyon afternoons when he and I huddled before the Motorola and rapturously absorbed the adventures of Lamont Cranston, known to crime-fighters and evil-doers alike as The Shadow, thrilling as one to that immortal mantra, "Who knows what evil lurks in the hearts of men? The Shadow knows!"

The process which resulted in this exercise began with a far more interesting premise. Peter had relocated himself and his family in the overpriced brownstone on the Upper West Side of Manhattan where he resides to this day, and on a two-day layover between arrival in New York and the flight to the Seventh International Congress on Studies in Popular Culture in Prague, at which I would deliver the seminal paper on "Barbie Doll, Bettie Page, and Vampira: the Rage Engendered of the Genderized," for which I was awarded my third "Atwood," I availed myself of the Straubs' hospitality, meaning that I was made to transport every single one of my bags, apart from those Peter found it in himself to transport for me, up five flights of stairs to the so-called "guest room," where the weary "guest" slept upon a fold-out bed and enjoyed the use of an inconvenient bathroom sporadically provided with warmish water. This comfortless cell was located on the same floor as Peter's office.

Grudgingly, my old friend took me to his favored watering holes after we had dispatched Susan's minimal evening repast, and I could not but notice his uncharacteristic preoccupation, even after the consumption of a great many glasses of the potion he was drinking at the time. I believe it to have been a mixture of cognac and champagne known as a "French 75," but I cannot be sure. These may have passed down the Straubian gullet on a later occasion, and he could have reverted at the time to gasohol. My enquiry as to his current project met with snarls, and after I had assisted him homewards and bade a fond good night to Susan, I made so bold as to sally into his office and rifle his papers in search of at least some clue to what he imagined himself to be writing. Papers I saw in great number, but these recorded only vestigial attempts at jump-starting a narrative. A foray into his hard disk—by this time I had been compelled to master the basics of "computing"—revealed more of the same, plus a great many of what I took to be elaborate jokes in the form of what I can only call faux-correspondence. I retired to the lumpy fold-out bed and the ungenerous bathroom in a state of the utmost concern.

On the following day, the hapless author informed me that he was indeed experiencing difficulties with his latest project and intended to address the problem by sequestering himself for a considerable period in a luxurious tropical resort. My alarmed reservations went unheard. Even Susan appeared to support her husband's scheme, no doubt on the grounds that a ruinous plan was superior to no plan at all. We went our profoundly various ways.

Perhaps a month later, rather I confess a-tremble that I might hear of a crisis requiring my immediate appearance in Manhattan, I telephoned my old companion to be informed that his sojourn at "Jumbled Bay," or whatever the place was called, had suggested a tale in the manner of Daphne du Maurier, whose autobiography he had stolen from the resort's library. He would write a story of identical twins and Doppelgangers and bring it to completion within the year. My relief at this statement cannot be overstated. Surely, the design suggested to him by his tropic excursion would bring about a return to the first principles of straightforward narrative, especially as represented by the example of Dame Daphne!

One shakes one's head, one shrugs one's shoulders before the perversity of authors. After stumbling upon an entirely workable notion he should have clutched to his well-padded bosom, after actually committing theft in aid of the notion, within a few short months Peter blithely ditched Doppelgangers and Daphne du Maurier to assail the fortress of the mystery novel. It was his assumption that the conventional reader would comprehend his title to be a pun, and that the secondary meaning of "mystery" would inform this reader's understanding of the book. One turns away from such delusions, remarking only that they are nowhere supported by the text.

Mrs. God

If I felt any honor in the association, I might be tempted to take credit for the original inspiration behind this deliberately meaningless bit of narrative perversity, but honor is about the last thing I feel when I am made to consider "Mrs. God." On a brief stay at vertiginous Straub Manor after my host's completion of *Koko* and toward the end of an evening, which, given my friend's unsociable notions as to meaning of "evening," means somewhere around 2:30 a.m., I had sufficiently relaxed, despite the incessant wailing of saxophones and pounding of drums which seem invariably to accompany Peter's lengthy "evenings," to recount an amusing anecdote concerning the odd conditions in which one of my colleagues, an Associate Professor in Popham College's English Department and a most eccentric chap in every way, found himself whilst engaged in research at a famous private library located within a magnificent country house in the north of England.

As ever preoccupied by the many "solos" he found compelling, constant telephone calls from thoughtless so-called friends and the several magazine articles he chose to skim during these hours, Straub appeared scarcely to attend to my anecdote. Yet when I had drawn rather irritated to its finish, he asked a number of questions about my eccentric colleague, his researches and the curiosities encountered during their pursuit. Was it actually the fact, he asked of me, that the young man was left utterly alone in the great house? And that gourmet dinners, prepared by invisible servants and invariably accompanied by an ever-rarer and more fabulous wine, had greeted his nightly appearance at the dining table? That one of the splendors of the library was the presence on its shelves of unpublished manuscripts by most if not all of the important Modernist writers? And that a visit to the village churchyard had suggested to my colleague some dark, unhappy secret in the history of the noble family which owned the great house?

Yes, yes, yes, I replied, all of that is true, wonderfully, puzzlingly true!

And is it also true, he asked of me, that this man went prowling through the cellars and discovered doll-houses of enormous size?

That, too, is the truth, I told him. "You know," I said, "you might make a tale of this, some intriguing little tale of horror concerning an accursed family and a visiting scholar." He rejected the notion out of hand—not his kind of thing, he said, too fey, too much like a million other stories. You mean, I remarked to myself, too much like what you know you should be writing, but said no more about for the remainder of my visit.

Imagine, then, if you can, my shock and dismay when coming upon the novella entitled "Mrs. God" in both its incarnations, that of the final piece in that sadistic oddity, *Houses Without Doors,* and that represented by the earlier version published by Donald M. Grant in a limited edition. Peter had incorporated nearly every detail of my anecdote into his tale! Not only that, he had made reference to my college, Popham, and inserted several unhappy incidents

I had long before described to him and had no connection to the anecdote in question! This outright betrayal was mitigated only slightly by those subsequent remarks made to me by some of my colleagues to the effect that they had (inexplicably) enjoyed the novella, especially its references to our beloved College, and were delighted by this proof of the substantial influence I apparently exerted upon its author! The mind, as they say, boggles.

If influence him I must, would that it were to the production of anything other than "Mrs. God." Peter admits that he wished to invoke the example of one Robert Aickman, whose laboriously mandarin efforts sensible readers have long deemed unreadable. This is Freudian mumbo-jumbo of a deliberate, willed incoherence. I gather it has something to do with a baby. Those who suppose they have understood it need not trouble me with their interpretations. "Mrs. God" represents no more than a foolish display of hostility not only to his readers in general, but also and quite shamefully to me. As their biographies repeatedly prove, the writers of fiction, those poor devils, are prone to this sort of thing. The title of the novella has no discernible significance whatsoever.

The Throat

The author of this volume recently confided to the undersigned, a buddy tactfully alert to overstatement, hyperbole, pretension, sentimentality, semi-mystical incoherence, and self-justification, that the title with which P.S. has afflicted his latest offering has nothing to do with necks, knives and wounds.

"It's not this," insisted Mr. Straub, drawing a forefinger across his well-padded neck. Apparently, he wishes us to overlook the frequent slittings, stabbings, mutilations, (six, by my count, not including the depredations of the post-modernist parody of his fellow Milwaukeen, Jeffrey Dahmer) in the present work. Of course, any such suggestion is absurd—*The Throat* is the slit neck, whatever the claims of its author. Despite protests to the contrary, Mr. Straub remains the special case of elevated theory and low practice so familiar to his readers.

How, then, does my friend justify his charmless title?

Firstly, this work has ingested *Koko* and *Mystery*, the two installments of his so-called "Blue Rose Trilogy." In that case, why not call the book *The Stomach?*

Secondly, Mr. Straub claims that he intends to refer to song, limitlessness of expression, the melody-crammed throat of a saxophone, such as that manipulated by his character, Glenroy Breakstone. This evasion we can dismiss out of hand. A book is not, nor ever will be, a saxophone. (Confusion of realms is typical of Straub. Instances may be found, pandemically, throughout *The Throat.*)

Finally, my old chum asserts that he refers to the utterance of suppressed, unsayable speech. Pity must be the most generous response to this oxymoron.

I prescribe frequent rereadings of simple, honest artisans such as Stephen King and Dean Koontz—our boy must learn to tell a story at least as well as his betters. And if he cannot learn to tell a story—from A to Z, without pointless complications—a story with clearcut heroes and villains—I intend to suggest during one of our frequent pub crawls that he take up the saxophone instead.

• • •

An addition to previous observations on *The Throat:*

To the above I should add only those few remarks forbidden by tact and ordinary good manners from inclusion in the "flap copy" of the Borderlands Press edition of this protracted and self-destructive assault in the form of an homage upon the classic detective novel. My most honest responses would have been acceptable to neither the deluded author nor the amateurish fantasts in charge of this vanity "Press," gentlemen so far out of touch with the conventions of trade publishing that they have yet to respond to my request for the modest honorarium of $450, a considerable bargain considering that I sweated over their copy for two full working days, revising my hard-won impressions into phrases more and more merciful.

The Throat

Set aside the hideous title, disregard the typical Straubian narrative clutter. Back and forth they travel, these Tims and Toms, through yet another vicious parody of Milwaukee in blatant imitation of Ross MacDonald's Lew Archer, an ancient but never completely outgrown enthusiasm of our author. Detective fiction routinely embraces outright absurdity, so we do not object that a present-day murderer has chosen to repeat the rituals of a serial killer of long ago; that our Tims and Toms solve the old murders in process of investigating the new ones has a pleasing generic familiarity. Less acceptable but still okay is the digression into the career of Jeffrey Dahmer inspired by Peter's affection for this creature. (In silence, I pass over the remarks in which he virtually took "credit" for the invention of Dahmer and his misdeeds.) False endings are cute, so, fine, I guess *The Throat*'s three false endings represents a tour de force of cuteness.

But…Please…If I may be so bold…might go so far as to state the all-too obvious…

No humble, artless, thick-fingered, genre-bound, two-books-a-year crime-writing pit pony, a type of writer heartily disdained by Mr. Straub, would dream of so betraying both story and reader as to leave his most interesting villain deposited invisibly in the past, where he may never be seen by the reader! And no professional "hack," to which dismissive category I am sure my starry-eyed friend assigns a good many of his colleagues, would make the fatal error of separating the first appearances of the second-most interesting villain from his final unmasking by such a great wad of pages that the average or even above-average reader cannot possibly remember the fellow.

Take a deep breath. Hold it for a count of ten. As you exhale, clear your mind of preconceptions and opinions concerning Mr. Straub and his work. Then, in the non-judgmental space you have entered, contemplate the perversity of recasting the weakest, most self-indulgent and self-consciously "literary" of Raymond Chandler's novels, *The Long Good-Bye,* as a Gnostic meditation upon detective fiction. Then, taking your life in your hands, imagine trying simultaneously to incorporate into the result of this process the Vietnam/trauma/grief/extremity themes from *Koko* and the "Hardy Boy" protagonist of *Mystery* once called upon to represent them, "intertextual" references to *Koko* and *Mystery* as well as to texts written by several of the novel's characters, among them a former Colonel of the Quartermaster Corps thrown in for no other reason than to parody Straub's conception of the military prose style, a sub-theme devoted to an utterly idealized and a mythical jazz musician addicted to cocaine, a second sub-theme concerning the "Nabi" painter Paul Ranson and, it pains me to add, yet more references to undigested portions of the author's autobiography. Finally, as if that were not enough, try to imagine doing all of this under the aegis of that evil dark star, Straub's most fatal influence, Vladimir Nabokov.

Disheartened, I sum up: a labored, exhausted effort at an exhaustive…

No, I give up, I surrender. This is a book I could not manage to read all the way through without frequent naps, vacations, and health-giving interludes spent in the company of writers clever enough to have less, in this sense meaning more, on their minds. I detect signs of extensive cutting, but the resulting moment-to-moment clarity of style serves only to heighten the reader's steadily intensifying unhappiness.

The Hellfire Club

On my return from the 1994 International Popular Culture Society's Annual Congress in the handsome old city of Barcelona at which I had the honor of accepting my fourth Elmer J. Atwood Award from the marmoreally pale, slender, long-fingered, in every way aristocratic hands of the Contessa Fabiana Paloma Therese de Ribas Loupo-Mondeale Allegro-Gonzaga y Gonzaga, the guiding spirit and generous patroness of our Mid-Iberian Chapter, I took advantage of Planet Hollywood Airline's overbooking my New York-Akron flight by the exchange of my seat for the delightful sum of $500 and a voucher for one night's lodging plus complementary sandwich and soft drink at the Reebok Airportland Hotel and Gift Shop. After rescheduling my return flight for three days hence, I telephoned Casa Straub and received the expected invitation to "come and set a spell," as we Midwesterners have it, for as long as I wished. The ointment was not without a complement of flies.

The note of resignation in Susan Straub's voice did nothing to soften my sense of having replaced a gracious environment with one distinguished by abrasiveness. The contrast between the Old World and the New, initially embodied in the Third-World chaos of John F. Kennedy Airport, was to be heightened by another exposure to the unpleasant rigors of Peter's comfortless dwelling, in effect an Alp made completely of staircases, after my recent experience of the welcoming chambers, galleries, ballrooms and other interiors of the dear Contessa's Palazzo, one of six such splendors located here and there about the world, or so I gleaned from an offhand remark my hostess whispered in the general direction of my awaiting ear while approving the Castilian flair with which her manservant Emiliano, a dangerous-looking, silver-haired chap whose air of ferocity was not quite domesticated by rimless spectacles, opened the latest but not last bottle of Dom Perignon upon the conclusion of her lavish opening night Reception for our Congress.

During the taxi journey from the airport, the sense of immersion into a dystopic favela was reinforced by the torrents of hostility projected backwards, once I had ventured a mild comparison between his vehicle and a public toilet, from the hunched shoulders, corrugated neck and misshapen head of the serial killer at its helm. After endangering my life during our charge into Manhattan, this thug, a Haitian conducting his life of crime under the unlikely "handle" of Labrousse St. Jean Labrousse, greeted with murderous rage my payment of the artificially-inflated fee of $34.50 and the generous tip of a voucher guaranteeing him free of charge one night's lodging at the Reebock Airportland Hotel and Gift Shop, not to mention the lagniappe of a complementary sandwich and soft drink. What a falling-off from the urbanity of Sigismundo Palp, Contessa Fabiana's chauffeur, whose drolleries had enlivened our forays in her Rolls Royce brougham (pronounced "broom," I had been advised, and of an intriguing brownish-red not unlike the color of Tabasco sauce)! The Haitian criminal refused to assist me in the removal and transportation to the curb of my bags, one of them bearing a nasty, still-glistening oil stain.

A distracted Susan Straub observed the Herculean effort of conveying my three weightiest, most essential suitcases up the torturous five flights to the barren "guest room" without offering assistance of any sort, and when I had staggered back down to the kitchen, attended fitfully to my tales of Spanish adventures and the Contessa's largesse. I believe Susan never quite grasped the magnitude of honor represented by my fourth "Atwood," especially when it was given to me by the Contessa herself, although I had gone to the trouble of carrying that splendid trophy downstairs with me and placing it on the kitchen table right in front of her eyes.

Such inhospitality of the part of my hostess may in nearly all cases be laid at the feet of her spouse, and when I inquired of Peter's state of mind and general well-being, the rule again proved true. He was suffering under a deadline, he was working night and day, he was grievously distressed. I love the way authors fret over their "deadlines." A deadline is an arbitrary matter, a convenience, and no one in the world of publishing, least of all authors, takes them seriously. Yet mention the approach of a deadline in anything less than, say, two years to one of these children, and he will begin sweating bullets. So it was with my old friend.

After eighteen months of drifting aimlessly behind his characters as they enjoyed elaborate meals, watched television, bickered, picked at their exhaustively-described navels, in short conducted themselves as his marionettes always do in the absence of any real function, Peter had at last recognized that a plot of even the most minimal order had failed to surface and thereupon entered into a panic. No one can wring the juice out of a panic like Straub, and he had clutched at a loathsome minor character absurdly named "Dick Dart" and forced him to commandeer the novel. Dart would rescue the book, he told me, well, he had to, there was no other way out. The deadline, the deadline, the deadline. There was no time to lounge about on his overpriced furniture and watch soap operas while permitting his characters to lounge about on their own overpriced furniture and watch the same soap operas to which he was addicted *(All My Children* and *One Life to Live)*, until some sort of story announced itself. No, no, this time he was desperate.

I wish my readers to know that Peter decided upon relinquishing his novel to the psychopathic Dart mid-point in his family's first-class flight to a luxurious resort in Puerto Rico. There, in the intervals between meals, he daily consolidated his plans by jotting notes while tanning himself in the comfort of two lounge chairs, one beside the resort's vast pool and the other on its even vaster beach. Many would be grateful to experience this version of desperation!

All of this Peter explained during those paltry hours, invariably so late at night as to be beyond any sensible person's bed-time, during which I was given access to the holy of holys, his "office," located on the top or fifth floor of his house and at the other end of the book-littered corridor from the guest room in which this old and valued friend had been installed. No doubt in jealous imitation of her husband, Susan Straub had compounded the inconvenience by claiming the so-called "guest room" as her own "office" and stuffing it with such a magnitude of computer equipment, files and stacks of reference materials that in the darkness of night the unfortunate guest could scarcely make his way to the adjacent bathroom without suffering painful bruises to hip, ankle, buttock, and other tender regions, not omitting those unmentionable in polite society.

During these few hours I was given—after Peter had detached himself from his computer, navigated his way downstairs to join Susan, his children and myself for an evening meal in a state of disorientation so profound that at least once a night he referred to each person present by every other person's name, so that I was "Ben," "Emma" and "Susie," Susan was "Ben," "Emma" and "Putney," Ben was "Emma," "Putney" and "Susie," Emma was "Putney," "Ben" and "Susie," and all of us were likely at any moment suddenly to be "Rainbow," the ponderous family cat, then plodded back upstairs gripping an enormous glass brim-full with an amber narcotic fluid to complete with many a groan whatever it was he imagined he had to complete that day and, then and only then, permitted me entry to the messy sanctuary—during the brief periods of coherent speech still left to him, he described the ghastly project.

The Hellfire Club, I learned, was to replicate the labyrinthine structure of a fantasy novel penned by one its own characters. Each of its parts would bear the part-titles of, and echo the actions of, the corresponding section of the fantasy novel, *Night Journey;* the fantasy novel would also provide hints, clues, suggestions and answers to the problems and mysteries of the novel which incorporated it. Many, though not all, of these problems and mysteries were directly related to the underlying fantasy novel, especially those related to its true authorship and the disappearance during the Pleistocene Era or thereabouts of a young female poet from a second-rate literary colony.

I tried, that's all I can say. I did my duty. I gave it my best shot. The man was too far gone to take heed. No matter how forcefully I drew his flagging attention to the incompatibility within the same narrative of his savior, Dick Dart, and these arid games, in spite of the eloquence I summoned when I jumped to my feet, leveled my index finger at his bloodshot eyes and condemned the absurd conjunction of thrillerish murders and literary investigation he proposed to set before the public, he would not correct his course. Peter met my denunciation of intertextuality with the innocently arrogant remark, "Put, that's what I like about the book." That, finally, is that, and no more can be said. The infection had reached the bone.

What, in the end, do we have here? From the general wreckage, might anything be salvaged? *The Hellfire Club* is one of those frustrating failures which contain passages of vitality sufficient to lift the glum reader's spirits over long stretches of text. After the languor of the first hundred and fifty pages, Dick Dart's kidnap of the heroine strikes like a bolt of lightning, and for a dizzy time we delight in the illusion that our author has cast his pretensions overboard and resolved to tell a story in the manner of his betters, honest entertainers such as Dean Koontz, John Saul, Frank Herbert and Mr. King. Alas, almost immediately one finds oneself swimming upstream against our author's usual flood of complexities, texts within texts, ancient secrets, inside jokes and jerry-built, if not actually, improvised constructions. The pace slows to a halt whenever food is put upon the table. Not only does the lazy novelist throw in a remote country house, a confusion of birth and a resolving storm, he cynically exploits every last cliché, as these particulars indicate, of the gothic genre the novel takes pains to ridicule. Unlike *Shadowland* or *Floating Dragon,* this book is not even good enough to be destructive. No, we must conclude, nothing can be salvaged from the wreckage. But one may conclude with the bittersweet observation that my old pal discovered at last how to write decent dialogue precisely when his other gifts abandoned him.

The dear Contessa Fabiana Paloma Therese de Ribas Loupo-Monreale Allegro-Gonzaga y Gonzaga, a fast friend, perhaps said it best after skimming through the copy of *The Hellfire Club* I had sent her as an ironic jeux in commemoration of our shared hours. The sophisticated reader will have little difficulty in hearing the nuances of her delightfully approximate English:

The Dearest Professor Putney, I have been reading all the way to the end the book written by your friend. This book is difficult for me on the account of my seldomness in reading fiction in English, except for the bon-bons of Mr. Herman Melville, Mr. Paul Auster and Mr. Thomas Pynchon, which so happily remind me of the tales I read in childhood. I think it is in your friend's book sometimes of more importance what is not said in the middle of so many words than what is said. Do you remember my chauffeur, Sigismundo? He has taken the book most eagerly away, but Sigismundo will be unhappiest to see no pictures. Could you send me now *Night Journey?* So sad, I will be in Mozambique when you tell me you can again represent yourself in Barcelona. In farewell, Contessa Fabiana

After reading a few pages, she gave the book to her chauffeur. The significance of the unsaid, indeed.

Mr. X

Professional writers of fiction, at least as exemplified by my friend of ancient days, do not so much transform as deform everyday reality. Confronted with the real world, they deface, *traduce* it, blithely. To all intents and purposes, these people shove reality into the dirt and pummel it to within an inch of its life. If these over-privileged fellows are anything like my friend Peter, they simply cannot be trusted with the truth. Mendacity, fabulation, prevarication, whatever you want to call it, and we might as well call it by its rightful name, lying, in fact lying of a sort to bring a blush to the cheeks of a confidence man, are second nature to them. If even the mildest, sweetest fiction-writer on the face of the earth should plant his right paw on the family Bible, elevate his left, and swear by all he holds dear that the sun is shining and the weather delightful, listen to me, button yourself into an overcoat and grab the umbrella before you leave the house. Fiction-writers, I have learned, turn truth inside out, compulsively, driven by reflexes beyond their control. I am not being harsh or judgmental here. As my old buddy is wont to say after he has finished tearing some acquaintance to verbal shreds, "It isn't a criticism, you understand, it's only a *description.*"

The above remarks are occasioned by Peter Straub's *Mr. X*, for which my fond, foolish hopes were of course shattered upon the adamantine, also reckless, selfishness so much a part, whether he knows it or not (and it is safe to say he doesn't, not at all, believe me) of my friend's character. I should have known better. Yet the origins and initial circumstances of the book now called *Mr. X* offered, I innocently imagined, a means by which my old pal might rediscover the first principles of his modest art and cleanse himself of those excrescences that have disfigured his work since the disastrously over-praised *Ghost Story*. For unlike his previous "novels," the project began with another text altogether, one written by someone else, a person my friend had never met and whose only work of extended prose, a touching although rather awkwardly written memoir, I surrendered into his all-too eager hands. We began in amity and ended in typically Straubian catastrophe.

I must sketch in the necessary background.

• • •

The year was 1995. Blissfully unaware of the currents destructively at work beneath the surface of my peaceful, productive, one might say all but idyllic existence as Chairman and only member of the Department of Popular Culture at Popham College in my cherished refuge over my past two decades and then some, little Popham, Ohio, I had visited the charming Provencal village of Sangue-sur-Rhone, site of the 19th Conference of the International Popular Culture Society. Despite the frustration of having been cheated of a tenth "Atwood" Award by one Rupert Dunst, a smirking, red-lipped androgyne equipped with a freshly-minted Ph.D., an expedient English accent, and a facile line in post-post-Structuralist vapor about, I forget what, something like Lesbian Colonialist Matrices in the "Nancy" Comics of Ernie Bushmiller, despite the *humiliation* of getting gypped out of an "Atwood" by this blatant fraud, I nonetheless knew the much greater satisfaction of having been honored with the Life Achievement Award of our governing body, the International Popular Culture Society. The IPCS's Life Achievement Award is no bauble, I assure you. The handsome object is made of a lead-titanium alloy cast into the shape of Grauman's Chinese Theater. It's at least twice the size and weight of an "Atwood." Without fear of exaggeration, I may claim that our LAA is to the field of Popular Culture what a Super Bowl ring is to the NFL, except that only one person gets it, not an entire team.

According to long-established custom, on my return from Provence, I telephoned the Straubs from John F. Kennedy airport. A soft-spoken female with what may have been an Iranian accent described herself as their "housekeeper" and informed me that my old friend and his life's partner had ensconced themselves for a month, presumably at ruinous expense, in the village of Sag Harbor, located in the region of Long Island known as "the Hamptons." I suppressed a groan of dismay and immediately dialed the number given me by the dulcet-toned Iranian. Susan Straub answered, politely attended to my account of triumph in Sangue-sur-Rhone, and for reasons of her own refused my offer to spend three or four helpful days at the Sag Harbor redoubt. Peter was fine, she said. Yes, really, apart from the ill effects brought on by an unusually hot and humid summer, factors I supposed beyond even Madame Straub's formidable control. No, I could not speak to her husband, Peter was at work in a studio located behind the house and unreachable by telephone. Good luck, congratulations, good bye.

With a heavy heart, I purchased a ticket on a connecting flight to dear old Ohio and the comforts of my ranch-style abode. I installed the cherished honor upon the mantel of my living-room fireplace and, some weeks later, beside it mounted an explanatory plaque provided from my own modest funds. With September came the Business Meeting of the IPCS, for which I was required to fly back to New York in fulfillment of my obligations as Trustee and Past President of that organization. New York is an extortionate city, prepared at every moment to extract whatever it can get from the visitor's wallet, and to my relief Peter and Susan responded to my tale of legal woes and a harrowing shortage of cash with an invitation to occupy either their "guest room," the cluttered, comfortless aerie on the fifth floor, or the fourth-floor bedroom of their son Benjamin, then beginning his Freshman year at the University of Southern California. "I'll take the lad's room, thank you very much," I responded, certain that Ben's doting parents had provided him with a bed vastly more agreeable than the creaking torture-device installed one flight up.

My legal difficulties, the product of a completely unjustified allegation of improper conduct leveled against me by a student in my Senior Honors Seminar, "Implications of Recent Trends in Scholarship Related to Popular Culture Issues," had distracted me from what would otherwise have been my concern for Peter's state of mind. That Susan had forbidden me contact with him augured ill, I knew. And his sojourn in the Hamptons, a hotbed of ostentation and snobbery, had been a troubling prospect on two different grounds, namely, (1) Peter's tendency to solve the unease aroused within him by any context in which he supposes he might sniff the possibility of rejection by throwing wads of money in all directions, and (2) the conjunction of the most merciless summer in decades, if not the entire century, with my friend's inability to do little more than whine like an infant and sweat like a plow horse when the temperature rises above 90 and the humidity keeps pace. The legal problems and consequent mental stress inspired by an unbalanced young Texan whose name I am forbidden to state by the terms of our settlement, so let us content ourselves with her initials and call her Ms. Neiman-Marcus Pedernales Blast, the hyphenate N-M consisting of two commonplace feminine handles, one of which rhymes with "fancy" and the other with "barely," P representing the squawk of a parrot in need of a cracker, and B a breed of short-legged, long-bodied hound, as I was saying, the turmoil inspired by Ms. Fancy-Barely Squawk Coondog kept me from the attention I would otherwise have given to my friend's plight, attention he sorely needed. (The fiendish N-MPB was not acting alone, either, I'm sure of that, evil forces within our English faculty have long yearned to undermine my authority, erase my entire department and get me reassigned to the humiliating drudgery of Freshman Composition, and will stop at nothing to attain their goals.)

In the end, personal integrity won a slender victory over calumny and hysterical falsehoods, and even that cost an unbelievable sum of money. My application for reimbursement from the College's General Funds was rejected by the Trustees, for which I in no way fault our President, Mr. "Bill" Liddy. President Liddy has been on my side since November 12, 1979, when at a heated gathering of the Dean's Extraordinary Affairs and Sensitivity Issues Committee I saved him from unwelcome Federal intervention by casting the deciding vote permitting female undergraduates, particularly those with singing voices located in the alto register, to join the famed Popham College Combined Men's Glee Club and Boy's Choir. (It pains me to note that very few of our young women have taken advantage of this opportunity, no doubt due to the formation on December 1, 1979, of the United in One Voice Willa Cather Empowered Wymyn's Choir, under the fatally sexist leadership of our Director of Women's Studies, Wilhemina "Call Me Willy" Frost.)

Be that as it may.

So it was at the end of a troubled September I took advantage of our annual Business Meeting to spend most of four days and nights in the Straub's vertiginous residence, a habitation in the form of a giant staircase from which little rooms sprout, at intervals, like mushrooms. (The Business Meeting generally takes up an hour at the most.) Susan Straub greeted my arrival with only a touch of weariness and held the door as I transported my many bags up the long, treacherous flight of steps from the curb where the usual surly driver had ejected them from the usual reeking taxi. Her husband, of course, was "working," but I could feel free to join him after I had deposited my luggage in their son's bedroom. Up I went, a monstrous bag in each hand, up and up to the fourth, or "children's," floor, through young Benjamin's doorway and into a chamber where the charm of gracious dimensions and a rank of windows upon the handsome facades across West 85th Street had been sabotaged by the savage graffiti sprayed on every surface, presumably by young Benjamin. At Popham, we respond to such vandalism with a stern hand, in the worst cases with expulsion and a hefty fine, but the Straubs must have encouraged their offspring's criminal tendencies, very likely under the delusion that he had been demonstrating an "artistic" bent. (I suppose the boy had been acting on the same artistic impulses back in 1980, when he responded to my first visit to their Westport mansion by delivering a brutal kick to my ankle, thereby giving me a nasty, dark discoloration I shall bear to my dying day—his first, most enduring *graffito*!) The sides and shelves of the bookcases, the sides and top of the little scholar's desk, the base of the chair, all these bore the repetitive, domineering slash-and-burn of the young urban hoodlum. I trudged down the endless stairs for the remaining bags in a state akin to shock, fearful that the symbolic violence rampant within the bed-chamber would destroy any chance of slumber. (I also felt a nostalgic twinge from the wounded ankle, my left.) When finally I had carried the last of my things upstairs, hung my suits, jackets, and trousers within the woefully inadequate closet-space, applied a cold compress to my forehead and stretched out on the young criminal's (admittedly quite comfortable) bed, I mounted the final flight of stairs, turned toward the customary uproar produced by saxophones, trumpets and drums screaming, wailing, and banging all at once, knocked forcefully on my friend's office door, and was granted admittance. Peter pushed himself upright off his couch and grunted hello. Then he mumbled something about going out for a drink.

Over the course of four, maybe five, gasohol-and-lime juice libations, Peter admitted having run aground in Sag Harbor. Instead of putting in the foundation-work so essential to a person of his modest but workmanlike talents, he had tried to jump into a novel-length fiction without benefit of preparation. He'd written the same ten pages over and over again, despairingly. He had no idea where he was going, and he spent most of the day asleep. "Don't worry about me, Put," he said, "I've been through this before. It's part of the process. That's what you academic *boyos* never really understand—the sheer, wretched misery of *process*." Well, I reposted, if you want to talk about misery, here's what happened to me since the last time we got together! Too self-absorbed to take in the crisis brought on by Ms. N-MPB, Peter signaled for another gasohol-and-lime. Soon I assisted him homeward, where Susan Straub served an evening meal of the hasty and functional variety. She paid scant attention to the color Polaroids of my LAA I had thoughtfully retrieved from my carry-on bag. Peter spent most of dinner frowning at his plate, though he did rouse himself long enough to announce, "Hey, Susie, listen, this Texas babe who was in Put's Senior Honors Seminar filed a sexual harassment complaint against him because he invited her back to his house to look at videotapes of the Dallas cheerleaders, and all it took to buy her off was a couple of thousand dollars."

"I've heard enough," Susan said. All parties retired early.

Early the next morning, the mystery of the Iranian woman was solved, though less than pleasantly. I had made my weary way downstairs to the sunny kitchen, where a red-haired young female personage with extremely fair skin was engaged in unloading the contents of the dishwasher. My hostess was nowhere in sight. My host, it goes without saying, was not going to lever himself out of bed for another five hours, and even then would be incapable of uttering anything but groans for a lengthy period. Deducing from her task that the girl was a domestic servant, I democratically introduced myself. In the soft voice and curious accent I remembered, she confirmed my deduction by declaring herself the Straubs' housekeeper and gave her name as "Linda Sign," an obvious alias devised to conceal her status as an illegal alien. I do not know if any Iranian females are named Linda, but I am sure that none are named Sign. Nor is anyone else. She had dyed her hair, and she was the lightest-skinned Iranian I had ever seen, but she could not pull the wool over my eyes. With a gallant wag of my finger, I said, "A likely story indeed, Miss, um, 'Sign,' but I assure you that your secret is safe with me. Let me congratulate you on your escape from the terrors of your Middle-Eastern homeland and request of you the favor of a nourishing breakfast, such as two eggs scrambled without the yolks, a slice of dry whole-wheat toast, two rashers of low-fat turkey bacon, freshly squeezed orange juice and a cup of good hot coffee, preferably French Roast." Astonishingly, the little minx laughed aloud, right in my face. She was employed as the housekeeper, she told me, not as the cook, and this was not a bed-and-breakfast. If it was scrambled egg whites I desired, I could jolly well scramble them myself, but the larder was bereft of low-fat turkey bacon and French Roast coffee. As an abstainer from coffee, Miss "Sign" hadn't a clue how the stuff was made, though she believed one of the shelves above the cats' litter tray contained a bag of black, oily-looking beans from Kenya, or it might have been Costa Rica, if I cared to grind them up. On the other hand, she was willing to prepare on a one-time-only basis the same breakfast for me that she was having herself. And what, may I ask, I asked, would that be? The Arabic baggage commanded me to sit down at the table and read the morning paper while she whipped up an Ultra SlimFast. My strenuous objections met with a second and firmer order to sit down. I sat. There came an ungodly clatter from what must have been a blender, located, like the coffee beans, above the cat litter. The minx thrust before me a tall glass filled with a brown, frothy liquid that looked for all the world like a milk shake. Much to my surprise, this concoction proved very tasty.

Ever since, I have enjoyed a daily morning beaker of Ultra SlimFast as an accompaniment or to speak more accurately a prelude to my customary breakfast of egg whites, dry toast and turkey bacon. Health-giving Ultra SlimFast does taste a good deal like a milk shake, but if you eat nothing else, starvation sets in well before noon. And over the past couple of years, I've been reducing my intake of fat during the cocktail hour by adding several jiggers of vodka to the blender, mixing a smooth, potent blend of alcohol, skim milk, and chocolate-flavored USF, thereby cutting out the need for salted nuts.

My old chum emerged from the bed-chamber a few minutes past noon. I had been ensconced before the graffiti-spattered desk on the floor immediately above, applying grace notes and lambencies to a ground-breaking article on the displacements of contextual framing devices in the Archie comics, vols I—IV, as echoed in the narratology of early Alan Moore, early Neil Gaiman, early Clive Barker, and the "Spenser" novels of Robert B. Parker, *passim*. Don't you think these people read Archie comics when they were children? Do you imagine for a second that they did not absorb, with the only barely-conscious *jouissance* of the childish artist-to-be, the false parallelisms established within the picture plane, subverted, punned upon, abruptly discarded only to re-appear, as they did, concealed in the details tucked beside the frame's abrupt right-hand closure? Why do you think Robert B. Parker ends so many chapters with one-sentence paragraphs? We are back in Pop's diner, that's why, and just beyond the caesura of the intervening white space, brilliantined Reggie Mantle is hurtling up in his overweening sports car to kidnap the narrative. There are times—please excuse this brief, in no way immodest outburst—when the sheer power of the insights delivered to this humble scholar all but drop him to his knees.

I heard, as I was saying, the bedroom door and the slightly uncertain tread of the Great Man making his way, muttering to himself as he went, downstairs to the scullery. Peter's day had begun. Having had nothing to eat since the Iranian's potion four hours earlier, I set down my faithful propelling pencil, cast an admiring glance at my latest emendation (it was, I recall, the replacement of a weak, passive *was moving* with the far more pungent *thrust itself)* and charged off in pursuit of my needy friend, not to mention a hearty luncheon.

Downstairs, Peter granted me a surly hello and polished off a glass of milk. Sound-effects emanating from Ms. "Sign's" quarters indicated that her limited experience of American culture had addicted the Iranian to one or more daytime dramas. Peter opened the massive refrigerator, contemplated its laden shelves, moaned piteously, lamented that there was never anything to eat around here, and said, "Let's go somewhere where they have actual grub." I seconded the motion. Out on the street, Peter rejected every dining establishment we passed within a four-block radius, retraced his steps and rejected them all over again, and at last chose a dim, Tibetan shoebox he called "Shogo Mo Fogo," not its name. We ordered soup with spinach and dumplings, dumplings with spinach, and buttered tea. Shogo Mo Fogo's few other patrons nattered away in language so deeply encoded by the mores of the Upper West Side of Manhattan as to be incomprehensible to the outsider. Peter bolted his buttered tea, demanded another, and devoured the soup course. Then, at last, he got down to the nitty-gritty.

"Hell, Put," he said, "all I wanted to do was write a nice little thriller about murders in Central Park. Because we were out in Sag Harbor, I decided to have the narrator be a Sag Harbor boy. His father was a war hero turned local kingpin who disappeared when the guy was just a kid. Turned out the father took off with a lot of municipal funds. All of a sudden, I'm dealing with World War II and stolen money. It's a mess, Put, that's all I can call it, a big, fat mess."

That day, and for the remainder of my visit, I did my best to remind my wayward friend that he had best work up an agreeable little plot that stuck to the point. "This is your chance to save yourself," I told him, repeatedly, in the restaurants we gloomily occupied after having found them (after Peter's having found them) unsuitable two or three times over, in questionable bars, in Peter's office, late at night, with the drums and saxophones. "Forget what you think you know and stick to what you can do. Begin at the beginning, end at the end, and don't go off the rails in between."

"Oh, God," he said, staring at the dumpling-spinach entrée, which in fact was called something very like Shogo Mo Fogo," do you have any idea how boring that would be?"

What I wanted to say was, *You call it boredom, but the rest of it the world calls it discipline.* Instead, silently, time and again, I acknowledged defeat. I returned to Popham with a heavy heart and a sense of having failed friendship's sternest obligations. A year went by. Peter, I gathered, alternated between the doomed attempt to yoke a breezy murder plot to hugger-mugger about the Italian Front and inventing jokes on e-mail, most of them composed very late at night. I had troubles of my own, which thank goodness had nothing to do with the accusations of sex-starved young ladies, although I am obliged to point out that our culture has gone sadly astray when a distinguished academic gentleman in his middle years may not seek to alleviate the loneliness of an attractive female student by inviting her into the safety of his ranch-style residence for a glass of Ohio chardonnay, a modest dinner, and an evening spent watching videotapes of her native city's football cheerleaders without risking personal disgrace, professional ruin, and financial injury. Ah, well. Let it pass.

My troubles concerned the publication of the ground-breaking Archie paper, which, maddeningly, was being rejected, thrown back, trashed, by precisely those journals that should most have applauded it. One after another, editors and their panels of judges, many of them colleagues I hitherto had thought of as old friends, either failed to grasp my argument or disputed my conclusions. It is bitter to find oneself threatened by knaves, worse to face the witless criticism of idiots once seen as valued peers. That, *that* is heartbreak beyond mere bitterness. After months of useless remonstration—the hard copies of which now fill three stout cartons and await eventual publication—I placed the article in a journal found on the Internet, *Eat This!: Comix & Other Garbage*, issued on a catch-as-catch-can basis from New Righteousness, Idaho, and which accompanied its remarkable letter of acceptance with several incendiary leaflets.

Not long after I had endured the annual crucifixion at the hands of the IRS, an utterly unexpected honor was given me. In its wake appeared my old buddy Peter. He was desperate. He was at the end of his tether. He was virtually begging for assistance. In my hand, which is to say, my locked left-hand bottom desk drawer, I held a bone in the form of a manuscript contained within a butter-soft leather satchel. What, given our long friendship, could I do but retract the treasure from its hidey-hole and offer it into his trembling hands, his slavering maw?

• • •

The above-mentioned honor consisted of an appointment to a one-year Fellowship to the American Academy in Rome. Yes, I was pleased by this recognition, which some might have considered long overdue, yet my gratification was shadowed by serious reservations. Acceptance of the Fellowship necessarily would involve the cancellation of my entire course schedule for an entire year, including my Senior Honors Seminar. In practical terms, the Department of Popular Culture at Popham College would have to close its doors for two semesters. Students who had clamored for entry into the Honors Seminar would be denied this valuable opportunity forever. Also, I would be unable to honor my obligations to the Committees on which I serve and the student organizations for which I am the Faculty Advisor.

Other reservations had to do with the American Academy itself. It was, I understood, and I was not in error, a mélange of young, essentially unproven artists and older academics of a deeply conservative stripe. Previously, the Academy had demonstrated a monolithic indifference to the field of Popular Culture and the radical innovations of its leading theorists. If I were to accept the appointment, would I be obliged to temper my firebrand ways?

Upon seeking private consultation with Our President, Mr. "Bill" Liddy, I was invited for a "spell of sittin' and spittin'," as he put it, within the sanctity of Fortress House, our Administration building. An hour later, still deep in dialogue, we repaired to an off-campus establishment known as Mr. Buckeye's House of Fine Cocktails Bar & Grille. "Bill" Liddy put my worries to rest. Yes, it was a pity that some fine young men and women should be deprived of participation in my Senior Honors Seminars, but "Bill" guaranteed them placement in the Honors Seminars of the Sports Management, Philosophy of Waste Disposal, and Science of Athletic Footwear Design departments, where their minds would not go to waste. I was assured that the relevant faculty Committees and student organizations would survive until my return.

"Putney," he said, "Putney, Putney, Putney. Good old Put. Put, my man. My man, Put. I want to say this. When you go to Rome, all of Popham goes with you. Please let me say this. Your distinction is our distinction. Having said that, please let me add this. Don't for a minute underestimate the impact of your magnificent prize upon our Development Program, Athletic Outreach Program, and Five-Year Greater Alumni Involvement Plan! Listen to me, Putney, and when I say listen, I mean listen. In terms of prestige, in terms of recognition, you have a chance to hit a grand-slam home run. Not only for yourself, but on behalf of the home team here at Popham! I want you take that opportunity, Put. Okay? Get your carcass over to Rome and shake up those stick-in-the-mud fuddy-duddies the same way you shook us up here at Popham. Hell, bring along a batch of those Atwood Awards, stick 'em in plain sight, and tell the Academy what's what! I know you'll do us proud, old buddy."

Here, I said to myself, *is inspirational leadership, here is vision.*

The following day I wrote back in acceptance of my Fellowship.

• • •

By mid-August I found myself installed within a bleak apartment and a ramshackle edifice atop an awkward hill and directly across the street from the grim Academy. There, a barren, third-floor office had been designated as my "work space." The narrow window of my lodgings provided a view of a back garden where the feral children of my frivolous, alcohol-addicted colleagues rioted day and night; the larger, more numerous windows of my office in the Academy looked across the Tiber to the filthy, crowded roofscape of central Rome, a spectacle I tended to ignore. The situation was unspeakable.

Let's not get into Rome. Rome is a nightmare. The streets are too narrow, the sidewalks are packed, and Italian hoodlums constantly buzz past on motorbikes, they're like monstrous mosquitoes. You think you will partake of spectacular meals, but as soon as you arrive, everyone tells you, "Of course, it's impossible to find decent food in Rome," and they're right, the food is dull, stodgy, and ridiculously overpriced. The only way to avoid the undercooked pasta is to subsist on sandwiches and the hearty fare available at the city's few German restaurants. To get to one of the legendary fountains, you trudge through one cramped alley after another. When at last you emerge from the final alley, dodge an aggressive taxi, bolt into the cobblestone plaza and thrust your way through a mob of Japanese tourists, the fountain is the size of a wading pool. The surrounding statuary is mostly broken. In the foreground, a Scandinavian adolescent dazedly plucks at a guitar, and from the rear approaches a gypsy-child with felonious designs on your wallet.

Ever-adaptable, I accommodated myself to the noisy, dirty, crumbling city and my dingy quarters. After all, I was not a tourist but a Fellow of the American Academy, and I had work to do, primarily a cutting-edge monograph on the Lacanian structures of language-systems in magazines targeted at the young female audience, such as *Jane* and *Marie-Claire*. (Fortunately, I had taken the precaution of shipping ahead a dozen cartons of these publications, because neither the public news stands nor the staid Academy library stocked them, not a one.) My relationships with my fellow-scholars soon proved amiable, even, I might say, warm, except for those who seemed incapable of remembering my name no matter how many times I introduced myself, and the young artists-in-residence quickly learned to value the helpful insights and criticisms I could offer about their as yet unformed but often quite promising "work." As my monograph progressed, word of its content spread through the Academy like wildfire, with the result that by the arrival of the unpleasant Roman spring, I had acquired amongst my peers a certain minor celebrity I found amusing but in no way inappropriate or uncomfortable. It was this unexpected development which led to my encounter with the young man henceforth known as "Ned Dunstan," therefore indirectly to Peter's egregious folly, *Mr. X.*

• • •

Temporarily resident in Rome in the course of a more extensive journey, Dunstan had accidentally or not run across several of my fellow-Academicians whose respect for my accomplishments, mentioned in passing during the enjoyment of espressos served beneath the umbrellas of sidewalk cafes, decided him to seek my assistance in a matter of considerable personal importance, of great delicacy also. He asked one of his new acquaintances if he might be introduced to this fellow of whom he had heard so much, and the acquaintance referred the request to me, but not before discussing the matter with a number of our mutual colleagues. There was a sense of disquiet, a sense of alarm—these people speculated, and I have to say it was sweet of them, that I might have acquired a "stalker," and one of my colleagues went so far as to suggest that I invoke the protection of the police.

Be reasonable, I advised, calm your anxieties and remember the propensity of "stalkers" to pursue the famous, a category not known to include Professors of Popular Culture from small colleges in the Midwest. Dear Putney, these friends responded, do not permit your instinctive modesty to underestimate the impact made upon the civilized world of your fearless and innovative work, not to mention all those "Atwoods" and your Life Achievement Award! You, dear Putney, they went on to say, are much more famous than you think, and here comes this unknown young man who lurks near the Spanish Steps and other points of interest, arranges random-seeming meetings with your fellow-Fellows for the purpose of spinning an improbable tale of a manuscript in need of professional assistance, asks questions about you, gives every impression of being desperate to meet you, why, he's got "stalker" written all over him, if you will not go to the police at least hire a bodyguard, please, Putney, please, if not for your sake then for ours.

I paid no attention to these distress-signals, for I sensed from the first that the young man in question, "Ned Dunstan," far from representing any threat to my well-being would instead exert a positive influence on my life. Mysteriously, I already knew that not only was there nothing to fear, I should experience what I can only call spiritual refreshment, a largess of spiritual nutrition, from my dealing with the unknown figure. (This certainty, I discovered, was of a decidedly Dunstan-ish nature. To the Dunstans, mystery, precognition, telepathic messages, all of that and more, was meat and drink.) At the simplest, most superficial level, this fellow had recently completed a sort of book-length memoir and wished to entrust it to someone capable of polishing his prose and arranging publication by a reputable firm. What he had heard of me indicated that I might be the answer to his needs, or at least that I would guide the manuscript into the proper hands. I was, I would: for reasons of propriety, I arranged for a trepedatious colleague to bring Dunstan to my office in the Academy late the following afternoon. At the appointed hour, the colleague rapped on my door, led within a young man distinguished by a remarkable physical beauty and carrying a soft, toffee-colored leather satchel, performed the introductions, and departed, not all that willingly. What then took place was undoubtedly the most extraordinary hour and by far the most extraordinary conversation of my life.

Ned Dunstan took the chair before my desk and clutched the satchel to his chest like a life-preserver. I can see him now, twitchy, haunted, unutterably sublime. He had no small talk; his attitude was that of a delicate, wary forest-creature pausing for a much-needed drink of water while in flight from an advancing fire. Beneath the hum of his anxiety lay a fine-spun network of nerves, a regal resolve, a steely assurance, a vast, speaking sorrow. He was, as I have said before, easily the most impressive man I had ever met. Yes, he said, he had completed a book, a memoir composed during his travels, and he had hoped that I might know someone, a professional writer, who would be willing to eliminate the rough spots and make all the necessary adjustments—for he knew himself no writer—after which I might be willing, of course at the customary fee, to attempt to place the manuscript with a publishing house. He would leave the addresses and whatnot at which he could be reached, but he could do no more with his book and wished to entrust it into my care.

I shall treat it as though it were my own, I assured him, I have the honor of personal acquaintance with several highly-regarded writers and many contacts in the world of publishing. May I ask for some description of your memoir's contents or subject matter?

Dunstan trembled. I feared that he would run from my office and escape for good. Instead, he slumped into the chair, displayed a smile of the purest, most heart-breaking sadness I have ever seen on the face of a fellow human being, and began to speak. The things he said startled me, electrified me, moved me nearly to tears, humbled me. He spoke simply, without affectation, opening detail by detail a world deeply Other and unfamiliar, yet deeply my own. All right, I know how that sounds. I *know* that, all right? I don't care how it sounds. This is what happened. Ned Dunstan smiled, opened his mouth, and, speaking in a steady, resonant, rational voice, expanded my vision of the possible. Foundations crumbled, walls collapsed, an old world fell in ruins and a new one rose in its place. Something like that. The earth shook. Something like that.

He surrendered the buttery satchel and left. The moment of his leaving, our handshake, the meeting of our eyes, his swift, quiet closing of my door, all of this was poignant. After composing myself, I took the elevator downstairs and copied the typescript. I brought both copies back to my wretched apartment and spent the rest of the evening and half the night reading Dunstan's book, which by a wide margin failed to match the effect of the version I had heard him tell in my office. It was awkward and self-conscious; it needed the touch of a professional.

For weeks, I sought to interest good writers, reputable writers, in the project. Most of them lacked the imagination to see the magnitude of the opportunity before them. My first choice, Tim Underhill, Peter Straub's sometime collaborator, would gladly have taken on the rewriting but could not spare the time. I despaired. Just at the point when I thought I would have to admit failure, my friend Peter left a message for me at the Academy. He and Susan were in Rome visiting Dennis and Lily Montresor, whose relationship with the Academy went back many years. Dennis had mentioned a mysterious young man and a manuscript entrusted to my safe-keeping. Could we get together?

My compatriot of the sandbox and the swingset appeared in my office that very evening. He took, far less gracefully than Ned Dunstan, the chair before my desk, and he whined, whined, whined. The tale of murder in Central Park was a dead duck, asphyxiated by narrative complications. His career was no less dead, kaput, extinct. He owed his publisher another book, but the well was dry. Desperation and self-pity roughened his voice and exaggerated his gestures. I believe he smoked an entire pack of cigarettes. Perspiration streamed from his shiny pate. Oh, the bills, the sheer, staggering fortune squandered on groceries, the private school tuition, the incomprehensible mortgage, the depredations of the IRS and the demands of the accountant who battled them, oh, the rising costs of cigarettes, triple-distilled vodka and other compensatory luxuries, oh, the price of Testoni shoes (his), Brioni shirts (his) and Armani suits (take a guess), oh, oh, sometimes it cost him five bucks in handouts just to walk around the block, shit, man, only frequent flyer miles had rescued him from the humiliating torment of a seat in steerage on the trip to Rome, hell, man to man, friend to friend and just between a pair of lifelong pals, if in fact there was anything to this story of Dennis Montresor's of a, a what, an unfinished manuscript, if that was true, you know, the part about looking for a writer, well, look no further, was all he could say. As a stopgap. To tide him over. In a professional sense.

I succumbed. I unlocked the desk drawer and passed across the desk the exquisite satchel containing the precious manuscript, as I did so admonishing my old friend that he content himself with merely brightening up the prose and smoothing the narrative flow. I told him, I told him *specifically*, not to turn this assignment into one of his laborious, wild-eyed fictions. "Just fix what needs fixing," I said, "and do nothing more."

"Putney," he said, "my dear old friend, the bulwark of my youth, you may depend, I guarantee you, on me. Cross my heart and hope to die."

Then Peter exited my office and disappeared for two years, over the course of which he violated every aspect of our agreement. By "disappeared" I do not mean "vanished from view," for he did not literally disappear. He disappeared in the sense of refusing to communicate anything of substance while single-mindedly gutting the precious memoir and rewriting it from start to finish. Narrative back-hoes and earth-movers, narrative chain-saws, narrative wood-chippers, nail guns and chisels came into play. Painted backdrops and artificial scenery came into play. So did pointless flashbacks, whimsical sub-plots, and the intrusions of colorfully instructive dreams, a sure sign of desperation on the part of a hard-pressed novelizer. He waded into that lovely memoir like an invading army and devastated it, utterly. When he had finished, air-castles of his own devise hovered unconvincingly over the smoking ruins. And when confronted with the fact of his treachery, he called upon that impervious mechanism, denial, which can be counted upon faithfully to reject the claims of rationality.

He said: No, I didn't. I'm telling you. I *didn't.*

He said: For God's sake, Putney, I just brightened up the language here and there.

He said: Putney, you are flipping out, old buddy, please take your medication. (I have never been under medication of any sort. Well, almost never.)

He said: You're kidding, right? Tell me you're kidding.

This is the voice of industrial-strength denial. Blind to the outrage he had committed, my friend Peter blithely treated my own outrage as an inexplicable delusion. Get a grip, Putney, stop yelling, Putney, calm down, I did what you told me to do and no more.

It was at this point that I recognized the absolute and involuntary mendacity of fiction-writers, and my fury began its slow devolution into wondering pity. You might as well berate a dog for hoisting its leg at bushes and nosing the excrement-cigars left behind by its helpless fellow-creatures.

At my insistence, Peter agreed to preface his crime with an Introduction written by myself and stating the facts of the case; in turn, I agreed that he might preface my Introduction with some self-serving Notes of his own. *Very well,* I thought, *let him babble—the astute reader shall get it instantly, and every reader shall have the option of whom to believe.* We wrote our introductory pieces, Peter with his usual verbose *élan*, I succinctly, and there the matter should have stood: his garrulous "Note," my truth-telling "Preface," then the hideous perversion Peter had entitled *Mr. X.*

The finished typescript went to my friend's editor. A month, two months, three, went by, much to impatient Peter's distress. Whine, whine, whine. My old playmate's anxieties at last induced somatic disorder in the form of excruciating back pain, for which he sought relief from chiropractic practitioners, acupuncturists, hypnotherapists, Oriental herbalists, masseuses, and specialists in aroma/aura balance maintenance. The editor promised to respond the moment she had dealt with the next season's list, and Peter responded to this sensible remark by deciding to undergo spinal surgery. A simple operation lasting no more than an hour, maybe two, put him out of commission for a season and a half. Whine, whine, whine, at epic length. In a fit of what I must call savage depression, he attacked his manuscript yet again and excised another two hundred, three hundred pages, I no longer remember, really, who cares how many pages it was…

…except that in the process, sneakily, without telling me, he also deleted our introductory matter, his Note and my explanatory preface. I blame the Vicodin tablets my old pal was shoving down his gullet, along with whatever else he used to medicate himself, but I blame him, too. He knew what he was doing, all right, despite the Vicodin. By excising all references to the history behind the text, Peter had completed its mutation into yet another of his "novels."

My objections were countered by a move of surprising subtlety. Peter had convinced a small press specializing in the horror genre to bring out our deleted introductions in the form of a chapbook. The press in question was called Underwater Books, Submerged Books, Buried Books, something of that sort. Yes, my account of meeting Ned Dunstan, his extraordinary tale, and the motives for my surrendering his memoir to Peter Straub were to find publication—in a subterranean edition from the Buried Underwater Press. When so impeccably literalized, irony is irony no longer, it is merely description.

As for the "novel" called *Mr. X,* whatever virtues it contains rightfully belong to Ned Dunstan. Peter did his best, but he could not entirely destroy this moving tale.

Wild Animals

Nothing more than Peter's heavy-handed method of sneaking his feeble darling, *Under Venus*, into print after he miraculously had accumulated enough clout to do so. Here at Popham, we have a term for such tactics, and the term is, well, perhaps not "bullying," but "strongarm tactics" comes near enough. The maudlin "Introduction" is at all costs to be avoided except in cases of severe sugar-deficiency. When his publishers graciously arranged for a mass-market paperback edition of the above-mentioned feeble darling, Peter responded in typical fashion, i.e. by moving to another firm or "house."

Houses Without Doors

From time to time, and not always, as the forgiving "fan" or admirer might suppose, in that expansively self-pitying condition any over-praised, over-indulged, largely unconscious scribe might be expected to attain late in the evening after the popping of many a cork and the dissolution of many an ice cube into the rich amber of the next-to-the-next-to-the-next-to-the last nightcap, my companion of old has taken the floor, seized the microphone and delivered to his devoted audience of one a lengthy diatribe centered upon the unreasonable demands made on his time and attention by those pushy editors of ridiculous anthologies (the editors are always "pushy," their anthologies ever "ridiculous") who daily, maybe even several times daily, write, telephone, fax or e-mail their urgent and heartfelt wishes that he submit a story for inclusion in their ridiculousnesses. These are invariably contemptible assemblages of tales devoted to themes and subjects—such as "Erotic but not overwhelmingly Perverse and if possible not Sadistic Relationships involving Vampirism," "the Other Women in the life of Jack the Ripper," "the Graves of the Great Psychic Detectives," "Zombies in the Sewers of

Joyce's Dublin," "the Chilling Fantasies Enjoyed by Your Favorite Serial Killer—and We All Have One!—During the Act of Masturbation," and the like.

"Why, Put," he asks, employing his forgiving auditor's childish nickname, "if you can tell me, and I don't suppose you can, didn't these fools bother me for their silly stories when I could have used the money? Why do they only come sniffing around now, begging for scraps like ragged tinker children, when they must know that I have long since ascended far above their grubby realm? And why should I squander entire minutes of my precious time when I should be refining and extending my ever-more-refined-and-expanding art, in the writing of polite but laborious notes justifying to these pushy nonentities my decision not to ennoble their ridiculous anthologies?"

To the first of these questions, I could, but do not, reply, because the fools in question were still unborn; to the second, because they thankfully have not recognized your massive narcissism; and to the third, Because no matter how bloated with self-importance you may be, you are still supposed to conduct yourself in a polite and civilized manner.

Despite his endless whining, Peter has at least now and again stirred himself to oblige some few of these despised supplicants with the stories they desired of him, and *Houses Without Doors,* which comes complete with an insufferably pretentious epigraph and an "Author's Note" stained with the deepest self-regard, represents his attempt to wring a bit more hard cash from the resulting efforts. None of the pieces are even third-rate Straub, least of all the gnomic "Interludes" with which he evidently wishes to unify his rag-bag, thereby elevating it above the general run of collections. Some of the stories here reveal the neurotic disposition in full bloom, gleefully exhibiting its symptomology while trampling all over more mature points of view. In most, that childish cliché, the "tortured

Artist," hogs center stage. An undigested mysticism pervades all, many times with hilarious and completely unintentional results. (See, for example, that virtual case study, "The Buffalo Hunter." On second thought, don't.) The worst story in this awful book, "The Juniper Tree," condenses every one of its author's shortcomings into forty-odd almost enjoyably psychotic pages.

lost boy lost girl

As I number myself among those who will always do what is necessary to aid a friend, no matter how impossible the task or difficult the friend, I must once again, even under these circumstances, take up the pen and offer some remarks for the dust jacket of the Borderlands Press edition of *lost boy lost girl,* Mr. Peter Straub's latest novel-length fiction. That this work incorporates into the usual Straubian murk several e-mail communications from a person no longer living more than justifies flap copy written by someone in the same position, i.e. one who has "passed over." Folded his hand. Departed. Not to put too fine a point on the matter, the author of these remarks passed over and folded his hand and departed the earthly realm some eighteen months prior to publication of this volume, and while I'm on the subject, I'm still mighty steamed about the witless, slanderous, insulting conclusions drawn by nearly all of my friends, acquaintances, and professional colleagues from the circumstances of the (extremely unpleasant) event.

It is true that Popham College, the reputation of which I burnished for nearly two decades in my ground-breaking tenure as Chairman and only member of its Department of Popular Culture, entered into a Bolshevik period upon the death of President Bob Liddy and put me, the most distinguished faculty member that gutless place ever had or ever will have the pleasure of underpaying, out to pasture via the mechanism of "forced retirement," which is the same as getting the axe, except you still keep getting your benefits and they don't cut off your pension, such as it is. I was obliged to leave my comfortable dwelling-place and take up lodgings in, ugh, the Block Flag Motel on Commere Avenue in the nearby town of Lead City. Therefore, it was my duty to remove from my former home all my worldly goods, very much including the trove of erotic journals discovered fanned out around my corpse at the bottom of the basement stairs, which is where I landed, already a goner, after suffering my fatal heart attack. The journals were research materials, not autoerotic stimulants!

In any case, the best one can say about this effort from my old pal is that it is at least mercifully short. His attempts to represent my present location, which he coyly calls "Elsewhere," are ludicrously misinformed.

In the Night Room

A great man is dead. A great man, a man of greatness. This must be said to the world at large, not merely within the deceptively leafy, ivy-walled, statue-haunted precincts of Popham College, where green, path-intersected quads luxuriate between handsome Georgian buildings. A mean-spirited treachery slinks along those paths, it continually conspires behind the closed doors of the English Department on the third floor of Poxey Hall, and of late it wrings its cold hands in triumph at the final defeat of its arch-enemy, Professor Putney Tyson Ridge, the former Chairman and only member of the Popular Culture Department. Now the Department lies in ruins, in less than ruins, disbanded and abjured. As a Popham graduate and former major in Popular Culture who reveres the memory of Professor Ridge and promises ever to honor his name, I seize the opportunity granted me by Elizabeth Monteleone and Borderlands Press to praise Professor Ridge by offering some few observations on this latest offering from the pen of Peter Straub.

In this task I humbly follow in the Master's footsteps, for my beloved Professor ("Put" to his friends and a very few favored students, myself gratefully among them) gave endless hours of his precious time selflessly composing brilliant "Observations" on every single one of his old friend Straub's works from the execrable *Marriages* to the lazy, self-indulgent *lost boy lost girl,* in that case posthumously! These revelatory mini-essays should be sought out and relished on Mr. Straub's web site, www.peterstraub.net, where the cunning author has tucked them into a sort of cul-de-sac, but you can find them if you persevere.

What, I ask the unresponsive heavens, would Professor Ridge have made of *In the Night Room?* It isn't really all that bad, if you want to know the truth, and I thought Willy Patrick was hot stuff, although the way Straub wrote about her was probably sexist. The stuff about sugar was interesting, too. I laughed at that part. But the ending was terrible. I didn't understand anything that happened and I felt cheated.

The one time Peter Straub came to Popham and spoke in the Warren G. Harding Temple of the Artistic Spirit, he just rambled on and on about himself, making it up as he went along. He didn't have anything prepared. I think he probably wrote this book the same way.

Ernie Tremple, Popham
Popham, Ohio